MW01244803

Jake Bernstein

SHORT-TERM

FUTURES
TRADING

Systems, Strategies and
Techniques for the Day-Trader

PROBUS PUBLISHING COMPANY
Chicago, Illinois
Cambridge, England

NOTICE
THE CFTC AND THE NFA REQUIRE WE MAKE THE FOLLOWING STATEMENT.

HYPOTHETICAL OR SIMULATED PERFORMANCE RESULTS HAVE CERTAIN LIMITATIONS. UNLIKE AN ACTUAL PERFORMANCE RECORD, SIMULATED RESULTS DO NOT REPRESENT ACTUAL TRADING. ALSO, SINCE THE TRADES HAVE NOT ACTUALLY BEEN EXECUTED, THE RESULTS MAY HAVE UNDER- OR OVER-COMPENSATED FOR THE IMPACT, IF ANY, OF CERTAIN MARKET FACTORS, SUCH AS LACK OF LIQUIDITY. SIMULATED TRADING PROGRAMS IN GENERAL ARE ALSO SUBJECT TO THE FACT THAT THEY ARE DESIGNED WITH THE BENEFIT OF HINDSIGHT. NO REPRESENTATION IS BEING MADE THAT ANY ACCOUNT WILL OR IS LIKELY TO ACHIEVE PROFITS OR LOSSES SIMILAR TO THOSE SHOWN. THERE IS A RISK OF LOSS IN FUTURES TRADING.

CONTENTS

CHAPTER SEVENTEEN

CHAPTER EIGHTEEN

CHAPTER NINETEEN

APPENDIX

A Brief Note From Jake Bernstein

In spite of its long history, futures trading has come of age only in the last 10 years. The popularity of stock index, currency, and T Bond futures has helped catapult futures trading into the realm of heightened public awareness. Along with increased trading volume and increased public participation there has been a proliferation of trading systems, methods, and indicators. This has, in part, been accentuated by new, more readily available and reasonably priced home computer technology. Today, virtually anyone with several thousand dollars can buy a computer and historical data. They can back-test and optimize various trading models and sell their systems to the public. There is much to be said about trading systems, their use, abuse and optimization. There is also a great deal to be said in favor of totally mechanical trading systems.

Yet, these are not the primary topics of this book. Jack Schwager, a man whose work and efforts I hold in the highest esteem, recently stated in an interview:

> The easiest thing in the world is to develop a system which makes 200 percent or 400 percent a year trading in the past. It doesn't mean anything except that you fitted the rules to exploit past price action. When you trade such a system in the future, expect a drastic reduction in performance.

In addition, Jack notes the following:

> You need intuitive skill to be a trader. There are people who have it just like great musicians have it. In their nature they're tuned into the markets so well that their instincts make them great traders. If you're

not one of those people, you need enough market experience to help compensate.*

You will find in these pages many ideas and techniques gathered from long and hard experience. They are curve-fitted or optimized. They are presented with the understanding that you, the trader, must study them and evaluate them within the constraints, limits, and scope of your ability. I have always believed that the human element is the weakest link in the trading chain. Some traders need mechanical systems to assist their discipline. Yet, many traders circumvent their systems when times get tough. On the other hand there are traders who seek to acquire the skills of futures trading. These skills only can be acquired through the process called learning. Some of the technical skills traders should consider in their search are contained in this book. There is no single source of ultimate market knowledge or skill. There is no single best teacher, system, or approach. The process of individual choice and growth as a trader will have ultimately its way. The purpose of this book is to facilitate your choices by offering a variety of alternatives.

Commodity Traders Consumer Report, 1713 Howe Avenue #149, Sacramento, CA, 95825. June/July

PREFACE TO THE REVISED EDITION OF *SHORT-TERM FUTURES TRADING*

The first edition of *Short-Term Futures Trading* was published in 1987. Since its publication, traders throughout the world have read, studied, and analyzed the trading ideas presented in this book. Thousands of copies have been sold and now, in 1992, the growing interest in short-term trading necessitates the publication of an updated and revised version.

The pages which follow contain much of the original material in the first edition. However, I have included more up-to-date examples, as well as several new trading ideas which have come to light as a result of my ongoing research and trading during the last few years. I hope you find the trading ideas presented herein to be useful, but moreover, profitable. I suggest that a good starting point for your own trading with these ideas is not necessarily to apply them *verbatim*, but rather first to research them in order to guage their current efficacy, second to determine if there are perhaps ways in which their performance might be improved, and third to determine how they best fit into your personality and trading style. It may be possible that the ideas presented herein can be adapted and developed in order to yield greater profits and more consistent performance. I can certainly claim no monopoly whatsoever on the development and research of new trading ideas. I perceive my role in this book to be one of direction giver and teacher rather than system promoter. Above all, remember that the effectiveness of trading systems is very much a function of the markets themselves. Some trading systems will work consistently well for many months—in fact, for many years—however, a time comes sooner or later which witnesses a deterioration in their performance. At times, systems enter a period of hibernation during which their performance is either lackluster or consistently negative. This does not mean that such trading systems, methods or ideas must be abandoned; rather, it means that they must be watched closely and monitored consistently, so that when their performance does begin to improve and they have passed through their dormant cycle, they may be once again deployed in real-time trading.

If I can be of assistance in your endeavors, please don't hesitate to drop me a line, either through the publisher or through my mailing address at P.O. Box 353, Winnetka, IL, 60093. I will attempt to respond to your letter as quickly as time allows.

Jake Bernstein

INTRODUCTION

When I wrote the first edition of this book the idea of short-term trading had just become fashionable as a function of increased volatility in virtually every futures market. Since then, the continued instability in international economics, politics, and the extreme fluctuations in international currency relationships have fostered a significant growth in short-term trading. This growth springs from wanton speculation and the need for institutions, banks, governments, and hedgers to protect themselves against losses which may be incurred as a result of price volatility. The purpose of the futures markets has been underscored, as they have provided a backdrop of stability which otherwise might not have been possible. One could easily be critical of the futures trading system, pointing out that futures trading itself has been the source of the intense volatility witnessed in recent years. This is, in fact, not the case. It is the instability of international economic conditions, as well as the uncertainty of political events (particularly in Europe), which have been responsible for the extreme gyrations in currency interrelationships, gold, silver, platinum, and a host of related markets. My work suggests that, had the futures markets not serve as a buffer against such fluctuations, the actual result might have been considerably worse. Be that as it may, the volatile conditions have provided a rich environment within which the short-term and day trader can operate. In having access to such volatile markets where large fluctuations create both great opportunity as well as risk, the importance of developing and implementing effective day trading and short-term systems becomes particularly significant. It is to this end that there has been a considerable increase in interest in the area of short-term trading, and in the market which serves the needs of short-term traders.

In 1987 this book was perhaps the only written source of information on short-term trading methods. Now there are a number of resources, both written and in video tape form, which purport to provide the short-term futures trader with effective systems. Unfortunately, many of the systems being offered nowadays are essentially worthless, supported with little or no backtesting, and based almost entirely on conjecture, market myth, and essentially minimal testing. The methods I've presented herein, on the other hand, have been examined, backtested, refined, developed, and adapted to real time application using real time trading methods. While I don't claim that these are the most effective trading systems available for short-term work, I do feel they are among the most consistent and offer traders the greatest opportunity for success. In reading what follows, I suggest you approach each chapter with the understanding that the orientation of the short-term futures trader, or speculator, is distinctly different from that of the position trader or the investor. While the position trader and the investor seek to profit from longer-term market moves, the short-term trader and day trader are interested in working only within their time frame. Events which may affect the market several months hence are essentially useless to the short-term and day trader. Events which may impact the markets on a minute-to-minute or day-to-day basis are the most significant events to the short-term and day trader.

The approach taken in this book is technical rather than fundamental. My more than 22 years of experience as a trader have convinced me that while fundamentals are very important to markets on an intermediate to longer-term basis, they are considerably less important on a short-term basis. This is not to say that fundamental developments will not impact markets in a significant way. It is to say, however, that technicals such as those described in this book, can allow the futures trader to enter and exit markets optimally, in most cases with little or no attention to fundamental developments. We also find in a vast majority of cases that technical changes tend to precede or predict changes in fundamentals and that fundamentals are usually consistent with the directions of the markets themselves. In short, it is possible for the technical trader to be on the right side of the market when important fundamental news develop, simply by following technical indicators rather than being concerned about fundamentals which may or may not be known, and which may or may not be important.

It is the nature of fundamentals to impact markets in different ways at different times. The same fundamental bit of news may result in Swiss Frank futures rallying sharply on one occasion, whereas an essentially similar news item ten days hence may have a negative impact on the market. The backdrop of fundamentals— international politics, economics, and behind-the-scenes operations— is so complex that is virtually impossible for the fundamental trader to have a grasp on all conditions which may impact prices at any one point in time. The true technician approaches the market from the vantage point of technical input only. The true technician feels strongly that if fundamental news is to impact the market, then the fundamental news will be known, in most cases, well ahead of time and will be taken advantage of by insiders who will, by their collective buying and/or selling, impact prices in such a way that the technician will find it possible to discern when changes are likely to occur and to act in advance of such changes.

As technicians and short-term traders, it is our job to find methods which will allow us to trade in advance of such fundamental developments. Certainly I can't guarantee that the techniques I offer in this book will always be successful or that they will be a panacea to the problems which plague the day trader and the short-term trader. We know from experience that if we can be correct in our anticipations and actions 60 percent of the time, then we can profit handsomely from our trading. It is not, therefore, my goal to provide you with methods which will allow you to be correct 80, 90 or 100 percent of the time. Such methods simply do not exist. Anything you may have read to the contrary, or anything you will be led to believe to the contrary by misleading advertising and claims, is simply false. Yes, there may be systems and methods which are correct 90 percent of the time; however, you must understand that statistics can often be misleading. A system promoter who has an expensive piece of software, or a book or trading program to sell you, may claim 80 percent accuracy without revealing the length of time over which such accuracy has been achieved, or for that matter the number of cases over which such accuracy has been achieved. A degree in statistics is not required in order to know that a system which has been 80 percent correct over a period of 500 observations is clearly a much more promising system than one which has been 100 percent correct over 5 observations.

In this book, you will find no claims whatsoever about accuracy of performance, no hard statistics about average profit, average loss, drawdown, profit to loss ratio, etc. You are free to research these on your own. I stress that the results which each trader can achieve through the use of the techniques described are as much a function of the trader as they are of the method or system. Ultimately, the trader must implement the systems and determine when to actually enter or exit markets, regardless of what trading signals or indicators may say. I have seen few if any traders who can religiously and mechanically follow a trading system.Trading is as much an art as it is a science—possibly, it is *more* of an art than a science. There are those who would argue otherwise. Some would claim that successful futures trading is 80 percent science, 10 percent skill and 10 percent good fortune. Even after my 22 years of trading, I do not have the knowledge or experience to provide a definitive answer to this question. However, I can state from experience that the trader and the system are of equal importance and that disregard for one or the other is sure to lead to failure.

Finally, just a brief word about computers and the growth of new technology which, I feel, will vastly change the face of futures trading in the 1990s. As many of you know, the availability of relatively inexpensive computer hardware and software, as well as the declining price of computer memory, has spurred the growth of increasingly complex and intricate software programs. It is now possible to achieve the same results using a personal computers which 10 years ago were only attainable using large computer systems whose price prohibited access by the general public. Today, several thousand dollars can allow the futures trader to enter the hi-tech world with sufficient computer power, historical data, and data analysis programs which will allow the development of profitable trading systems and methods. The same relatively inexpensive hardware and software also allow for the development of artificial intelligence programs and for their availability to the investing and trading public. I am referring specifically to neural network programs which, over the next several years, will likely render virtually all traditional trading methods and systems obsolete. A neural network is an artificial intelligence program which attempts to mimic the stimulus response and analytical connections of the human brain. It is, in effect, a program which can not only "think for itself", but also "learn from its mistakes". The applications of neural software in industry and in economic analysis have proven extremely promising and highly effective. Neural network technology has been applied in virtually every area of the physical sciences, is being applied to the social sciences, and, in recent years has also found its way into the trading arena. While software developers have been able to achieve great successes in the physical and social sciences using neural networks, the application of neural networks to the problems of the investor and trader have not yielded similarly promising results until recently.

Using a neural network, the trader can input a host of market variables, both price and non-price related, and instruct the computer to ascertain and implement pattern recognition studies which will take into consideration all of the permutations and combinations of price and price indicators. In effect, the neural network's "brain" analyzes all of the inputs and, in a quasi-thought process, determines which relationships and which indicators have been operative and to what extent they have been operative at major market turns. Neural networks may well prove to be the systems of tomorrow. But no matter how good the networks may be, they will not replace the trader who is, was, and always will be the weak link in the chain.

This is why I have attempted to give you a well rounded market education—not one limited by the tunnel vision which is an unforunate side effect of too much concentration on systems and not enough focus on the trader

CHAPTER ONE

SHORT-TERM TRADING IN FUTURES

UNDERSTANDING SHORT-TERM TRADING

To understand the nature of short-term trading one must first understand the difference between the short-term trader and all other
traders. There are many different types of short-term traders.Let's first
deal primarily with one particular type—the day trader. Day traders
are actually in a class by themselves. Their expectations, techniques,
and personalities are different than those of traders in all other time
frames. And the philosophy of day trading is markedly different from
all other trading philosophies. Day trading, by its very nature, differs
radically from all trading that results in a position being carried into
the next day's trading.

SHORT-TERM TRADING GOALS

Until the late 1970s and early 1980s, most intraday trading was carried
out by floor traders and those known as "upstairs traders." The upstairs
trader is usually an intraday trader who trades not on the trading

1

floor, but rather in "upstairs" offices usually in the exchange building, trading as if he or she were on the floor. New traders who have entered the world of day trading in the last few years are now pursuing the same trading goals which professionals have long sought to achieve. Specificallythey attempt:

1. To enter and exit positions on the same day.

2. To trade frequently, seeking out smaller, more reliable moves.

3. To strictly limit losses and maintain a winning end result each day.

4. To pay minimum commissions.

5. To trade only in markets that characteristically have reliable intraday price moves sufficiently large to permit consistent profits.

6. To avoid thin markets even though they may characteristically exhibit large intraday price moves. And,

7. To enter and exit as promptly as possible and at the best possible prices.

In order to achieve these goals, the day trader must strive to achieve the following:

1. Total commitment to the market throughout the trading day, exiting most positions before the day's close.

2. The ability to accept losses quickly.

3. The ability to take profits quickly when necessary.

4. A reasonably objective or mechanical trading system.

5. A willingness to trade contrary to news and, on occasion, contrary to existing trends.

Above all, the day trader must approach markets with a totally mercenary attitude, seeking to make each day a winning day, even if only by a small amount. On the other hand, the short-term trader willing to carry positions overnight has the luxury (some would call it a necessity) of not being forced to make a decision, or for that matter many decisions, before the end of each day. In some respects this is positive; in others, negative. Consider one of the most common market blunders, that of staying with a losing position. The day trader who is totally committed to exiting positions at the close of the market (at the latest) will be forced to liquidate a losing position by day's end. The short-term trader who may carry a position from three to five trading sessions may be tempted to carry a losing position beyond his or her original anticipated risk level. Ultimately, this could prove very harmful, especially if the speculator continues to carry the position as the result of unwillingness to take a loss. The day trader, on the other hand, will have minimized the loss by the enforced restrictions of his or her time frame. In a circuitous fashion, the day trader may actually be at an advantage by not carrying positions into the next trading session.

TRADING TOOLS

The distinction between the day trader and the short-term trader is as significant as that between the short-term trader and the long-term trader. Yet all three types of traders, could employ the same basic market tools. Many of the tools differ only in their application and resolution. In other words, all three types of traders use the same technical indicators, but do so in significantly different fashions and with significantly different results. This does not mean, however, that there are no specific tools unique to day trading.

Since the focus of this manual is exclusively on intraday and short-term tradinghor, I will address the issue of technical indicators for long-term trading only briefly, or as it relates to a specific example relevant to the current topic.

Let it be understood at the outset that the short-term trader and the day trader must abandon certain predispositions, biases, and expectations in order to gain a proper perspective on the markets. This perspective, once developed, will facilitate effective implementation of the timing tools discussed in these pages. Another *caveat*: remember that complex interactions between trader personality, market time-frame orientation, personal factors affecting the trader, timing indicators, and many other influences may yield markedly different results in each case. There are artists, good artists, and great artists; although it is likely that all have learned the same history of art, the same basic techniques, and the same methods, each produces art that ultimately depends upon an individual understanding, interpretation, and integration of many factors. Traders are not unlike artists. Many claim to follow strictly mechanical systems, but nuances in the structure and application of their systems are significant variables in their ultimate success or failure.

CHAPTER TWO

AN INTRODUCTION TO STOCHASTICS

My ongoing search for effective technical trading indicators has led me to study myriad systems. Over the years I've received so many calls and letters from individuals claiming to have the "perfect" trading system that I've become convinced of one fact: *the perfect trading system does not exist, and it never will.*

On occasion, however, though, a method or technique is developed that has excellent *potential* as the basis for a wholly new trading system and/or which may serve as an adjunct to existing trading systems. So it is with stochastics. This chapter introduces the concept of stochastics in broad terms, discusses its basic construction, its application, assets, and limitations. It should be understood that the stochastic methodology I describe is not a self-contained trading system, nor does its use guarantee profits or the avoidance of losses. It has some distinct limitations—distinct liabilities. The following discussion reflects only *my personal adaptation* of the technique. Other analysts and traders undoubtedly use it in their own particular ways.

The origin of the stochastic indicator (SI) is somewhat obscure. My first contact with stochastics was through the work of George Lane.[1] After studying SI, I concluded that there were some extremely interesting and potentially profitable applications of this approach to market timing. I discovered that using the SI with cycles was a very effective approach Therefore, I studied the technique further and developed several worthwhile applications.

THE BASIC INDICATOR

The stochastic indicator (SI) consists of two values, %K and %D. The basic formula for Stochastic is as follows:

1. Assume you want to run a 10 time-unit SI. Take the highest high and the lowest low of the 10-unit period. Subtract the two.

2. Take the low of the 10 units and subtract it from the current close. Divide the difference by the figure arrived at in Step #1.

3. The next increment plot is calculated by dropping the oldest data point and recalculating according to the above steps using the most recent data as you would do for a moving average.

4. The second line (called %D) is a 3-period smoothed moving average of the first figure (%K). (This completes the calculation for "Fast" Stochastic. The charts in Chapter 2 show "Slow" Stochastic.)

5. Slow %K is the Fast %D and Slow %D is a 3-period smoothed MA of Slow %K.

The indicator tells you when the market is "overbought and likely to turn down" (75 and above) or "oversold and ready to turn up" (25 and under). *This does not mean that a market will definitely turn once it enters the critical areas.* It must do some "price and time work" first, *and* the SI must then turn as well. SI is considered a type of trend-following method since it tends to give signals *after* tops and bottoms have been made. Figures 2.1 through 2.7 illustrate SI and price relationships in various time frames. You can see how closely the highs and lows correlate with overbought/oversold readings on the SI.

Figure 2.1: Stochastic Indicator (SI) Showing %D and %K—14 Periods

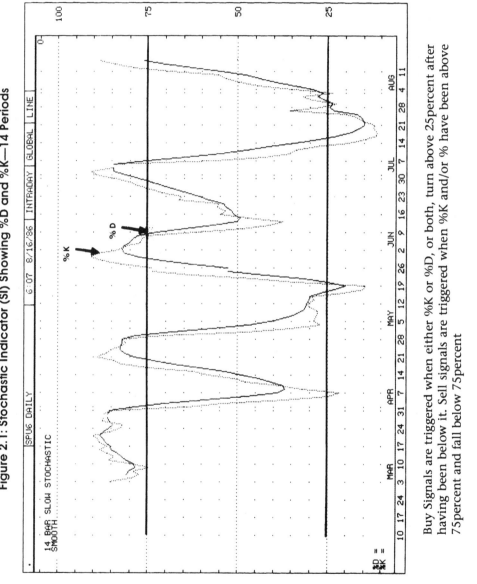

Buy Signals are triggered when either %K or %D, or both, turn above 25percent after having been below it. Sell signals are triggered when %K and/or % have been above 75percent and fall below 75percent

Figure 2.2: SI on Daily Chart

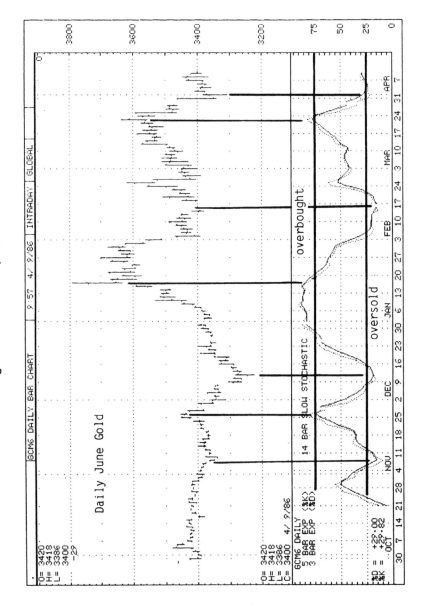

This chart illustrates the high correlation between price tops and bottoms and "over-bought"/"oversold"readings on the 14-period exponential SI.

Figure 2.3: SI on Weekly Chart

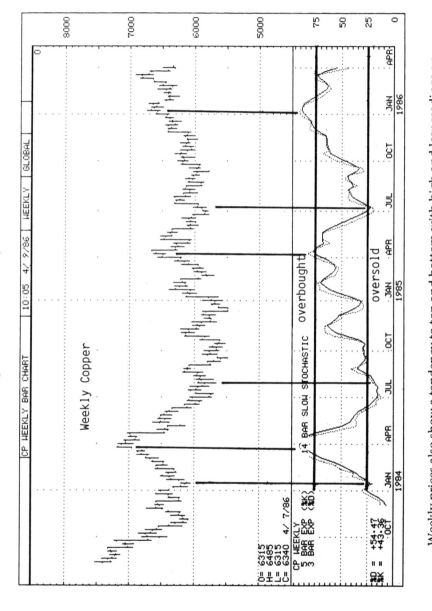

Weekly prices also show a tendency to top and bottom with high and low readings on the SI.

Figure 2.4: 1/2 hour T Bond Futures and 14-Period SI

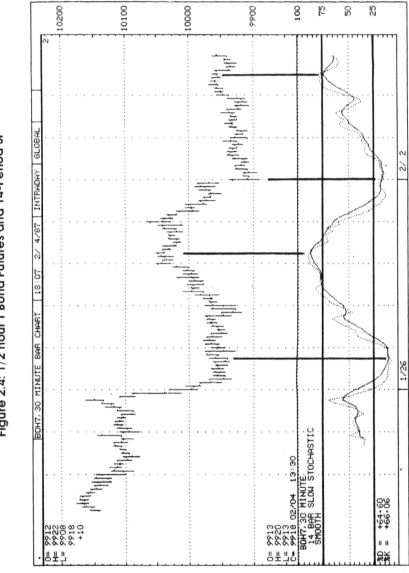

The SI is also useful on intraday charts since it tends to correlate well with changes in trend.

Figure 2.5: Hourly Chart of T Bond Futures and 14-Period SI

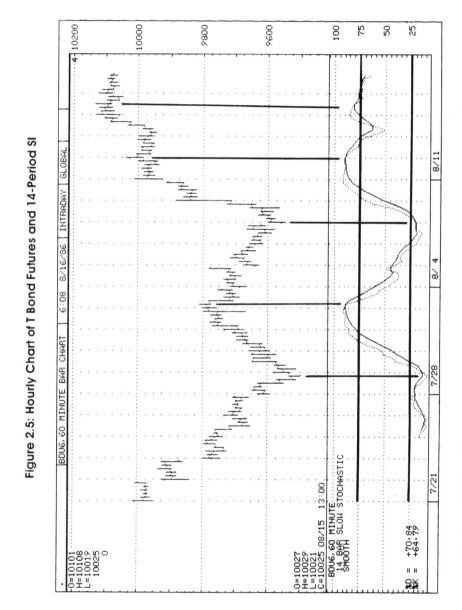

The hourly T Bond Futures chart clearly illustrates the relationship between SI readings of under 25 percent and lows and SI readings of over 75 percent and highs.

Figure 2.6: 14-Period SI on 30-Minute Swiss Franc Chart

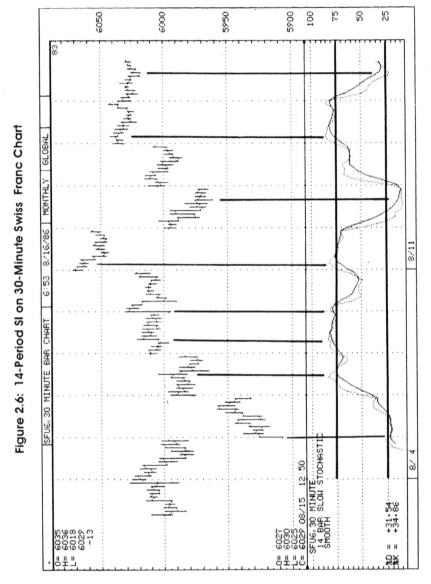

Even markets as volatile as the Swiss Franc can be studied with the SI. It is important to remember that the SI can remain above 75 percent or below 25 percent for extended periods of time. SI is frequently used in conjunction with other timing tools.

Figure 2.7: SI 30-Minute Chart: Lows and Highs

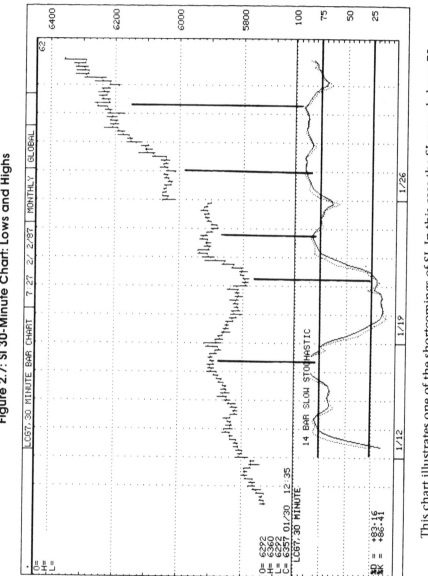

This chart illustrates one of the shortcomings of SI. In this case the SI moved above 75 percent on 1/26, but prices continued higher for several more days. This is why SI should be used with other indicators.

SI Time Frames

As mentioned earlier, the range of SI application and utility extends from ultra-short-term analysis (that is, five-minute intraday) all the way to monthly analysis. My preference is a time segment of 12-16 units for short-term trading—this includes all time frames from five minutes up to and including one day. Time frames, of course, will vary according to individual needs. The goal in selecting a proper time frame is to provide as smooth and clear-cut a turn as possible. Figures 2.8, 2.9, and 2.10 are daily and intraday charts with various lengths of SI. Examine my notes and comments.

USING THE SI AND ITS VARIATIONS

The two lines on the SI chart are essentially different computations of the same data. They're like two different lengths of moving averages. Ideally, you'd want both lines moving in the same direction between 75 percent and 25 percent. As long as they are, the current trend is likely to continue. Prices are neither overbought (high) nor oversold (low), and the trend should continue in its current direction. When the two lines cross or when their separation narrows (as in Figure 2.11) it is often a sign that the trend may soon change, or that it has, in fact, already changed. In short: the two lines tend to confirm trends and trend changes.

I suspect that every indicator has as many uses as there are traders and market analysts. While I am certain that my ways are not the only ways, the following applications of stochastics seem to me to have good potential:

SI as an index of overbought/oversold. Figure 2.12 illustrates a classic implementation of the SI using the indicated methodology. The trick is to wait for a turn from the extremes, because the SI can stay in the overbought (OB) or oversold (OS) area for quite some time. The intraday chart in Figure 2.13 shows how this can occur. *Therefore, if you are going to use the SI for the purpose of selling and buying on such extremes, you must wait for the cross to occur from OB back under 75 or for a cross above 25 from OS before you take a position.* The SI itself does not tell you where to put your stop losses or where to take your profit.

Figure 2.8: SI Too Short (Too Sensitive)

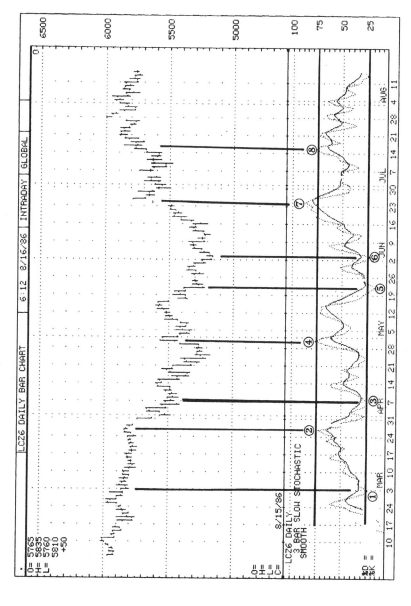

If the SI is too short (i.e; too few time periods), too many signals may be triggered, and their accuracy may be questionable. Compare this with an SI that is too slow (long) in Figure 2.9. Note that the stochastic indicator was extremely low and turned from bottoms 1,3, 5, and 6. Conversely, tops marked 2, 4, 7, and 8 all occurred in very close proximity to stochastic readings of 75 percent or higher.

Figure 2.9: SI Too Long (Too Insensitive)

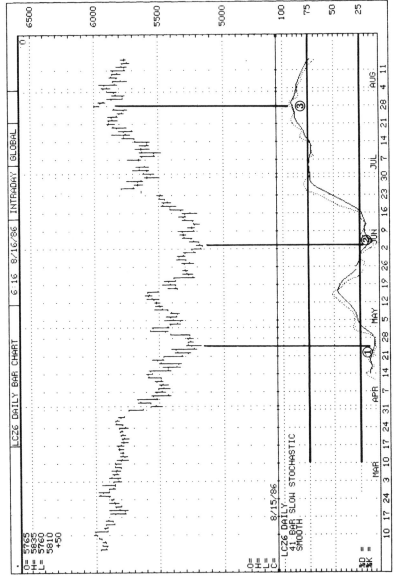

Though the 41-period SI shown here provided only two important lows and only one significant top over a span of four months, the market turns were very clear. To an active trader the 41-period SI is too long. Bottoms 1 and 2 both came in close correlation to extremely low stochastic readings, however, crosses over the 25 percent level did not occur until a number of time periods thereafter. Similarly, top #3 occurred in very close proximity to the stochastic peak, however, the actual sell signal did not develop until many days thereafter. A stochastic length of 41-periods is, therefore, too long for the purposes of a short-term futures trader.

Figure 2.10: SI "Just Right" Fit

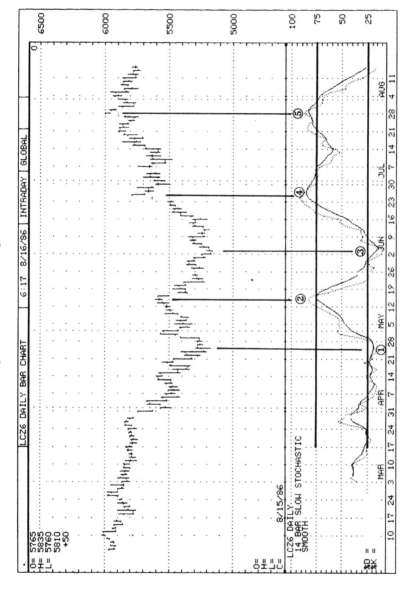

The 14-period SI, however, is a better fit. Five market turns were indicated, compared with other SI lengths which were either too "fast" or too "slow." You will note that price lows 1 and 3 occurred within several days following extremely low stochastic readings. Similarly, price peaks 2, 4, and 5 occurred within several days prior to stochastic sell signals. A sell signal which is triggered by stochastic crossing below 75 percent would therefore have been a perfect fit using a 14-period slow stochastic indicator. Note also that in this case we are using the smoothed version of the 14-bar SI.

You must use your other methods or your own judgment. As always, you must be prepared to take losses when necessary, without excuses and without adding to losing positions just because the SI is heading in a given direction. *The SI is not infallible!*

As an aid to spotting cycle turns, the SI has excellent potential. Assume that you are waiting for a cycle to bottom, and that you are in the low time-frame. You consult the SI. It should be getting oversold. Once it turns back above 25 you have reasonable confirmation that the cycle has turned higher. The reverse would hold true at expected cycle tops. Assume you are waiting for a top. The first thing that will happen is that the SI will become overbought by going above 75. *This does not mean that a top has been made;* it merely means that one is likely. Tops and bottoms can take a relatively long time to form. Once the SI drops below 75 there is good reason to believe that a top has been made. Figures 2.14 and 2.15 illustrate the SI in conjunction with cycle highs and lows. For day traders, the use of stochastics with cycles is of no particular advantage. It is mentioned here, however, since position traders and short-term traders could benefit from its use.

Divergence in price versus the SI can also be a helpful tool. Assume, that price makes a new high but that the SI does not achieve a new high, though it still reads OB (above 75). Even though price has made a new high, the SI suggests that relative strength is not as strong as the price alone implies. The resultant downturn should, therefore, be quite strong. The reverse would happen at market bottom divergences. Divergence is indicated in Figures 2.16, 2.17, and 2.18 .

Using SI with traditional chart methods is another way traders can take advantage of the SI. Figure 2.19 (page XX) shows a half hour T-Bond futures chart with support and resistance lines, and SI. You'll observe that when you use the SI with chart support/resistance lines, you can filter "false" signals on the SI. I've marked the chart with my notes to demonstrate how this can be done. Note that even though the SI entered a long period of overbought, the chart support line failed to give way. This might have prevented premature short sales.

Figure 2.11: SI Convergence and Crossings (60 Minute T Bonds)

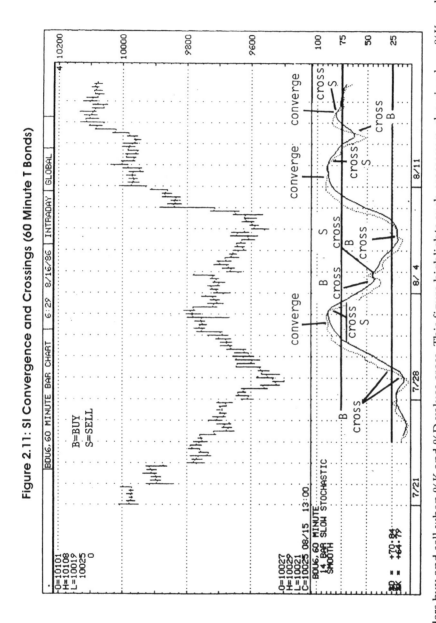

Some traders buy and sell when %K and %D values cross. This figure highlights such crossovers, showing how %K and %D first converge and then cross to yield Buy signals (B) and Sell signals (S). You will note that the convergence and divergence of %K and %D has a very close relationship to crosses of %K and %D. A good technique, therefore, would be to calculate the difference between %K and %D, using this as an oscillator of the stochastic indicator to time market turns.

Figure 2.12: Daily SI Buy/Sell Signals using the 75 percent/25 percent Method

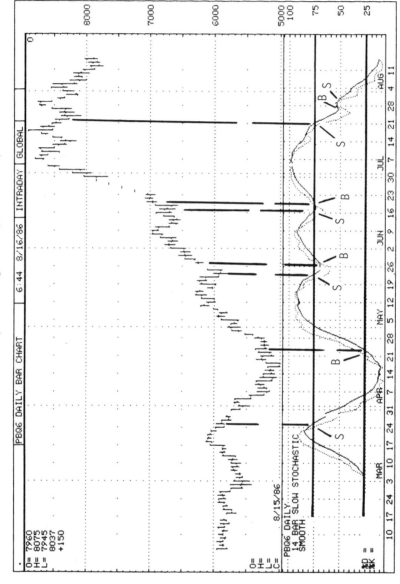

Another approach to SI is to buy when %K or %D cross the 75 percent line or 25 percent line respectively. See the chart notations. If a Sell is triggered, the position is reversed and the SI lines cross, and vice versa for a Buy signal. Although I have chosen the 75 percent line and 25 percent line as indicators of sell and buy respectively, these values are not written in stone. Some traders may prefer to use 80 and 20, 90 and 10, or even 80 and 35 as their points. The best way to determine the optimum stochastic crossover points is through empirical research.

Figure 2.13: SI Can Stay Overbought or Oversold for a Long Time

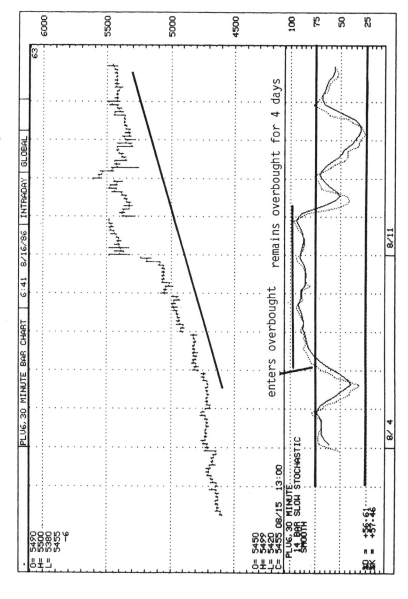

As indicated earlier, SI can remain in one mode for a relatively long time while prices continue in a strong trend. The traditional use of the SI would have required other indicators as confirmation. Since the SI indicator can remain in an overbought condition for many days, simply selling when stochastic rises to 75 percent or higher is not an effective procedure and can lead to considerable losses. Conversely, a stochastic reading can remain at 25 percent or lower for many days or even weeks. Therefore, buying simply because SI is at 25 percent or lower is also a procedure certain to lead to losses.

MORE ABOUT THE MATHEMATICS OF STOCHASTICS

In addition to the basic SI formula given earlier, there are a number of other ways in which the SI may be calculated. According to the Commodity Quote Graphics (CQG) technique, the SI is calculated as follows:

1. Assume you want to run a 10 time-unit SI. Take the highest high and the lowest low of the 10-unit period. Subtract the two.

2. Take the low of the 10 units and subtract it from the current close. Divide the difference by the figure arrived at in Step #1.

3. The next increment plot is calculated by dropping the oldest data point and recalculating (according to the above steps) using the most recent data, as you would do for a moving average. You have now calculated %K.

4. The second line (called %D) is a three-period smoothed moving average of the first figure (%K). This completes the calculation for "fast" stochastic. Figures 2.20, 2.21, and 2.22 show "fast" stochastic.

5. Slow %K is the Fast %D and Slow %D is a three-period smoothed moving average (MA) of Slow %K.

LIMITATIONS AND POSSIBLE DETRIMENTS IN USING THE SI

Perhaps the greatest limitation regarding the use of SI is the fact that it can give false signals in markets that are very weak or very strong. As can be seen in a number of the charts in this chapter (see illustration in Figure 2.13), it is very possible for the SI to go above 75, then to turn lower, and for prices to continue higher while the SI remains below 75 for a prolonged period. The opposite can happen as well. The

Figure 2.14: SI With Cycle Highs and Lows (Weekly)

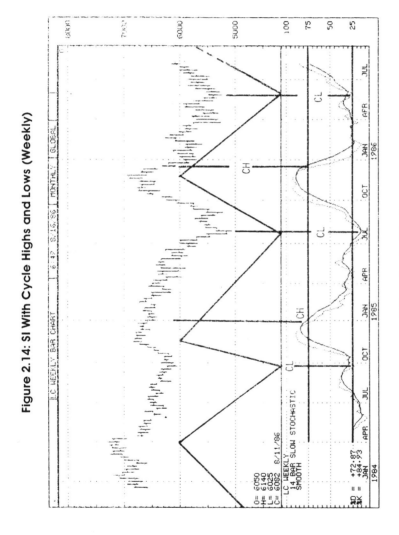

CH = Cycle High
CL = Cycle Low

The chart above illustrates how cycles and SI can be used in conjunction. Here, the approximate 9- to 11-month cycle in live cattle futures is shown. Note that highs and lows of the cycle do not correlate perfectly with the SI; however, the approach has merit.

Figure 2.15: SI With Cycle Highs and Lows (Daily)

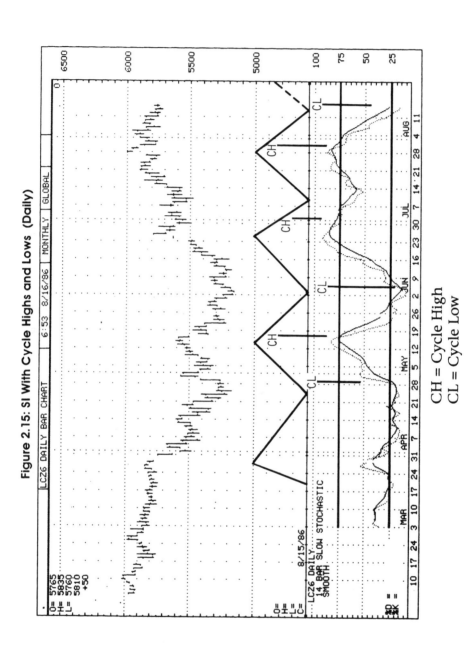

CH = Cycle High
CL = Cycle Low

The approximate five-week cycle in Cattle Futures and SI Signals (75/25 method) illustrate that the combination of cycles and SI is a viable and useful one.

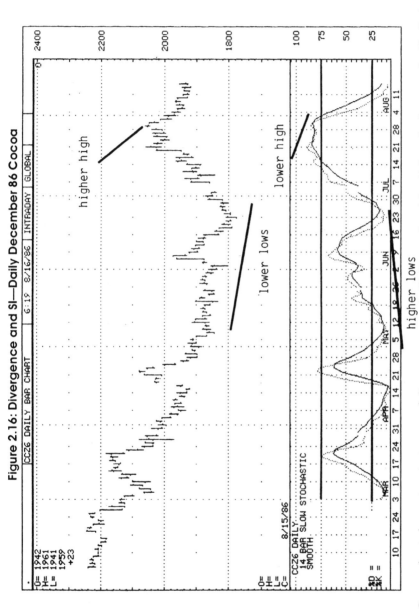

Figure 2.16: Divergence and SI—Daily December 86 Cocoa

The Daily Cocoa chart shows two instances of divergence, one bullish, one bearish. Although the period of bullish divergence took many weeks to develop, its ultimate result was a substantial price move-up. The bearish divergence only took a period of several weeks to develop and resulted in a declining market. Typically, bullish divergence tends to take longer periods of time to develop than does bearish divergence. Although bullish and bearish divergence are very effective indicators, they are, unfortunately, not totally mechanical nor are they easily defined in operational terms.

Figure 2.17: Divergence and SI—1/2 Hour Swiss Franc

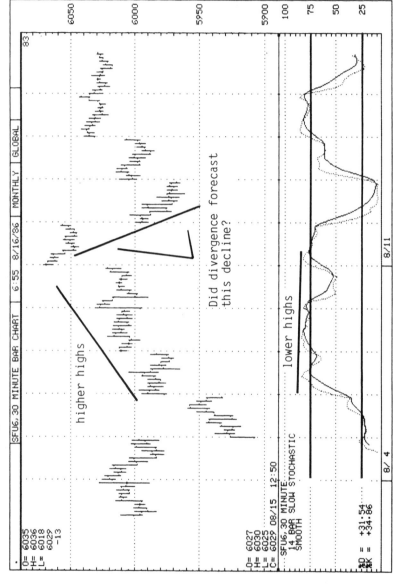

Divergence between SI and price can be seen even on intraday charts. Note the decline following divergence between SI tops and prices tops. You will note that there were three instances of lower highs on the stochastic indicator and three instances of higher highs on price. There is no limit to the number of successive higher highs or lower highs which can occur as divergence develops. In this instance a simple timing indicator would have been sufficient to confirm a top in the market. Divergence can be a powerful indicator, however, it does not always forecast an immediate top or an immediate bottom. It is frequently helpful to use confirming indicators.

Figure 2.18: Divergence and SI—1/2 Hour S&P

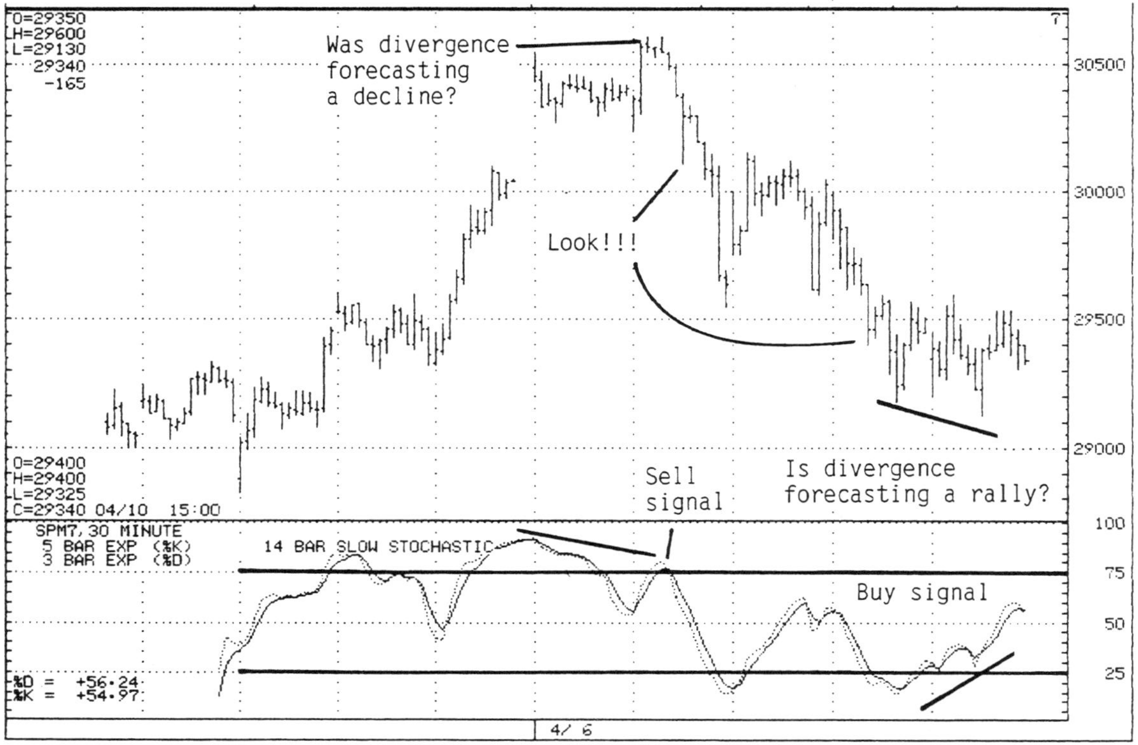

Note that second top on SI was lower than first top, thereby not confirming the new price high. Also note that Buy Signal resulted from new low in price not confirmed by new low in SI. This is another classic example of bearish divergence forecasting a significant price decline in stock index futures. Even a simple timing indicator such as a moving average or trend line would have been sufficient to forecast the drop which occurred subsequent to the bearish divergence. As you will also note, the later part of the chart indicates the development of bullish divergence which could easily be confirmed with the addition of a simple timing indicator.

Figure 2.19: SI and Support/Resistance—30-Minute T Bonds

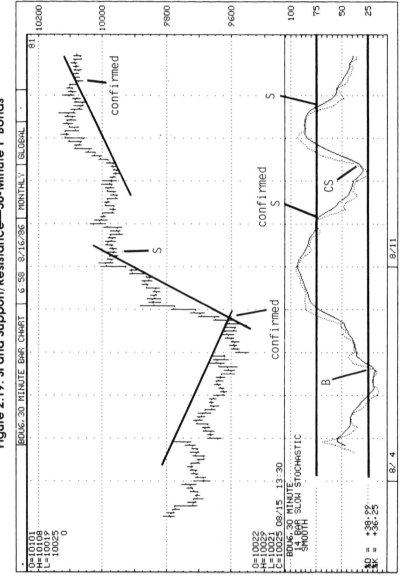

SI also can be used with trendline penetrations. Note the Buy and Sell Signals (B) (S). Also note that the trendline/SI combination can signal reversals in position and position liquidation without reversing position. Unfortunately, the combination of trend line, support/resistance, and the stochastic indicator does not lend itself easily to mechanical signals. It is therefore more of a technique than it is a trading method.

trader who continues selling or buying on such extended periods of false signals can run up a considerable string of losses. Some markets can remain overbought or oversold for days on end. Figure 2.23 shows how the SI acted hour by hour, remaining overbought with prices not falling.

Another limitation is that the SI *will not tell you how much of a move you'll get.* It often happens that the market will be down for an extended period of time, the SI will give an indication to buy, the market will rally only slightly, and before you know it, the SI will be overbought. The reverse can happen at bottoms.

Finally, the SI does not help you with money management or stops; this must be achieved with other techniques. Generally speaking, it is advisable to use a stop beyond the extreme high or low of the move.

Use of SI with Other Techniques

To repeat: the SI works best when used in conjunction with other methods. Therefore, I suggest you take a close look at your present systems and/or methods—they often can be greatly enhanced by the SI.

Is a Computer Needed for SI?

No, not really, unless you want to follow a large number of markets daily, monthly, weekly, and intraday, as I do. If this is the case, there's no way you can do without a computer.

Special Applications of Stochastics

Chapter 3 covers the stochastic "POP" method. Please refer to it for further details on using stochastics for short-term and day trading.

Figure 2.20: "Fast" SI

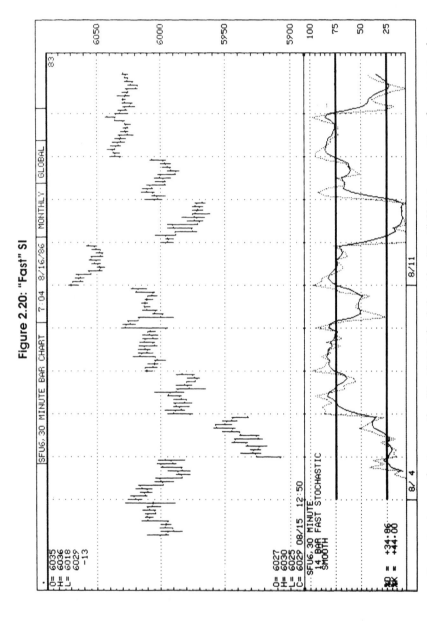

Some traders prefer to use the "Fast" SI. I find that the "Fast" SI is too sensitive for most traders. As you can see, the "Fast" SI is extremely variable and tends to signal many tops as well as bottoms. While the use of "Fast" SI can be helpful to some traders, it tends to have the same limitations as does "slow" SI and frequently yields false signals at significant tops and bottoms.

Figure 2.21: "Fast" SI

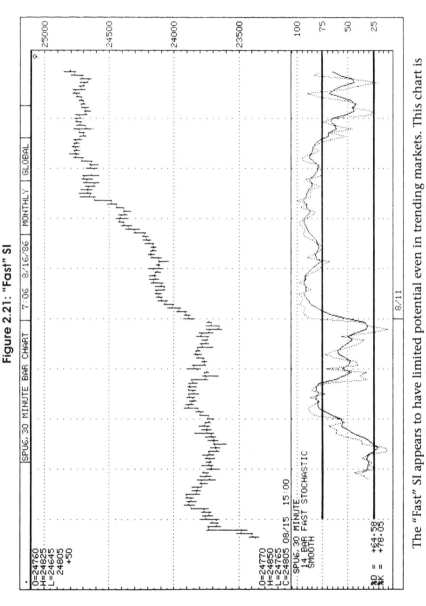

The "Fast" SI appears to have limited potential even in trending markets. This chart is a classic example of how the "Fast" SI can remain above 75 percent for an extended period of time while the underlying market trend continues higher. It is therefore difficult to use the "Fast" SI for trading purposes.

Figure 2.22: "Fast" SI

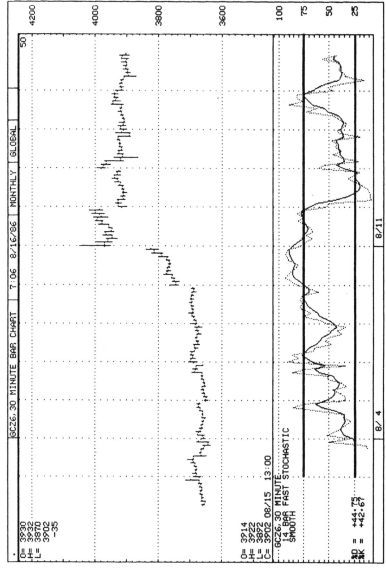

Here is another example of how the "Fast" SI can vary greatly during sideways markets and thereby yields numerous trading signals which ultimately generate more heat than light.

Figure 2.23: Stochastics Can Remain at an Extreme Level for Many Hours

(see arrow)

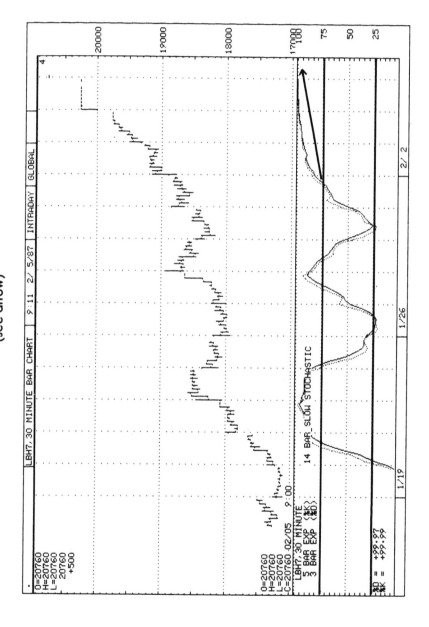

This underscores the necessity of using SI with other indicators. The chart shown here is a classic example of how the "Slow" SI can remain at an extremely high level for many time periods. The trader who sells simply because SI is 75 percent or greater would have done so on 2/2 and would have maintained a short position which would have resulted in a substantial loss over a period of several days.

Practice Charts

Figures 2.24 through 2.30 are SI charts illustrating various SI signals and indications, along with my analysis. Study these in order to acquire a better understanding of how the many different aspects of the SI can be applied.

NOTES

[1] George Lane, *Investment Educators*, 719 South Fourth Street, Watseka, IL, (815)432-4334.

Figure 2.24: Practice Chart

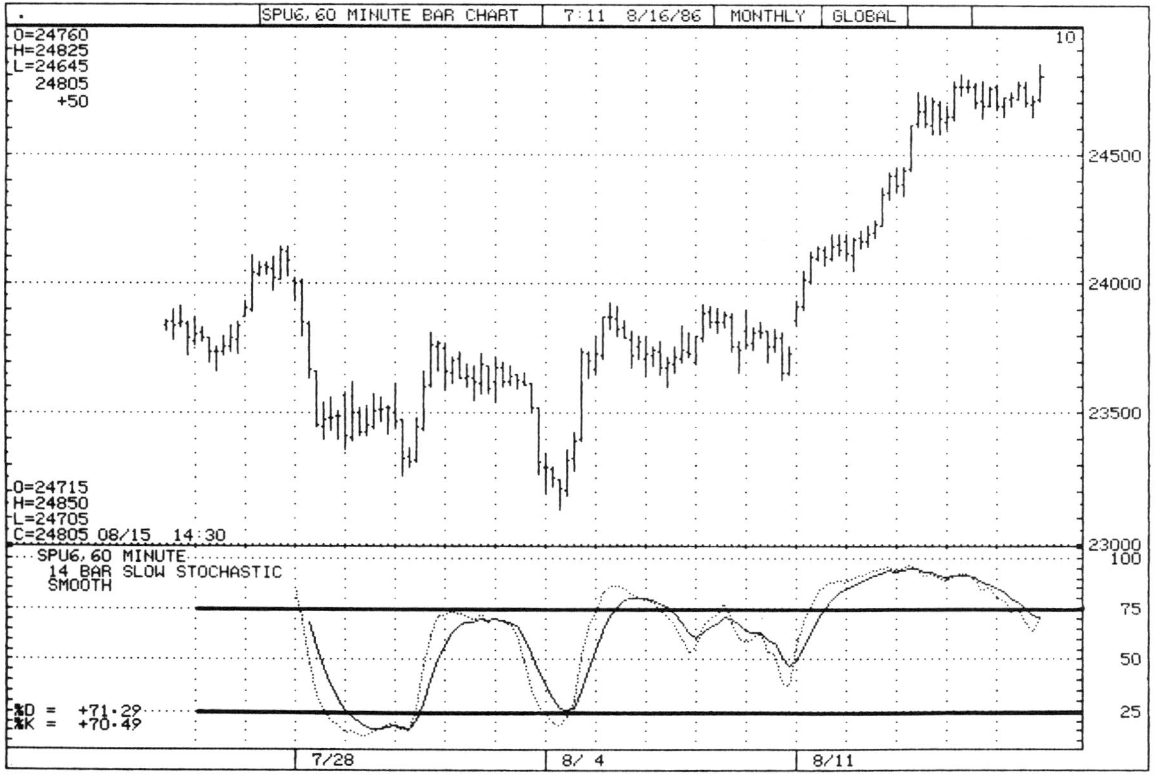

This practice chart shows a number of important SI signals. Can you find the SI sell signals? Can you find the bearish divergence at the top? Can you find the lengthy period of overbought SI while trend continued higher? Can you find the one instance of bullish divergence which occurred between 7/28 and 7/30 and then again between 7/30 and 8/4?

Figure 2.25: Practice Chart

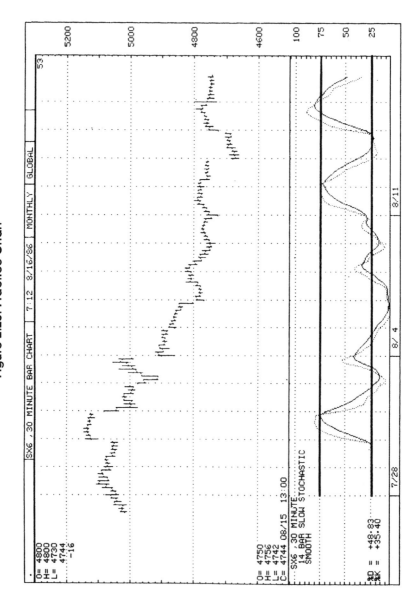

This chart shows not only several instances of bullish divergence but, in addition, several classic SI sell signals. Can you find them?

Figure 2.26: Practice Chart

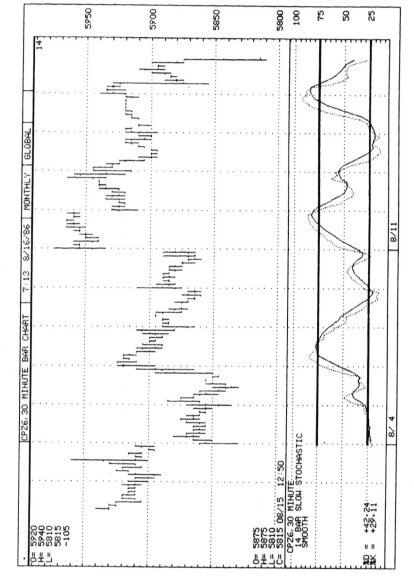

This chart shows three extremely accurate stochastic sell signals as well as two very profitable buy signals and one mediocre buy signal. Can you find them?

Figure 2.27: Practice Chart

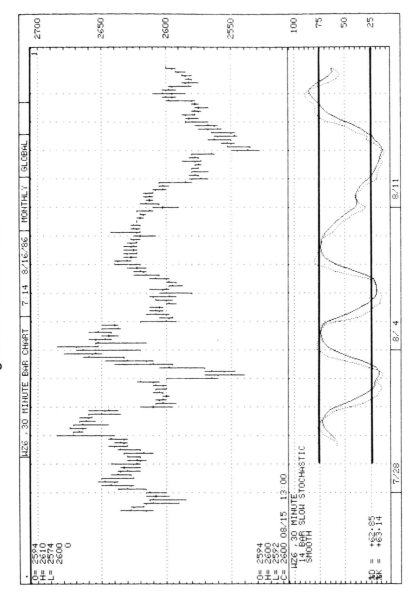

This intraday chart shows several instances of buy signals, which occurred very close to important lows and three sell signals, at least two of which we know would have been profitable.

Figure 2.28: Practice Chart

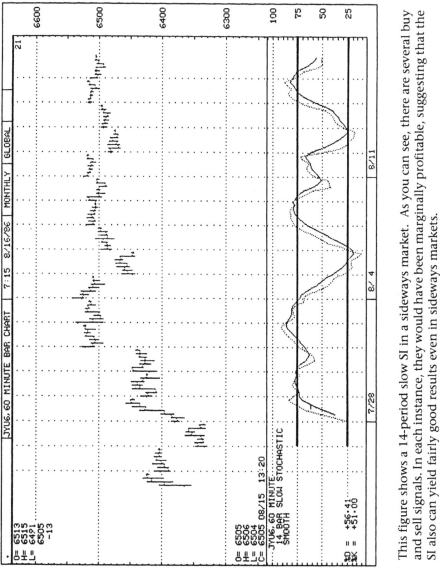

This figure shows a 14-period slow SI in a sideways market. As you can see, there are several buy and sell signals. In each instance, they would have been marginally profitable, suggesting that the SI also can yield fairly good results even in sideways markets.

Figure 2.29: Practice Chart

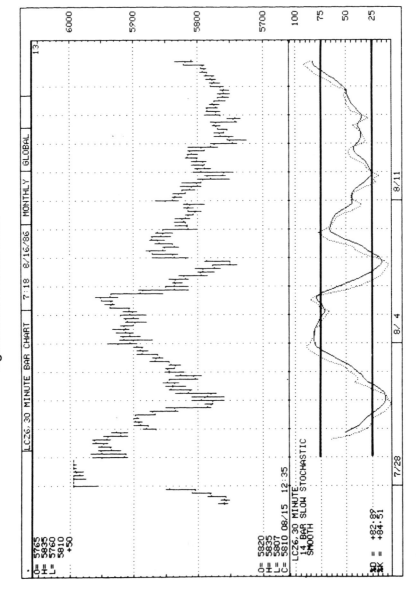

This figure shows a classic example of bearish divergence at a significant top as well as bullish divergence at the low which occurred subsequent to 8/11.

Figure 2.30: Practice Chart

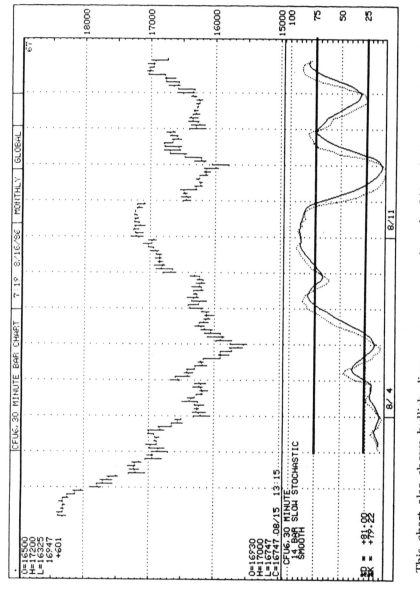

This chart also shows bullish divergence on approximately 8/4, which was followed by a substantial rise in prices prior to an SI sell signal which occurred on 8/11.

A NEW TWIST ON STOCHASTICS

We tend to interpret market indicators according to a belief in absolutes: the market is either bullish or bearish. When a market becomes "oversold," we are afraid to go short. When bullish opinions prevail, we are afraid to go long. When the market is "overbought," we are afraid to buy. When prices are too low, we are afraid to sell short, and so on. Our thinking colors our actions: perceptions and preconceptions often prevent us from seeing things as they really are.

As a most illuminating example, consider the stochastic indicator discussed in Chapter 2. One of many ways of using the SI is to buy and sell on crossings of %K and %D. Another way is to sell short after a market has crossed from overbought (above 75 percent) to below the critical 75 percent line, or to buy after a market has become oversold (under 25 percent) and crossed back above 25 percent. Both strategies have promise. Yet I have found that a different approach, one which seems to fly in the face of logic, also has potential. Why not buy a market when it becomes "overbought" and sell a market when it becomes "oversold"? *Why not?* Just as a body in motion tends to continue in one direction, so money tends to follow an up or downtrend. Naturally, you must exit the position at the slightest

43

Figure 3.1: The Stochastic POP Method

S = Sell Signal, B = Buy Signal, CL = Close Out Long, CS = Close Out Short

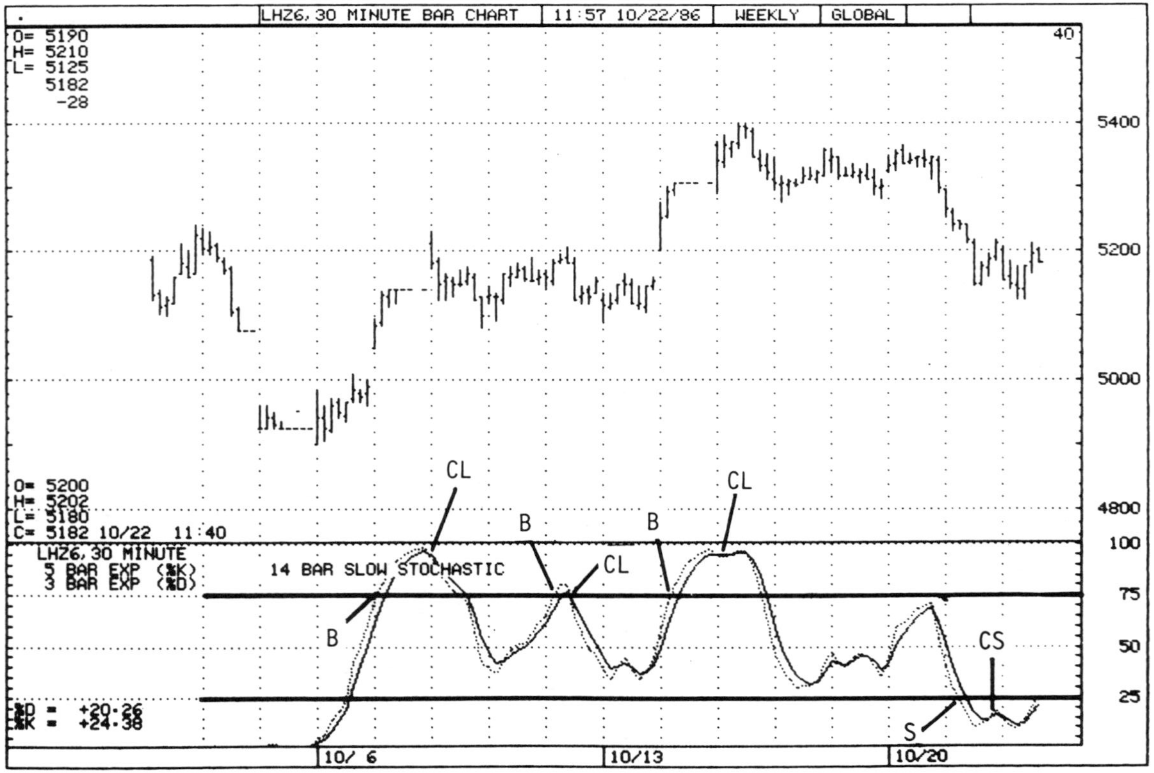

The Stochastic POP (SP) seeks to capitalize on high probability moves which occur at price extremes.

Figure 3.2: The Stochastic POP Method

S = Sell Signal, B = Buy Signal, CL = Close Out Long, CS = Close Out Short

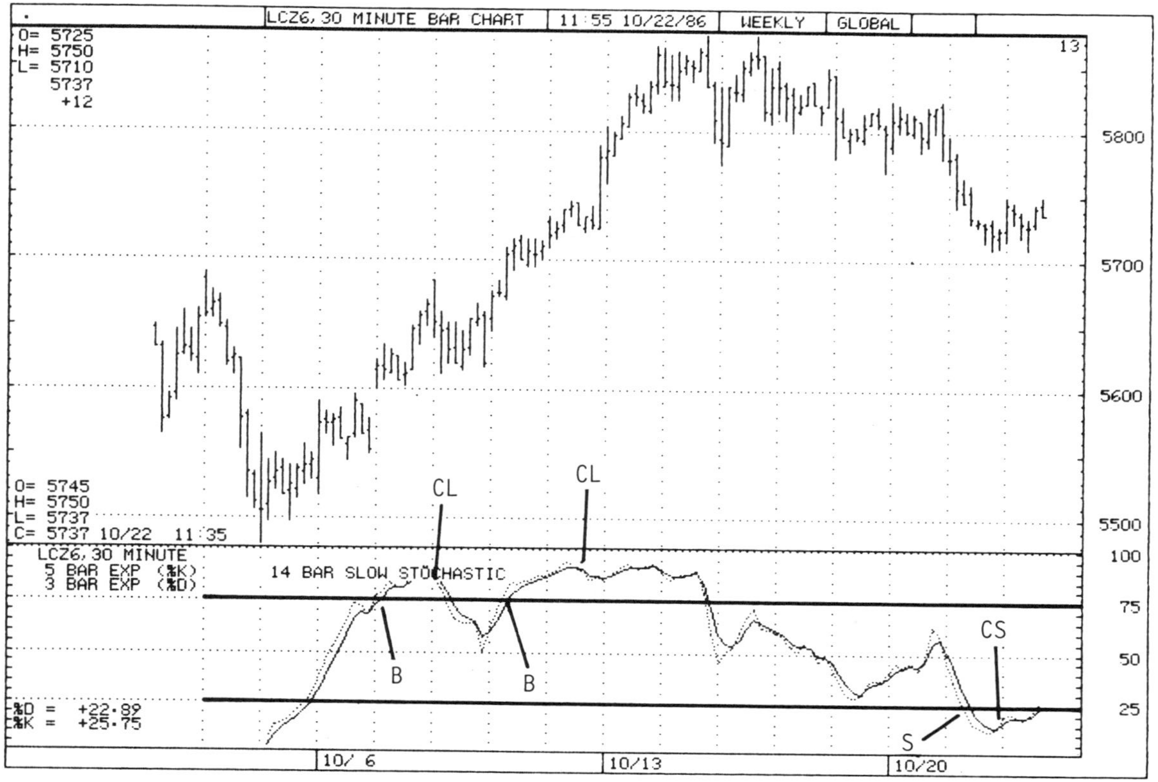

Note that the SP tends to signal market exits very quickly.

Figure 3.3: More Stochastic POP Signals

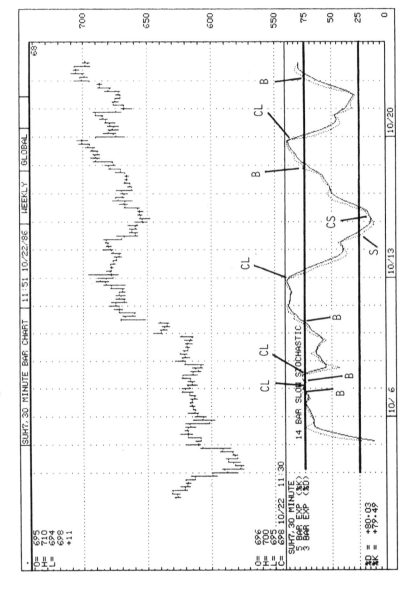

In markets characterized by frequent price swings, the SP method is still a valid indicator.

Figure 3.4: More Stochastic POP Signals

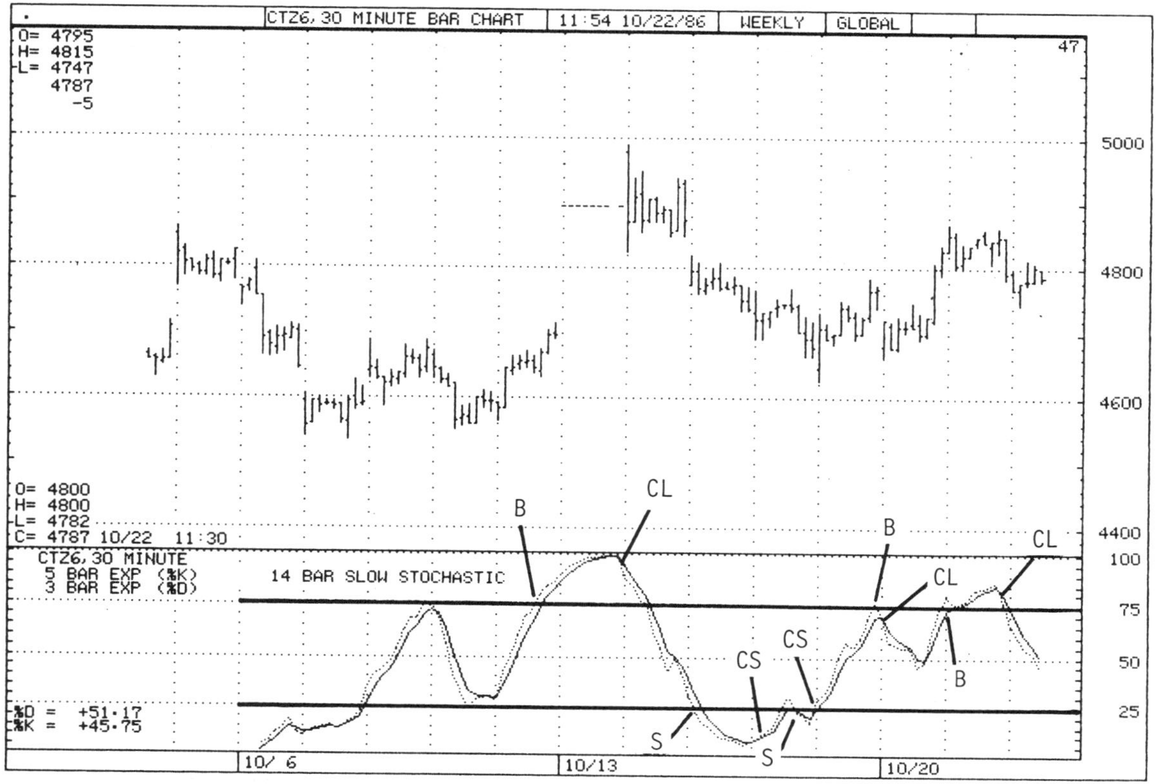

Figure 3.5: A Closer Look at 30-Minute Stochastic POP Signals

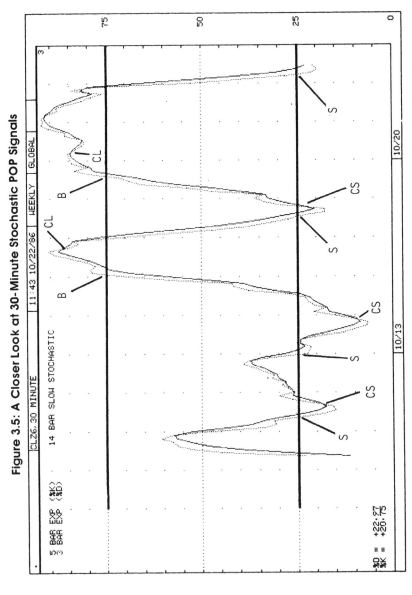

This chart shows 30-minute stochastic POP signals. As you can see, the ideal procedure calls for selling short when SI has reached 25 percent or lower and covering short positions when %K and %D cross. Conversely, the procedure vies when SI has reached 75 percent or higher and liquidates positions when %K and %D cross. The SI POP indicator will show similar signals on all charts regardless of time frame.

indication of a turn. However, be aware of the fact that a market can become overbought or oversold and *remain that way for extended periods of time.* Some of the largest moves, up and down, in recent history have happened *after* markets have become overbought or oversold. Many traders are afraid to take positions once overbought or oversold levels have been hit. See Figures 3.1 through 3.5 and my comments. You might begin to wonder about the wisdom of adhering to traditional approaches to the stochastic timing.

THE STOCHASTIC POP METHOD

This interesting new application of stochastics may well become one of the most potent short-term trend indicators I've ever developed. The POP technique triggers long entry when a market becomes overbought on stochastic (75 percent and above). When a market becomes oversold on stochastic (25 percent or lower), "POP" goes short. This approach is contrary to what many analysts advocate, yet it makes sense because it should keep you in the strong moves. Figures 3.6, 3.7, and 3.8 further illustrate the stochastic POP method. These charts merely show the raw signals on a number of time frames. *When combined with the trading rules I've developed, the POP achieves its true greatness!* Figures 3.9, 3.10, and 3.11 further illustrate POP signals. POP rules are discussed below.

POP Entry and Exit

As soon as %K and %D rise above 75 percent on a closing basis, you go long. You stay long until the two lines cross. It doesn't take much for %D and %K to cross when the market is overbought—it occurs as soon as a market shows even a slight amount of weakness. When this happens, don't sell short; just liquidate your long. Each entry and exit is "at the market." Indicators are calculated on a closing basis. The optimal time period I've found for the POP is the 30-minute segment. There also appears to be good potential on five-minute

Figure 3.6: Signals on 60-Minute Stochastic POP Indicator

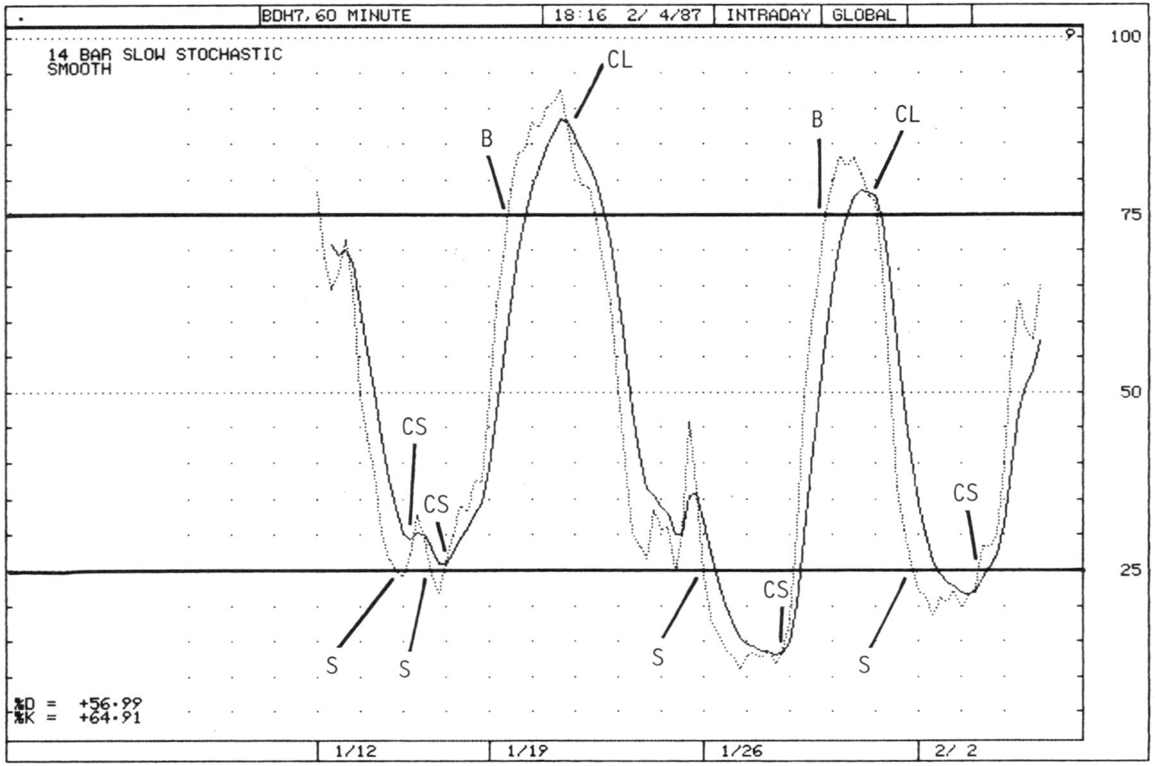

Figure 3.7: A Closer Look at Stochastic POP Signals—60-Minute Data

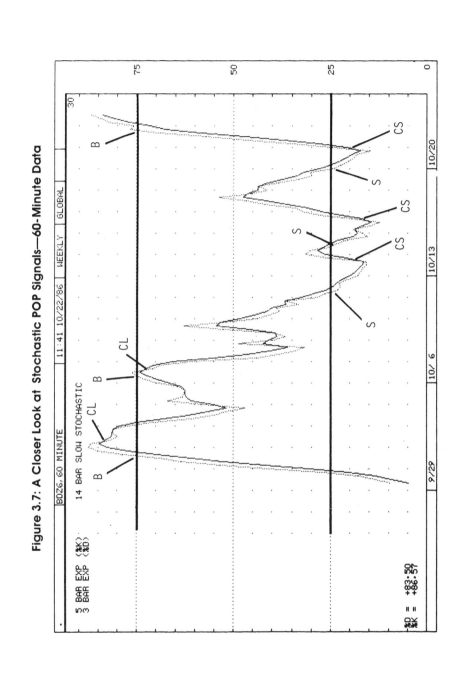

Figure 3.8: Stochastic POP Signals—30-Minute Data

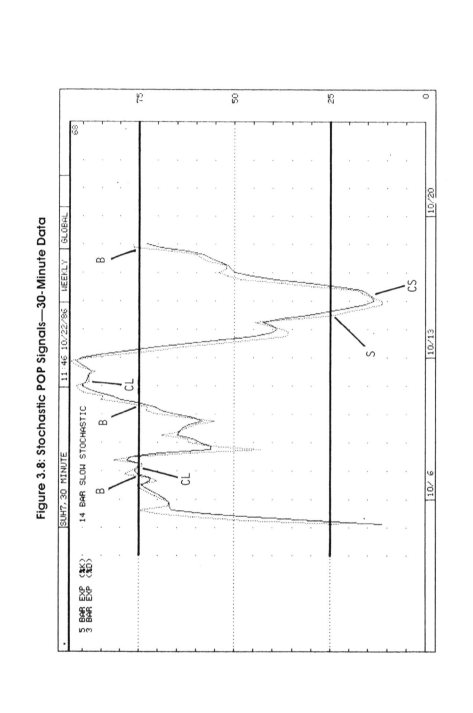

Figure 3.9: "Popping" Pork Bellies—Stochastic Signals and Price

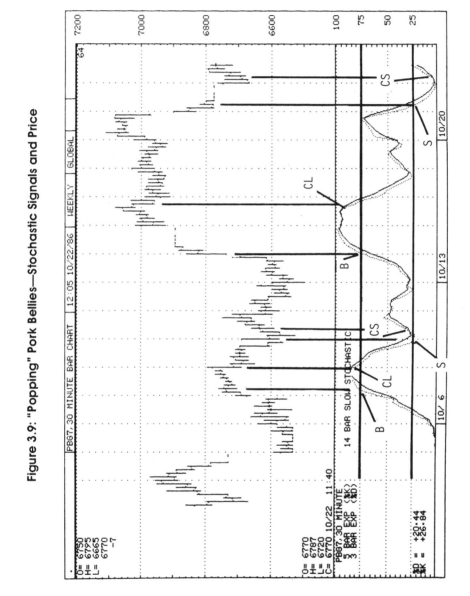

The pork belly market, in spite of its volatility, appears to have good potential for SP trading.

Figure 3.10: Daily Pop Signals and S&P Futures

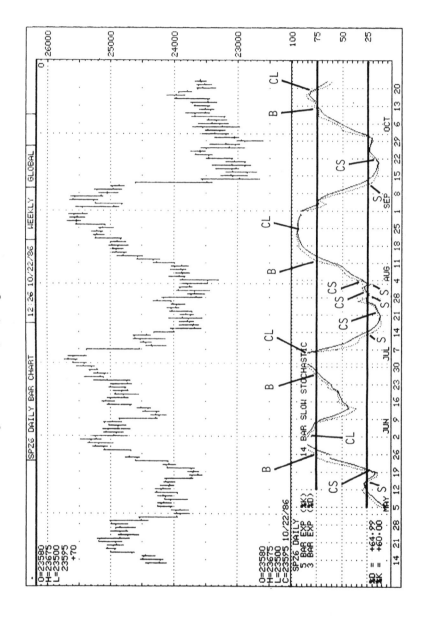

SP signals can be observed and used on daily data as well as on intraday data (see also Figure 3.11).

Figure 3.11: Daily Pop Signals T Bond Futures

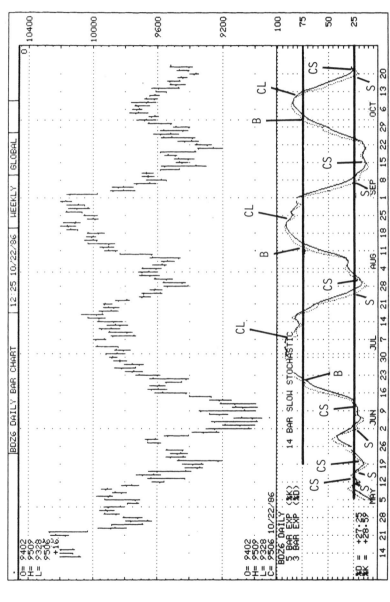

Although this figure, as well as Figures 3-10 and 3-9, show SI POP signals on charts ranging from 30 minutes to daily, the SI POP signals also can be effective on weekly and monthly charts. SI POP signals are not time frame specific. They appear to work in all time frames, regardless of length. I would caution you, however, to be particularly careful when using SI POP on time frames of less than 30 minutes since there can be numerous false signals and relatively small moves which may not make the technique worthwhile, given slippage and commission costs.

charts, but research remains to be done on this. My notes on Figures
3.9 to 3.11 should help you understand the mechanics and implementation of the POP method. Keep in mind that it is best used for
short-term moves in active markets, although POP also has potential
on hourly, daily, and weekly data. Remember that you cannot enter
or exit a POP trade until the time segment you are using has been
completed. In other words, the POP is not calculated on a tic-by-tic
basis, but on the basis of the time segment you are tracking (i.e.,
hourly, half-hourly, five-minute).

CHAPTER FOUR

MOVING AVERAGES

Moving averages, originally introduced by Richard Donchian in the 1950s, have been popular with futures traders for many years. They are among the most widely followed techniques in futures technical analysis. The advent in the Eighties of widely available low-cost computing power has fostered many complex variations on moving averages. Whether these variations ultimately will be of much value is still difficult to assess. However, to the extent that moving averages impose discipline on the trader, they have been helpful. More often than not, moving average systems are the most simple to track, execute, and test. Moving averages, as used in the traditional fashion, are relatively simple to compute, easy to explain and comprehend, and allow entry into strong trending markets. The longer the period of the moving average, the less frequently it will trade.[1]

THE TRADITIONAL USE OF MOVING AVERAGES

The single moving average (MA) is the most elementary example of the traditional use of moving averages. Simply stated, a long position is established when price closes above the moving average for any given period of time. Some traders prefer to see two closing time periods above or below the moving average; others prefer to see a certain percentage closing price above or below the moving average line. This is done in an effort to eliminate so-called false signals. Another variation of this system holds the requirement that one complete price bar (that is, open/high/low/close) be above or below the moving average plot in order to trigger an entry. MA signals are illustrated in Figures 4.1, 4.2, 4.3, and 4.4. Slightly modifying moving average entry minimizes the number of false starts so characteristic of moving averages. This frequency of false starts—or "whipsaws"— constitutes the weakness of all moving average systems. Figure 4.5 illustrates several such occurrences on a short-term basis. Figures 4.6 through 4.10 show the basic signals.

The concept of moving averages certainly has validity in a trending market. However, MA systems tend to get into trouble in non-trending markets or in markets that fail to show a definite direction. In such cases, the MA systems give many signals, and most of these result either in breaking even or in a loss. Figure 4.6 is a half-hour chart showing two different moving averages. My work suggests that a moving average period of less than three time units may be too short for most applications and that a moving average period of more than 30 is likely to be too long for most applications. Based on initial indications, somewhere between 12 and 18 time units seems to work best; an 18-unit period is one of my favorites.

In sideways or trendless markets, moving average systems tend to take most of their losses, which all too often prove greater in their sum total (including commissions) than all the money made during trending markets. Hence, technical analysts have spent considerable effort and funds attempting to improve their systems by optimizing, or finding "best fit" moving averages to the markets. Whipsaws also have led technical analysts to employ additional moving averages as checks and balances and to impose specific initial dollar risk levels as stop losses. Figures 4.11 to 4.13 introduce a technique using two MAs, one as a trend indicator and the other as a timing tool. (More discussion about this later on.)

HOW MAs WORK (TRADITIONAL USE)

The traditional approach for one MA is incredibly simple and specific. The common rules are: (1) go long when the close of the time frame

Figure 4.1: 18-Period Moving Average Signals: Intraday Chart

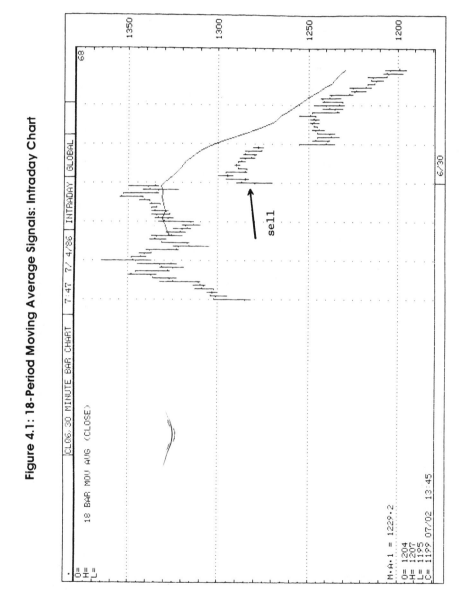

A 30-minute price closing under the 18-period MA triggers a Sell signal.

Figure 4.2: 18-Period Moving Average Buy and Sell Signals: Intraday Chart

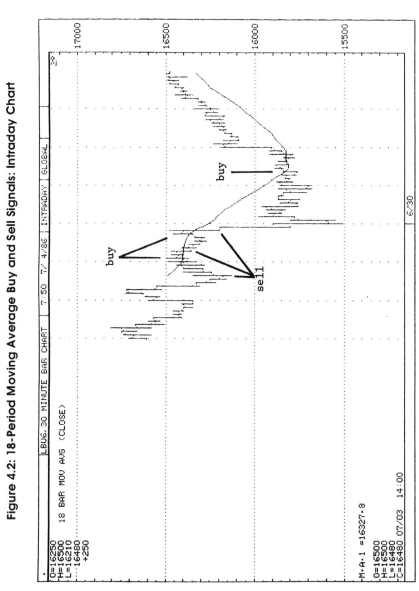

Buy signals trigger on a 30-minute close above the 18 MA; Sell signals on a close below the 18 MA.

Figure 4.3: 18-Period Moving Average Buy and Sell Signals: Intraday Chart—60 Minutes

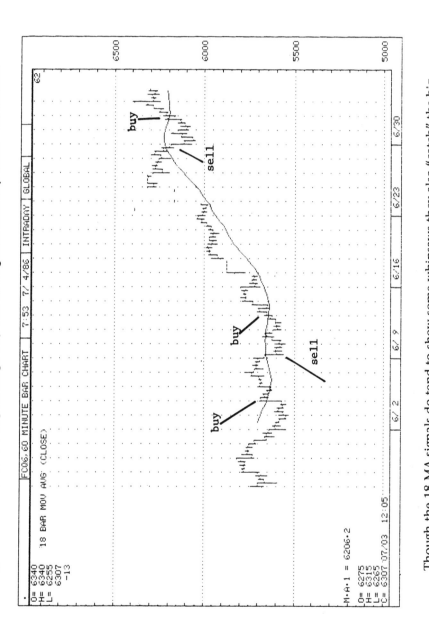

Though the 18 MA signals do tend to show some whipsaws they also "catch" the big moves.

Figure 4.4: 18-Period Moving Average Buy and Sell Signals: Intraday Chart—30 Minutes

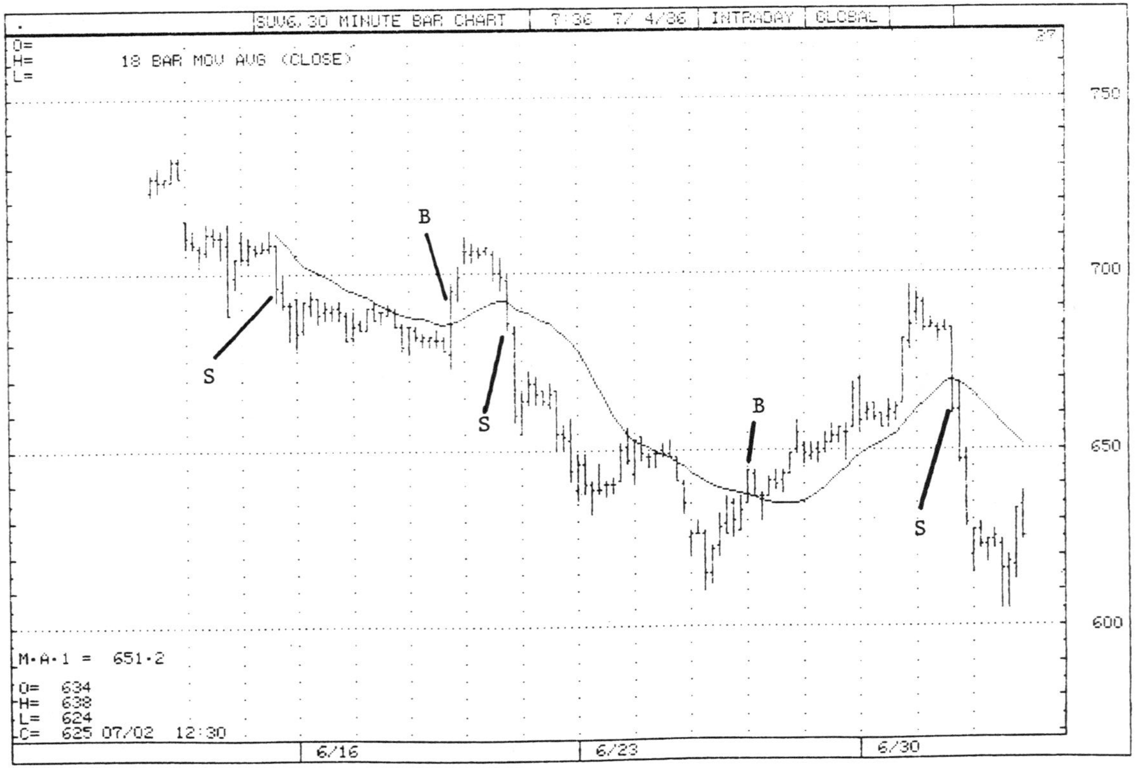

Figure 4.5: Moving Average Signals showing Whipsaws at (a), (b), and (c)

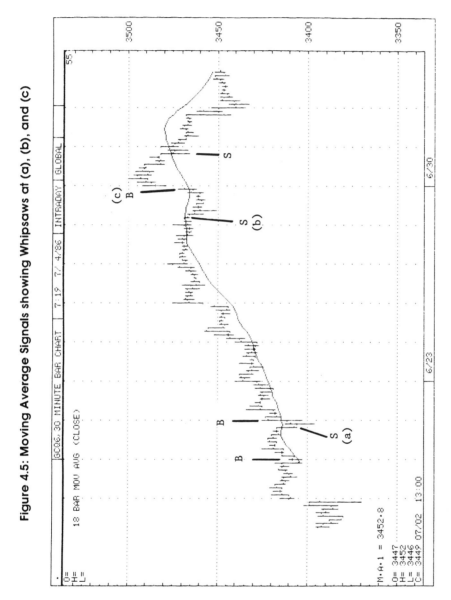

Perhaps the single most serious drawback of simple MA systems is the large number of whipsaws.

Figure 4.6: 2 Moving Averages and 1/2-Hour Chart

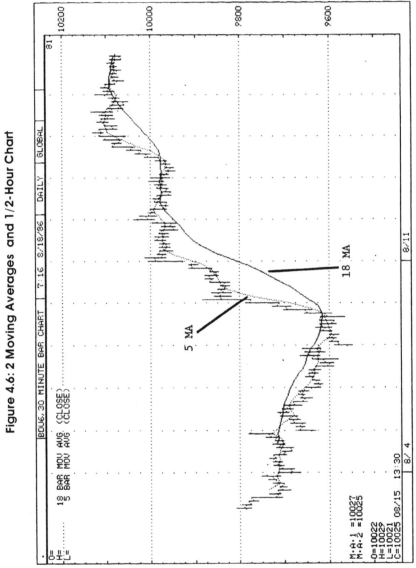

The use of two MAs can filter out some whipsaws. In this case, signals occur when price bars close above or below both MAs.

Figure 4.7: Traditional Moving Average Signals. Note Whipsaw at (a)(b).

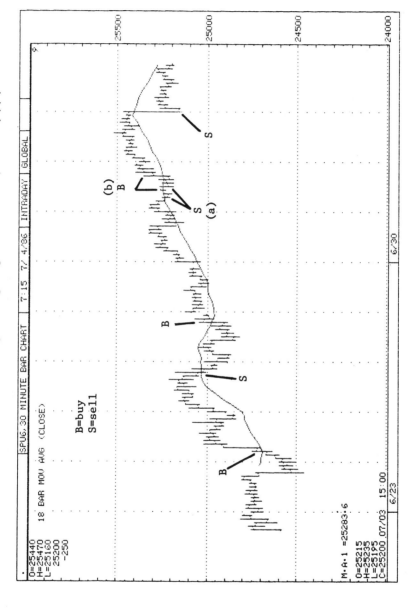

This chart further illustrates the one important drawback of traditional moving average systems.

Figure 4.8: Traditional Moving Average Signals Showing Propensity for Whipsaw Signals

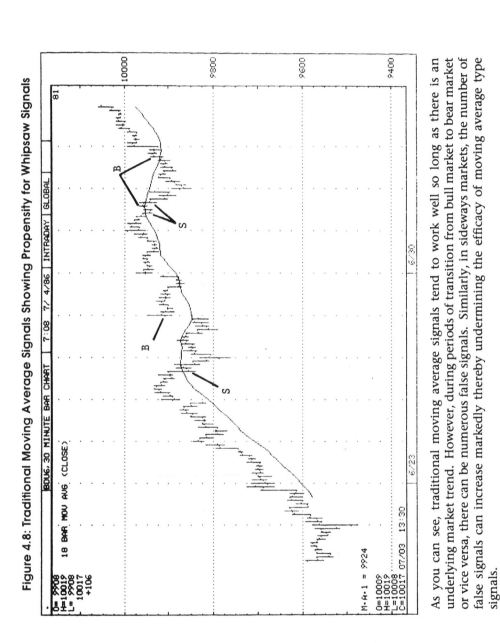

As you can see, traditional moving average signals tend to work well so long as there is an underlying market trend. However, during periods of transition from bull market to bear market or vice versa, there can be numerous false signals. Similarly, in sideways markets, the number of false signals can increase markedly thereby undermining the efficacy of moving average type signals.

Figure 4.9: Traditional Moving Average Signals During A Strong Uptrending Market.

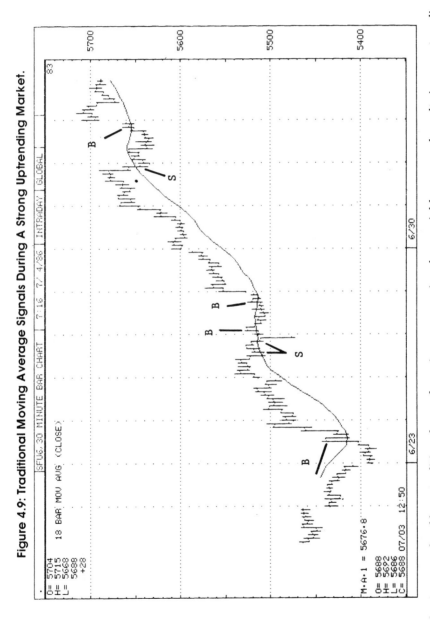

Here is a classic example of how traditional use of moving average signals can yield very good results in an uptrending market. Naturally, this is an ideal situation, one which shows moving averages at their best. Ideally, traders will experience or encounter such situations relatively infrequently. The more realistic situation would be one during which there are numerous losing signals during periods of transition or sideways market movement. It is these situations which much be addressed when critically examining any trading system whether moving average-based or not.

Figure 4.10: Traditional Moving Average Signals During a Strong Downtrending Market. (Note the absence of whipsaws)

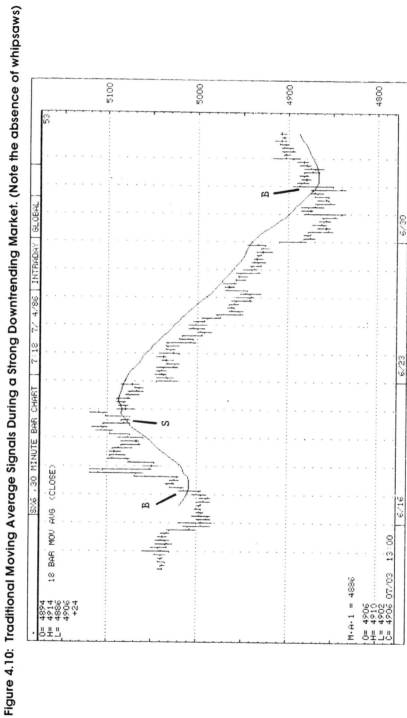

Figure 4.11: 18-Period and 5-Period Short-Term Trading Approach

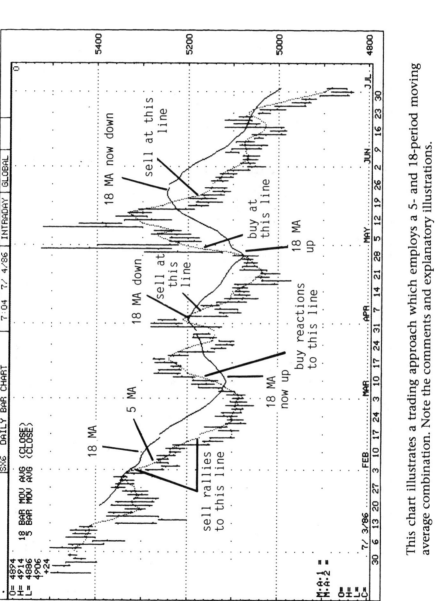

This chart illustrates a trading approach which employs a 5- and 18-period moving average combination. Note the comments and explanatory illustrations.

Figure 4.12: 18-Period and 5-Period Short-Term Trading Approach

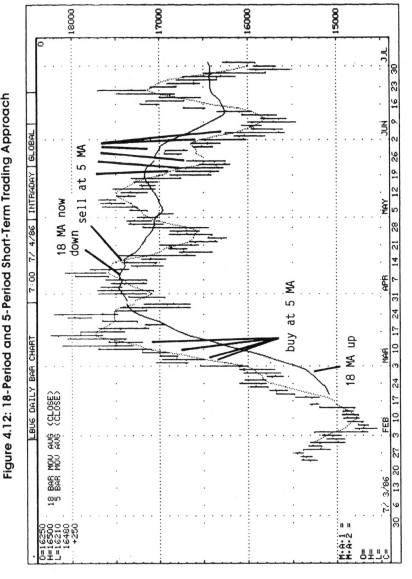

Another look at the 5/18 period approach shows that it can yield many trading opportunities for the active trader. Note the abundance of trades (not all trades are marked).

Figure 4.13: 18-Period and 5-Period Short-Term Trading Approach

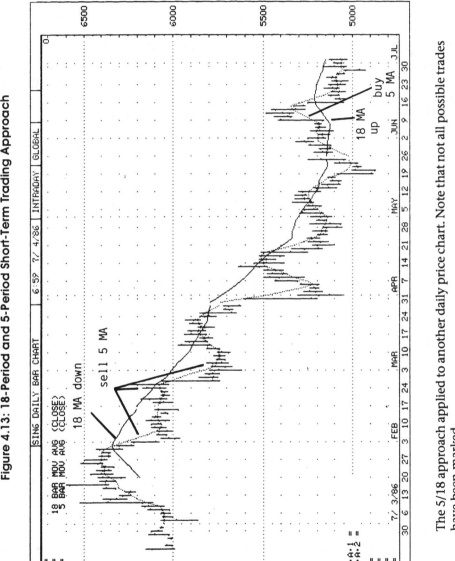

The 5/18 approach applied to another daily price chart. Note that not all possible trades have been marked.

is greater than the close of the moving average for that time frame, and (2) reverse your position when the close of the time frame is less than the close of the moving average in that time-frame. Simple as they sound, there are many ways to pervert or abuse these rules. Figures 4.1 through 4.5 and Figures 4.7 through 4.10 demonstrated the implementation of these guidelines in various types of markets. I have selected markets showing bull trends, bear trends, and sideways or whipsaw trends so that you may see the assets and liabilities of this approach.

Having studied many MA systems, I've arrived at a few interesting twists that have potential for the day trader and the short-term trader alike. The ideal time periods for the day trader are likely to be one-minute, five-minute, and/or 30-minute durations. Any time-frame longer than 60 minutes would not be ideal for the short-term trader. Most short-term traders will find half-hour time frames to be ideally suited to their needs.

Using Moving Averages as Support/Resistance and Trend Indicators

An interesting variation on the traditional use of moving averages is their use as support or resistance levels. In uptrends, which, by definition, show price above moving average, the day trader could use the moving average value of the half-hour charts at which to buy in the event of a downside reaction. Conversely, in a downtrend, when prices are below the moving average, the day trader could use the moving average plot as a level against which to sell in the event of a rally. In such approaches, the moving average plot serves as support and/or resistance. Yet this technique, too, can yield many false signals.

A more feasible approach, mentioned briefly in an earlier section, uses two moving averages. One determines the trend and the other determines the ultra-short-term or intraday buying or selling level. Consider this possibility: An 18-unit time period MA is used to determine the trend. If price is above the 18-unit period MA, the trend is assumed to be up. If the price is below the 18-unit MA, the trend is assumed to be down. A second moving average—for example, of five units—could be used as the trigger point against which to establish positions. In a downtrend (based on the previous definition) the five-unit MA could be used as a price level against which to sell, in the event of a rally. This approach previously has been shown in Figures 4.11, 4.12, and 4.13. This technique appears to be more sensible than using one moving average for the purpose of buying into support or selling into resistance. It should keep you trading with the trend. It allows you to make quick moves in the markets, and it allows you to day trade on reactions within the trend. You know the trend at the start of each day, and you also know the exact price at which you want to establish your position. The only thing you might not know is exactly where you want to get out. There are ways of dealing with this situation as well, some of which will be discussed shortly. The benefit of this dual MA method is its specificity and comparative objectivity.

Moving Average Channel (MAC)

Consider the possibility of using the moving averages of highs and lows rather than the moving averages of closing prices. A moving average of highs and lows can be graphed as a price channel—the Moving Average Channel (MAC). This channel has specific characteristics which vary with the number of time units assigned to the averages. If, for example, we use a moving average channel comprised of 10 time units of highs and eight time units of lows, then the MAC plotted against price would appear as shown in Figures 4.14 through 4.16. By studying these figures you can see that certain characteristics of the channel become rather evident. To summarize them:

1. Bull trends are defined as those in which price is above or returning to within the MAC.

2. Bear trends are those in which price is below or returning to within the MAC.

3. Markets turn from bearish to bullish when price bars begin to appear outside the top of the MAC. Let's call the top of the MAC the Moving Average of Highs (MAH).

Figure 4.14: MAC and Price on 30-Minute Chart

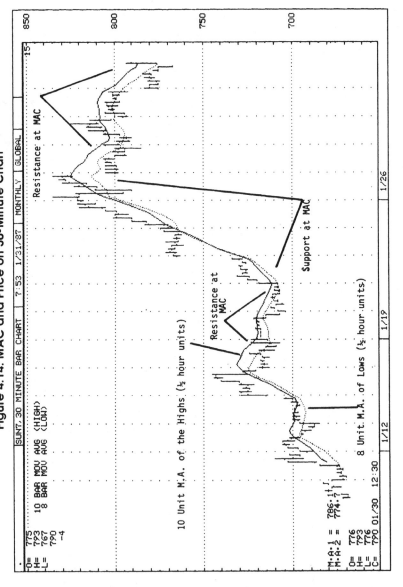

Note resistance in the MAC in downtrends and support in the MAC in uptrends. Observe what tends to happen when price bars fall completely above or below the MAC. Although I have been studying and using the MAC technique for many years now, I still have not found a simpler or more effective method of determining support and resistance. For those who are inclined to trade with the trend, the MAC offers outstanding potential to determine succinct buy and sell points according to the rules I've outlined in this chapter.

Figure 4.15: MAC and Price on 60-Minute Chart

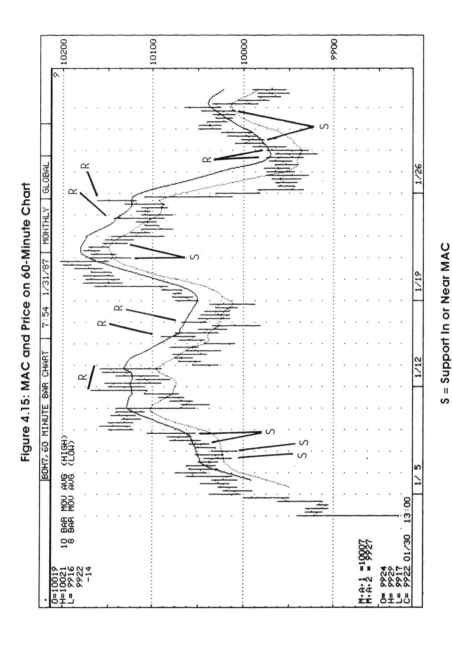

S = Support In or Near MAC

R = Resistance In or Near MAC

Figure 4.16: MAC and Price on 5-Minute Chart

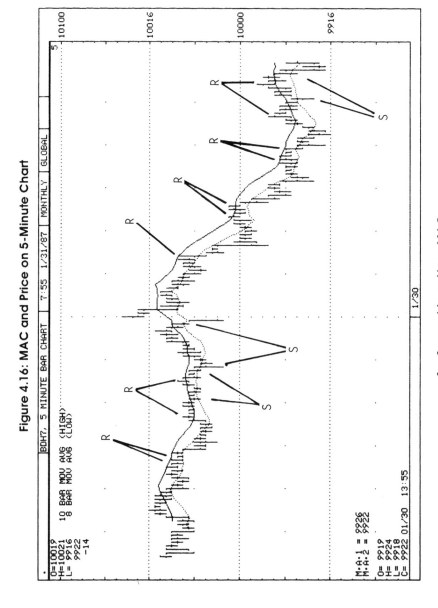

S = Support In or Near MAC
R = Resistance In or Near MAC

Although the MAC is shown here on five minute data, I do not recommend its use on charts of such short duration. I've found the MAC technique to work best on time frames of 30 minutes and higher.

4. A market turns from bullish to bearish when price bars begin to appear outside the bottom of the MAC or the Moving Average of Lows (MAL).

5. Strong bull trends are evidenced by the fact that no portion of the price bar touches the MAH for extended periods of time.

6. Strong bear markets are characterized by the fact that no portion of the price bar touches the MAL for extended periods of time.

7. In bull trends, a return to within the MAC often results in support and, therefore, an opportunity to go long consistent with the trend.

8. In bear markets, a rally to within the MAC often constitutes a rally to resistance and, therefore, an opportunity to go short consistent with the trend.

Illustrations of various techniques using the MAC are shown in Figures 4.17 through 4.19.

The MAC, as a moving average technique, has the same drawback (false signals) as all other MA approaches. Yet, for the purpose of determining trend support and/or resistance, as well as for the purpose of isolating major moves on a short-term basis, the MAC seems to have good potential with fewer false signals. The MAC can be used more objectively by adding a third moving average, which can be varied in length to yield fewer or more trades. A three-unit period moving average of the close, used with the MAC, can yield some very interesting results—see Figures 4.20 through 4.22 . These figures show a channel consisting of 10 units of the high, eight units of the low, and three units of the close. When the three-unit period MA of the close closes above the MAH, a buy signal is generated. When the three-unit period MA of the close closes below the MAC, a sell signal is generated. Such an approach is best used as a reversing system (always in the market). Its best feature is that it is objective and can be relegated to a totally mechanical implementation. This approach is superb in trending markets but, I hasten to remind you, it is not without its problems in choppy markets. As illustrations of choppy

Figure 4.17: Possible Trading Application of MAC on Intraday Chart

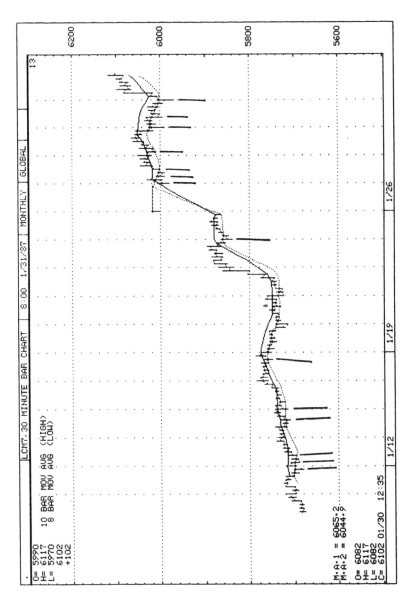

Pointer shows buying on reactions to bottom of MAC (i.e., buy at the MAL). Note: not all buys are shown.

Figure 4.18: Possible Trading Application of MAC on Daily Chart

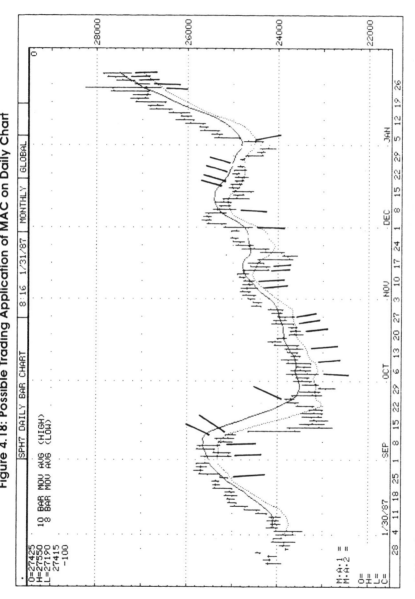

Pointers above MAH show selling on intraday rallies in bear trend. Pointers below MAL show buying on intraday declines in Bull trend—both buys and sells are for short-term trades only. Not all signals are shown. As you can see from the use of the MAC on daily data, the opportunities to buy on reactions to MAC support and sell on rallies to MAC resistance are numerous. As indicated above, not all signals or opportunities have been shown. I suggest you track the MAC on daily charts and intraday charts in order to observe more closely its outstanding potential.

Figure 4.19: Possible Trading Application of MAC with Price Probes and Spikes

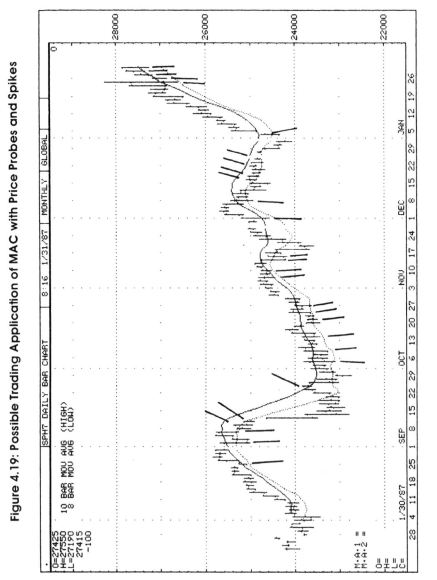

(See Chapter 10 for explanations). Arrows show Sells (S) at PPU and MAC and Buys (B) at PPD and MAC

Figure 4.20: Ideal Buy and Sell Signals on the 10/8/3 Channel

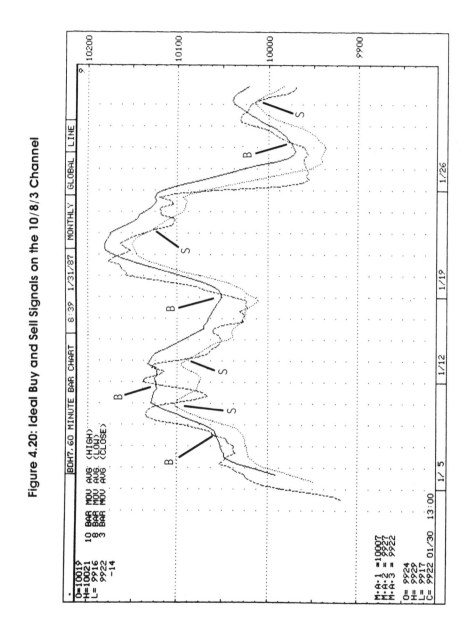

Note that only the MA lines are shown in order to clearly illustrate the signals.

Figure 4.21: Buy and Sell Signals on 10/8/3 Channel Including Price Bars: Intraday 30-Minute Lumber

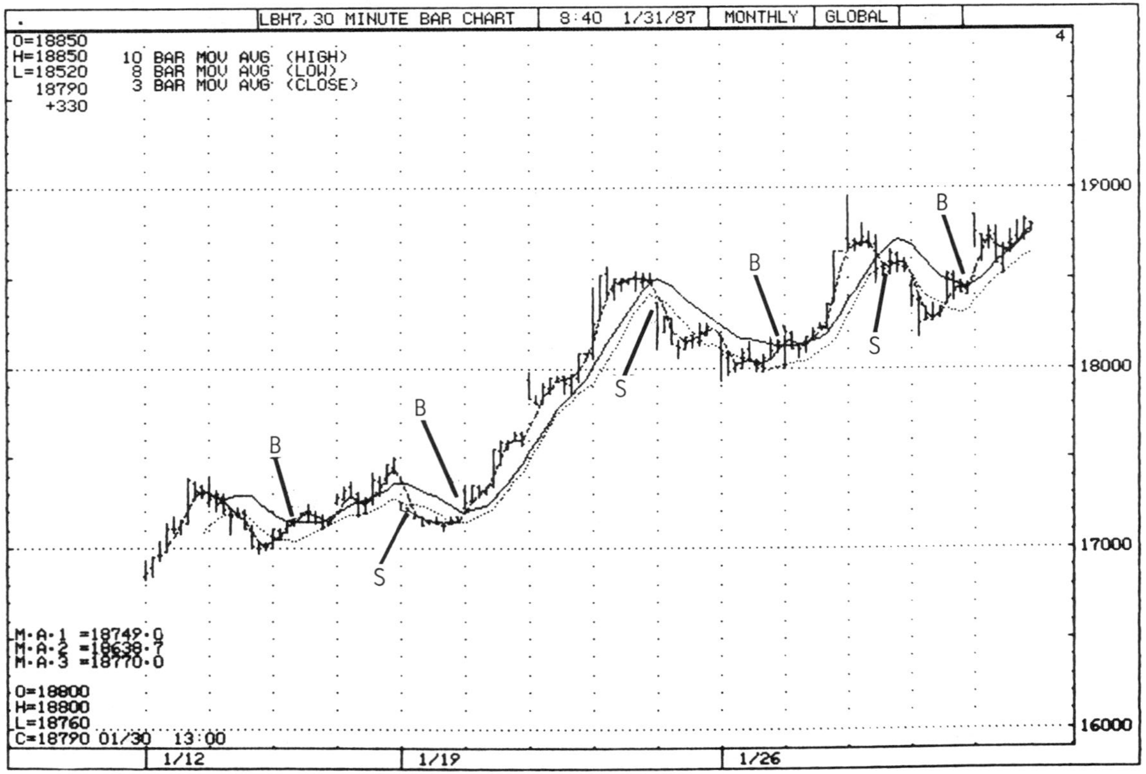

Figure 4.22: Buy and Sell Signals on 10/8/3 Channel: 60-Minute Lumber

markets, I include for your observation and study Figures 4.23 and 4.24.

NOTES

[1] I assume my readers understand how moving averages are computed. If not, then I refer you to my book, *Facts On Futures*, published by Probus Publishing, Chicago.

Figure 4.23: The 10/8/3 Channel in A "Choppy" Market

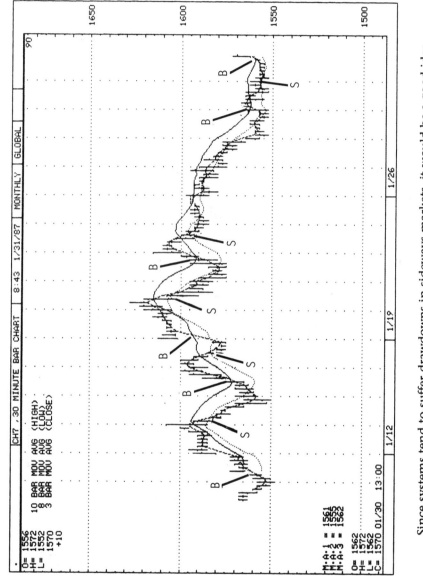

Since systems tend to suffer drawdowns in sideways markets, it would be a good idea for you to examine the shortcomings of 10/8/3 in a "choppy" or inactive market.

Figure 4.24: The 10/8/3 Channel in A "Choppy" Market

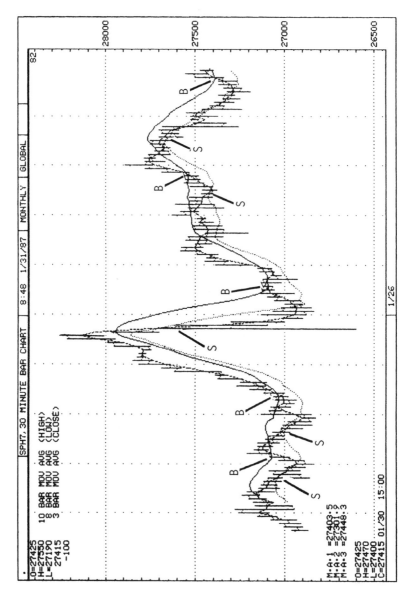

Though 10/8/3 can generate whipsaw signals, it seems to do a good job in catching big moves.

CHAPTER FIVE

CRITICAL TIME OF DAY (CTOD)

Futures traders have long sought to establish intraday parameters that will alert them to potential upside or downside breakouts during any given trading day. Back in the 1970s, I began some fairly intensive research on intraday price/time relationships. I searched for ways in which speculators—particularly day traders—might establish the direction of the market for the balance of the day, or for a fairly good intraday move based upon the market's behavior during the early part of the trading session (i.e., the first few hours.) I made a most interesting discovery: active markets appear to have a critical price frame that is often established during the first two hours of trading. I call this time period the critical time of day (CTOD). It is during these first two hours that ideas of support and/or resistance develop. Once these support or resistance levels are penetrated, price frequently tends to have a fairly good move in the direction of the breakout. Mind you, this is not always so, but it happens often enough and with sufficient magnitude to warrant consideration as a day trading indicator.

CTOD can be used in several different ways, and with several different objectives. I am not entirely certain what makes CTOD a viable methodology, nor am I certain how often you can rely on it.

Whatever its inherent or fundamental value, the fact is that CTOD has alerted me to some of the largest intraday moves, up and down, in the history of the markets.

CTOD DEFINED

The critical time of day is an upside and downside price parameter consisting of the five-minute high and five-minute low "closing prices" in an active futures market. I define an active futures market as having a minimum of 600 price tics (that is, price changes, not total contract volume) during the average day. An average number might be used instead (that is, an average of 600 tics per day during any given week). The five-minute closing high and the five-minute closing low are relatively easy to determine. Note that there may be some minor differences from one quotation system to another. The ideal method for determining these price levels is to use the official ticker from the exchange and the closest possible price to the five-minute closing.[1]

Entry Rules

The entry rules for CTOD are very simple. After the initial two-hour CTOD period ends, a buy signal is triggered on a five-minute close above the five-minute closing high during the CTOD period. A CTOD sell signal will occur if there is a five-minute closing below the lowest five-minute close that occurs during the CTOD period. Typically, when a buy or sell signal has been triggered, there tends to be good follow-through to the upside or downside, most often in the direction of penetration. See Figure 5.1.

An Illustration of CTOD

Figure 5.2 shows how the CTOD works in an ideal situation on the buy side. Figure 5.3 shows how it works in an ideal situation on the sell side. Figure 5.4 shows CTOD trading on both sides during the same day. Examine my notes here as well. It is possible for CTOD to

Figure 5.1: Basic CTOD Model

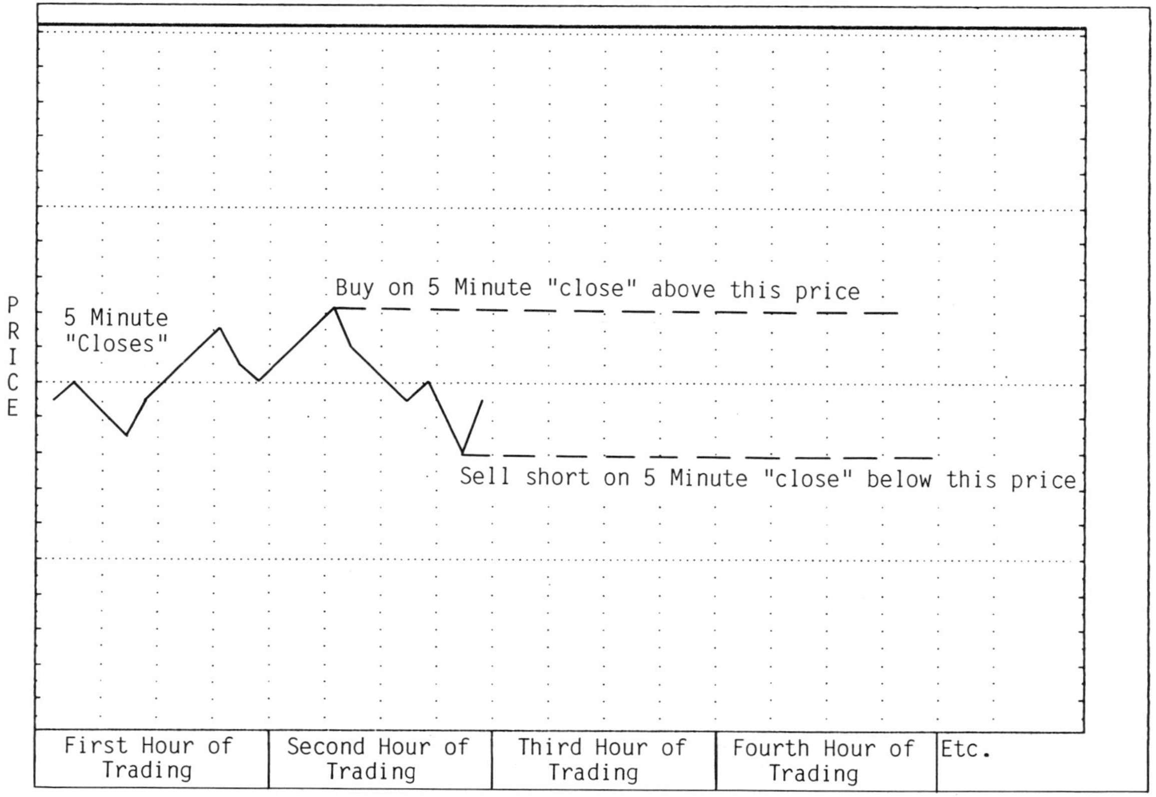

Figure 5.2: CTOD Ideal "Buy" Signal (B)

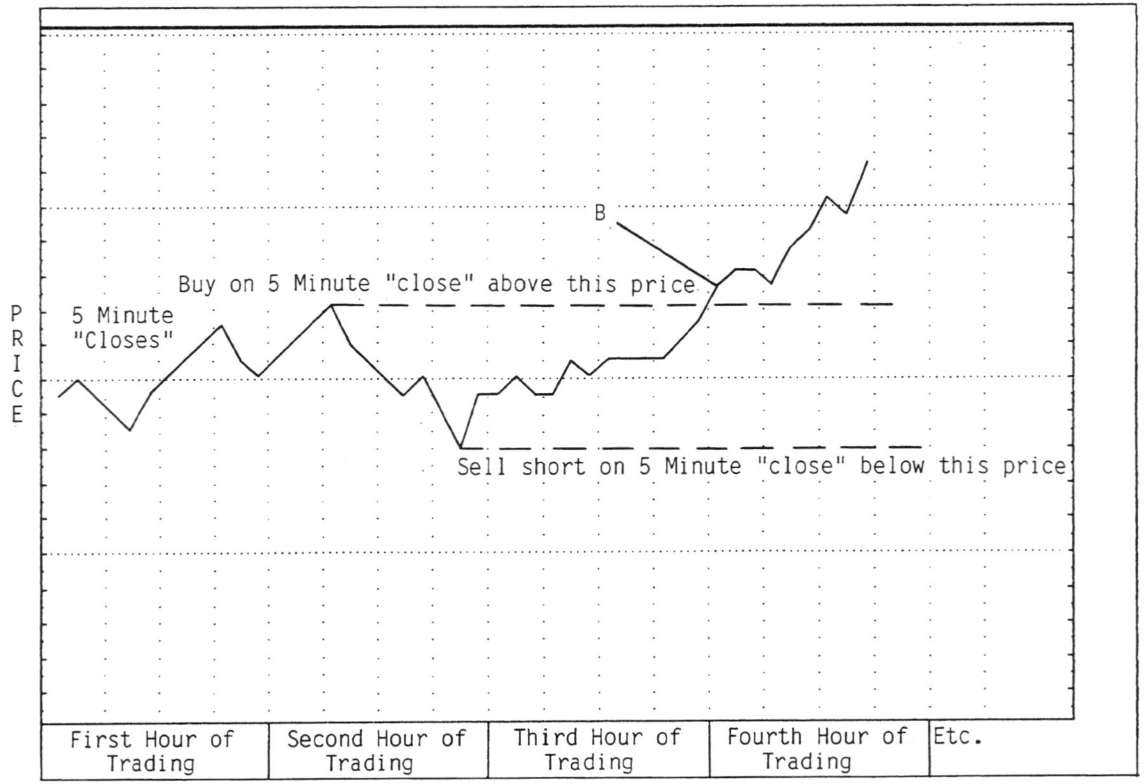

Figure 5.3: CTOD Ideal "Sell" Signal

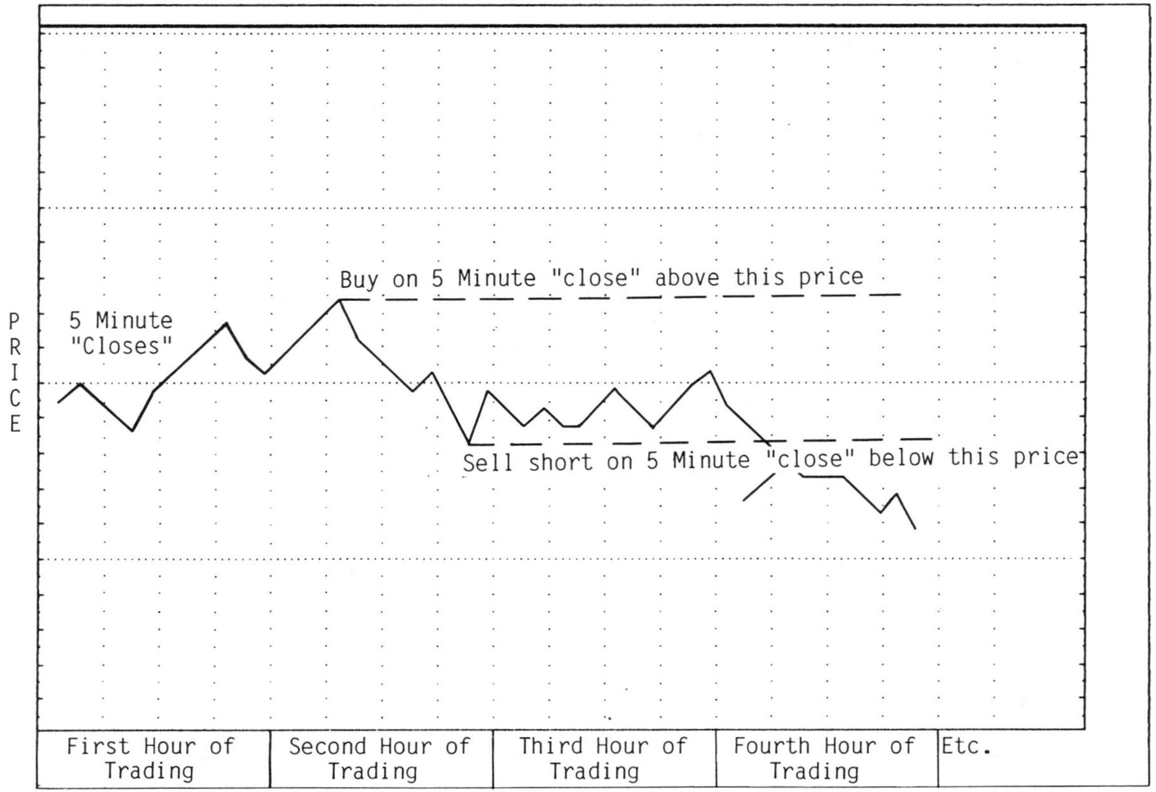

Buy on 5 Minute "close" above this price

5 Minute "Closes"

Sell short on 5 Minute "close" below this price

PRICE

First Hour of Trading	Second Hour of Trading	Third Hour of Trading	Fourth Hour of Trading	Etc.

Figure 5.4: CTOD Signals on Both Sides of the Market During Same Day

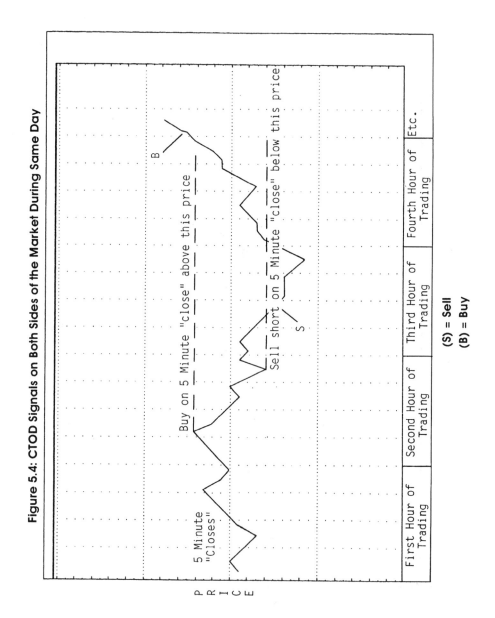

(S) = Sell
(B) = Buy

trigger only two trades per day, but more often than not there will be only one trade per day. If a buy signal occurs first and is followed by a later sell signal, this is valid. The sell should be taken. If a sell occurs first, followed by a later buy, this too is valid. However, once there has been a buy signal, it is the only buy signal possible that day, and vice versa for a sell signal. Many traders have asked me how to re-enter once a trade has been closed out. Using the CTOD in the fashion I have described, I know of no way.

How Often Does CTOD Work?

On the basis of follow-through in the signal direction, regardless of magnitude or duration, I roughly estimate that CTOD will trigger the expected direction more than 70 percent of the time. This is probably a conservative estimate, but remember that follow-through is not as important as is the magnitude of the follow-through. This will vary from one market to another. The astute trader will want to employ other techniques for market exit in order to maximize the potential of CTOD. Figures 5.5 through 5.8 are illustrations of CTOD in a number of markets with different results. Observe my comments and notes. Refer to the following section, "Other Aspects of CTOD," when examining these figures.

When the original version of this book was published in 1987, the futures markets were not as volatile as they have become in the 1990s. This is particularly true in the foreign currencies and stock index futures markets. If you plan on using the CTOD technique, then I suggest you followup your positions once they have been entered with fairly close stop losses and/or use another methodology to allow for trailing stops in order to lock in as much profit as possible. It is not unusual for market to move very strongly in the predicted direction once the CTOD signal has developed, but later in the day to erase its gains due to the immense volatility which has been characteristic of the currency markets in recent years. Another method for capturing the greatest amount of profit possible is to use multiple positions on initial entry which would allow you to take a profit on part of your position while holding the balance of your position strictly in accordance with the exit rules provided herein. I would like to stress very strongly that CTOD is a technique and not a trading system per se. While the CTOD can offer many opportunities to enter

Figure 5.5: CTOD Signal

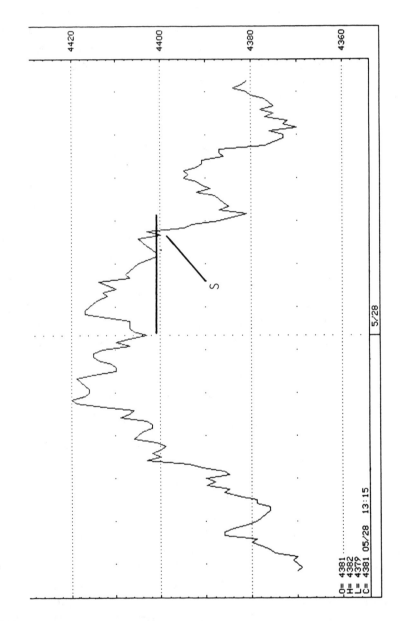

Note that Sell signal was triggered when five-minute "close" fell below the two-hour, five minute "closing" low. Note also follow through to the downside.

Figure 5.6: CTOD Signal

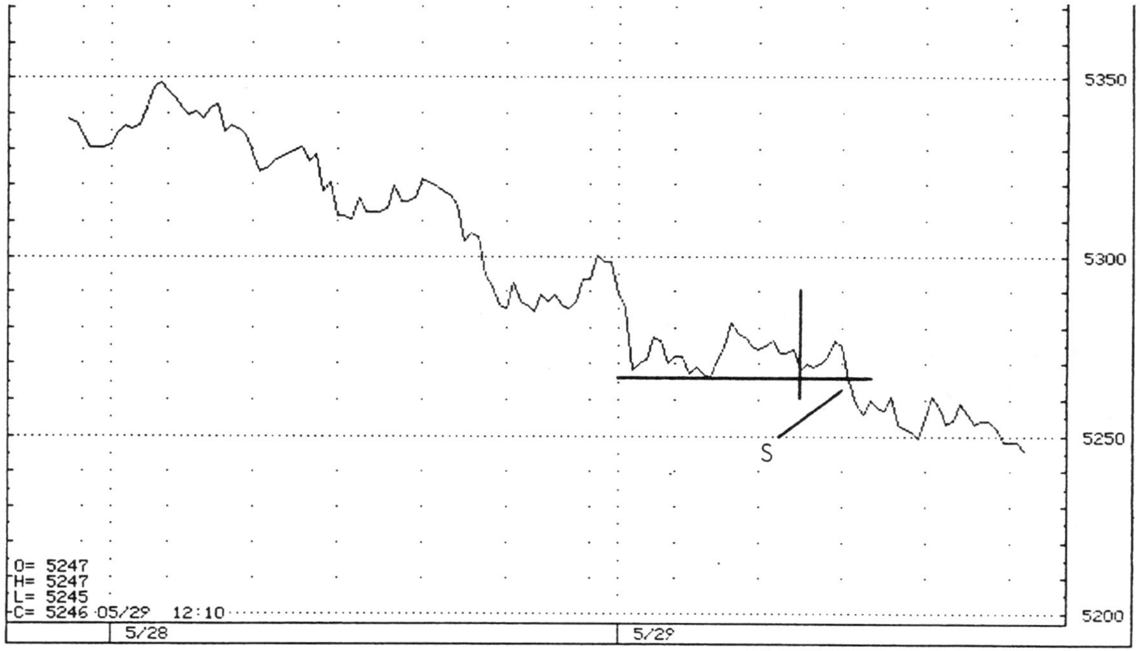

(S = Sell)

Figure 5.7: CTOD Signal

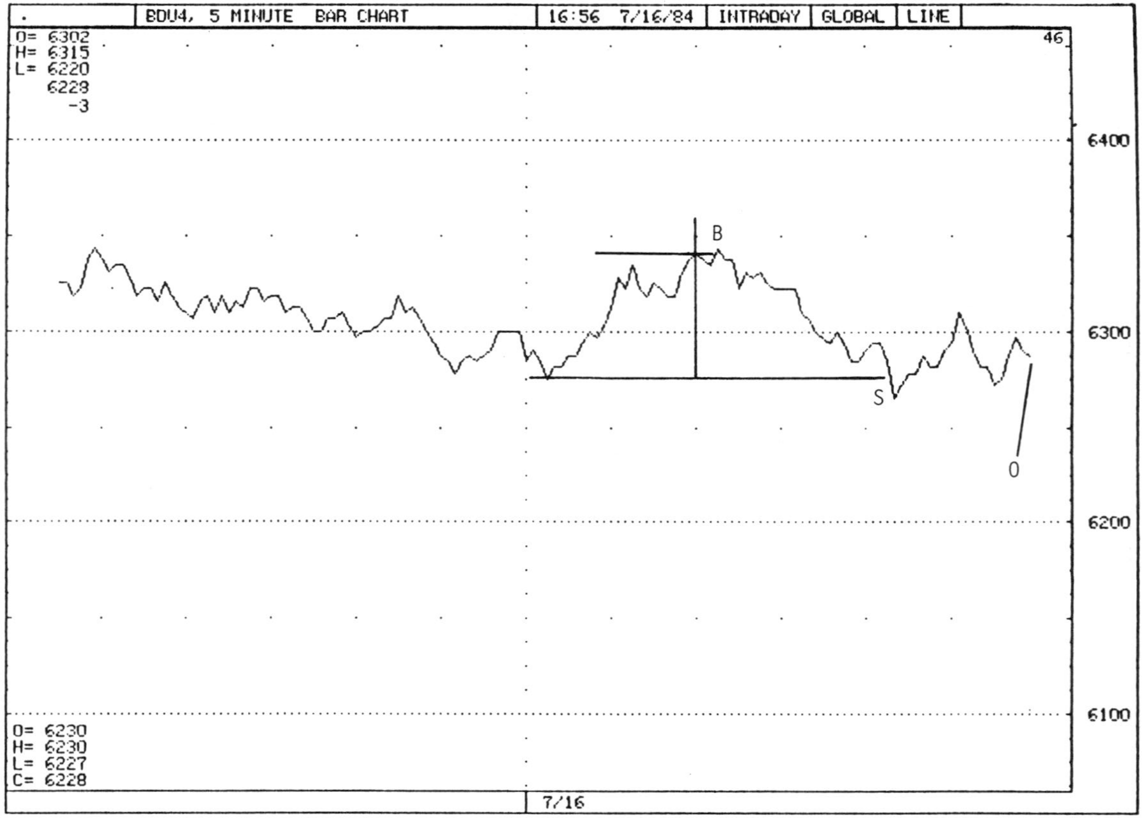

Note that first signal was on long side. The market failed to move up. The next signal was a Sell signal which also failed to produce a profit.

Figure 5.8: Actual CTOD

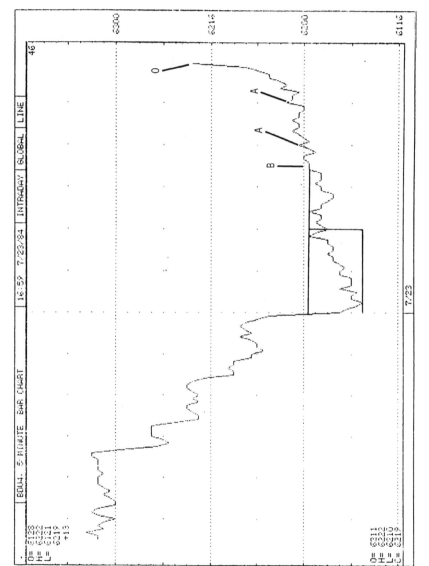

Procedure for going long and adding contracts as original trade becomes profitable.

both the long and short side early in the inception of major market moves, it is, as I have stressed previously, a technique which must be refined and incorporated into the trading style of each individual speculator. In your work with CTOD, you may be able to develop rules which willserve you well. Although I have traded very frequently with this technique, I have developed only the most general rules other than those presented herein. A certain amount of art is necessary in applying this technique successfully.

OTHER ASPECTS OF CTOD

When a CTOD signal has occurred, a number of things tend to happen. They are as follows:

1. On a CTOD buy signal, the market is apt to close higher than the price level at which it penetrated. On a CTOD sell signal, the market is likely to close lower than the price level at which it penetrated. There are exceptions, particularly if the market is at or near limit up or limit down. I will discuss some of these situations shortly.

2. Prices are apt to continue, even if only briefly, in the direction of their penetration.

3. Some very large intraday price moves have been triggered by CTOD signals, particularly on days during or after which major reports have been released. A bearish report the previous afternoon may result in a sharply lower price opening. Prices could trade in a very confined range for the first-two.hour period. Thereafter, they could yield a CTOD buy signal. In such a case, the market could not only gain what it lost from the previous day's close, but could also move plus on the day or even limit up! There have, indeed, been such days.

4. After a CTOD signal, price tends to be higher each subsequent hour or lower each subsequent hour than it was on the penetration, depending upon which way the penetration occurred. In the case of a sell signal, the high for each hour typically

tends to occur early in the hour, with the low coming late in the hour. The reverse tends to hold true for penetrations to the upside. The aggressive trader could conceivably add to a position at the start of each hour, therebymaximizing return from the existing signal.

SOME IDEAS FOR STOPS

Stops, money management, risk—all of these factors—should be considered by all traders when they research a trading technique. Here are some ideas for risk management with CTOD:

1. **Don't execute a CTOD signal that occurs during the last 30 minutes of trading.** There is simply not enough time to realistically enter a trade, exit a trade and make a profit in such a short period of time, in most cases.

2. **Trade for specific price objectives.** Calculating the average price move (up or down) following a CTOD signal during the last 10 to 15 trading sessions will give you an idea of what you an expect in the current market. This will give you a price objective. Thereafter, you can either take the profit or actually put in a stop/loss that will cover your commission and make a small profit as well (providing the market has traveled far enough in the expected direction).

3. **An initial stop upon entry could be used at a predetermined dollar risk level consistent with your account size.** A five-minute closing stop loss below the previous hour's closing low is often an effective risk-management tool for longs. For example, if T Bonds give a CTOD signal to go long on the hour from noon to 1 p.m., a good stop would be a five-minute close below the five-minute closing low of the hour from 11:00 a.m. to noon. the reverse would hold true for stops on sell signals.

4. **A stop could be moved to each previous hourly five-minute low or high at the end of each hour.** Another

method of following up a CTOD trade is by adjusting the stop loss each hour after the trade has been initiated. You can employ any of three techniques, depending upon the specific opening time for the market(s) you are trading. Some markets open for trading each business day on the hour or half-hour. Grain futures, for example, begin trading at 9:30 A.M. central time, while T Bond futures open for trading at 8:00 A.M. central time. For these markets the stop loss procedure is simple. After you enter the trade, use a stop loss that is one tic below or one tic above the previous clock hour low if you are long, or the previous clock hour high if you are short. The stop loss should only be triggered by a five-minute close or posting beyond the hourly low (if long) or high (if short). In other words, a stop loss cannot be placed with your broker, as there is no way of knowing what the five-minute plot or closing price will be. You may find this a bit confusing, but if you think about it a while it becomes quite clear. Remember that we are not considering anything that transpires between five-minute time segments.

A second technique can be used for markets that do not open on the hour or half-hour. Swiss franc futures, for example, begin trading at 7:20 A.M. central time. In this case you could consider the trading hour as beginning at 20 minutes after each clock hour and adjust the stop loss accordingly. As a third alternative, you can consider the first 10 minutes as a separate segment, beginning with 7:30 A.M. as the first hour for stop loss purposes. Whichever technique you choose, employ it consistently. Remain with whatever choice you originally make in order to avoid confusion.

The CTOD indicator is a very powerful tool. I have found its ability to pick major intraday moves to be quite uncanny. I could present chart after chart, day by day, illustrating its effectiveness. But heed this important note: CTOD is not a trading system—it is merely a method of market entry. You must develop other ways to help you exit positions. These include the use of intraday moving averages as a stop, the MA envelope method, and oscillator methods. But mind you, there are many more possible approaches than the ones I have cited. Use your ingenuity and creativity to develop these.

SOME CAVEATS

Like any other methodology, CTOD is far from perfect. It is merely a method of going with the flow of the market once the market has given some indications as to the direction it will take. It is, in effect, a trend-following approach. Here are some precautions, gained from personal experience, to keep in mind when you attempt to use CTOD:

1. Days on which the first two-hour five-minute closing ranges are rather narrow tend to produce the most surprises and, frequently, larger moves.

2. Be sure to use a method of follow-up (some of which are discussed in other chapters) to get out of a CTOD trade.

3. Make certain that you are out of your CTOD trade by the end of the trading session, win, lose, or draw.

4. Once a CTOD trade has moved in your favor, do your best to ensure that the profitable trade does not turn into a loss. As a rule of thumb, once a trade has moved in your favor by about $150 (an arbitrary value, which you may decide to change over time) you should make certain that you'll be able both to pay your commission and make a small profit as well if the trade turns against you. (As you know, the cost of commissions is significant.)

5. If a market has made a large move up or down by the time a CTOD signal occurs, evaluate how much potential there may be in the direction of the given signal. For instance, if a CTOD buy has been triggered with the market only a few tics away from a limit up, then the upside potential for the trade is limited. The day trader might do best to wait for the possibility of a CTOD sell signal instead of taking the buy.

6. Study, track, and observe CTOD until you feel comfortable with it. This technique is not for everyone and, as I've stated, it has its weaknesses. One should not overestimate its potential or follow it blindly simply because it has shown some spec-

tacular intraday performance in the right kind of market. On the other hand, the technique should not be discarded simply because it is not as objective or as mechanical as one might prefer.

7. Trade in active markets only and remember that CTOD tends to work best when intraday trading ranges are large.

8. Develop your own style with CTOD. Some traders prefer a "hit and run" approach, entering and exiting quickly. Other traders want to be more methodical, entering on a signal, using a trailing stop, or otherwise attempting to maximize profits on each trade.

9. Because there is often a small setback following an immediate response by the market in the direction of the CTOD signal, some traders may find it beneficial to wait for a bit of retracement once a CTOD trade has been triggered. Though the technique of waiting for a setback has merit, it also has one clear-cut drawback: the setback might not come.

Let me add in closing that I have spent many, many hours studying and researching CTOD, and I encourage my readers to do likewise. Ultimately, each individual must define how much risk he or she is willing to take, determine where and when the profits should be taken, and implement the system accordingly. Though they do exist, ideal situations—those in which one's path is clear—should not be expected; nevertheless, it is possible to gain a good sense of how to use the CTOD approach regularly and profitably. Finally, there may be other CTODs that have even better potential than the two-hour period. I suggest this as a possible direction for the reader's own research.

NOTES

[1] It should be noted that there is no official five-minute "closing price." I define this price as the price at the end of each five-minute period, or that price closest to the end of each five-minute period.

CHAPTER SIX

THE DUAL EXPONENTIAL MOVING AVERAGE (DEMA)

The Dual Exponential Moving Average (DEMA) consists of two indicators. The first is an oscillator, and the second is a moving average of the oscillator. The oscillator is calculated by computing two exponential moving averages and subtracting them. An exponential moving average of the oscillator is then calculated. The result yields two values. Mr. Gerald Appel of Signalert[1] has done considerable work with what he calls MACD (I call it DEMA), particularly in the area of stock index futures. MACD stands for "Moving Average Convergence/Divergence." DEMA, as I use it, can be applied to intraday, daily, weekly, and monthly charts.

The basics of the DEMA are simple:

1. The DEMA is a reversing indicator; when a long is closed out a short is established, and vice versa, if you plan to use DEMA as a system.

2. Signals are generated when the two DEMA values cross.

Figure 6.1 is a chart of the DEMA without price. I have marked the buy and sell signals accordingly. Figure 6.2 is the same DEMA plot with price above it and with buy/sell signals. Though I am still working on the uses of this indicator, I have found it especially helpful on the daily and intraday charts, as well as in the analysis of spread charts. I suggest you examine the DEMA as a potentially valuable tool for optimizing cyclic timing.

CALCULATIONS AND FORMULAE

DEMA can be calculated according to the following formulae and procedures:

1. Determine the length of the exponential moving average. The first step is calculating the coefficient using this formula:

    $$\text{COEFFICIENT} = \frac{2}{n + 1}$$

    where n = number of time units in the moving average. (For the sake of example, we'll choose nine periods.)

2. Compute the MA as follows:

    VALUE = (closing price - MA × coefficient) + previous VALUE

3. Compute the second exponential average, using the same procedure.

4. Subtract one from the other. This gives you the OSCILLATOR value.

5. Calculate an exponential MA of the oscillator. This gives you the AVERAGE value.

The oscillator and average values are compared with each other for the purpose of generating buy and sell signals. As demonstrated above, anyone with a bit of mathematics background can easily calculate these values.

Those who have a Commodity Quote Graphics system can input these values and obtain the readings. The intricate mathematical computations of DEMA are worth the "clean" signals it tends to

Figure 6.1: DEMA on 30-Minute S&P Chart Showing Buy and Sell Signals

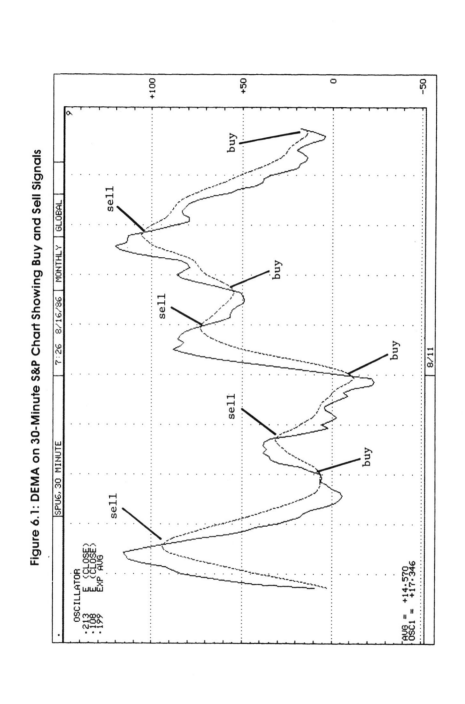

Figure 6.2: Same as Figure 6.1 Showing DEMA and Price

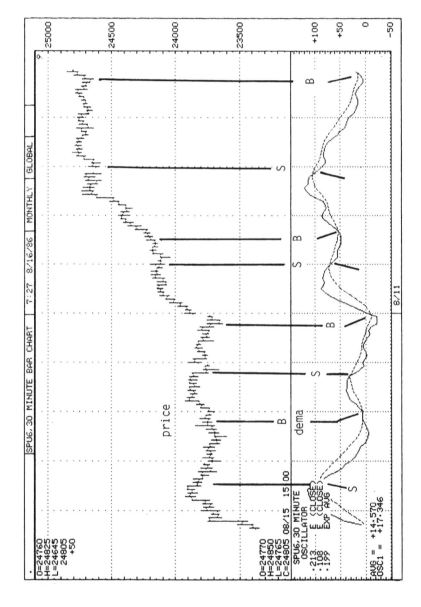

Note that DEMA is a sensitive indicator, not prone to many whipsaws.

generate. DEMA tends to turn quickly at tops and bottoms. It frequently avoids whipsaw-type signals that could bump you out of the market before a trend has changed direction. Furthermore, the DEMA does not become "overbought" or "oversold." It can yield buy or sell signals at virtually any level.

DEMA does not require the use of a chart for spotting signals; you need only look at the numbers to see when the values cross. Figures 6.3, 6.4, 6.5, and 6.6 are intraday DEMA charts, along with data printouts to illustrate how the signals develop using the DEMA values alone.[2]

USING THE DUAL EXPONENTIAL MOVING AVERAGE

The precise values used are critical to the sensitivity of the DEMA. I use the following values on my Quote Graphics System: .213 exponential MA, .108 exponential MA and a .199 exponential MA of the difference of the first two MAs. The result is a two-line indicator that generates buy and sell signals on closing crossovers. DEMA, like all timing indicators, is not perfect. When a market has made a sharp move, up or down, the oscillator values tend to signal a turn in the opposite direction while the market fails to respond as expected. This is, of course, where money management and risk limitation come into play. Figure 6.2 shows the basic signals generated by the DEMA. I've found that the use of the DEMA in combination with stochastics, cycles, and traditional trendline analysis nets better overall results than does its exclusive use. (In fact, this combination appears to improve the results of all the indicators I've mentioned.) Examine the intraday chart in Figure 6.7. It shows DEMA and stochastics in combination. Also examine Figures 6.8, 6.9, 6.10, and 6.11 which show the combination of stochastics and DEMA. The merit in combining various indicators should be obvious. The combination is not infallible—astute money management remains a necessity. With this perspective in mind, I think you'll find Figures 6.12 through 6.15 and the accompanying text of interest.

In his *Computer Trading Tutor,* [3] Bruce Babcock discusses the use of DEMA (or MACD) as a timing indicator. The DEMA has been heralded in recent issues of the *MBH Weekly Commodity Letter,*[4] as a very effective timing tool when used in conjunction with other

Figure 6.3: DEMA on 30-Minute Swiss Franc Showing Buy (B) and Sell (S) Signals

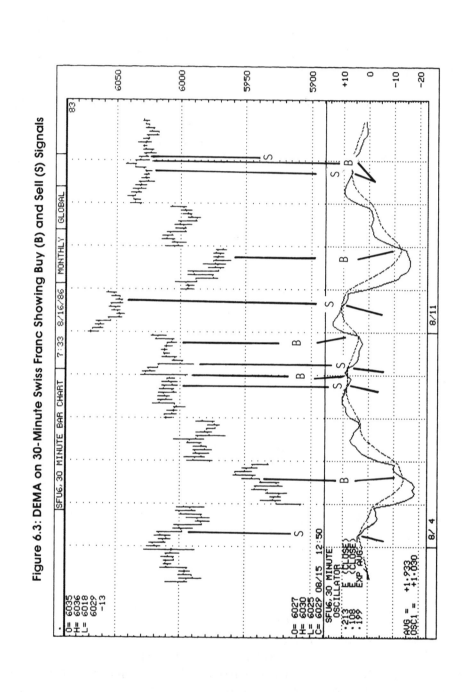

Figure6.4: DEMA on 30-Minute T Bonds Showing Buy (B) and Sell (S) Signals

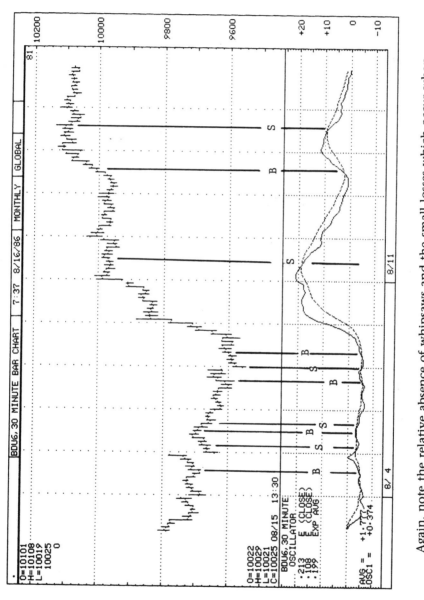

Again, note the relative absence of whipsaws and the small losses which occur when there are whipsaws.

Figure 6.5: DEMA on 30-Minute Silver Showing Buy (B) and Sell (S) Signals

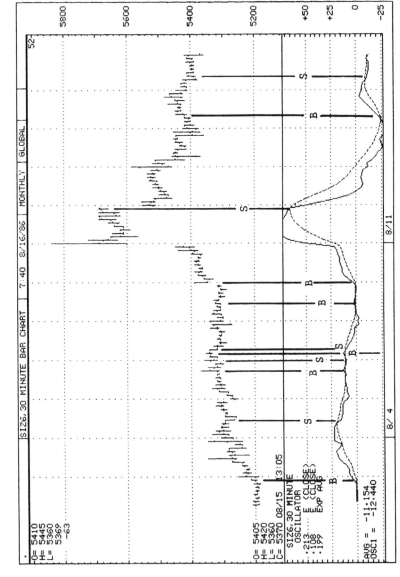

Note the ability of DEMA to signal large moves, which more than compensate for the frequent but small losses on this chart.

Figure 6.6: DEMA on 5-Minute S&P Showing Buy (B) and Sell (S) Signals

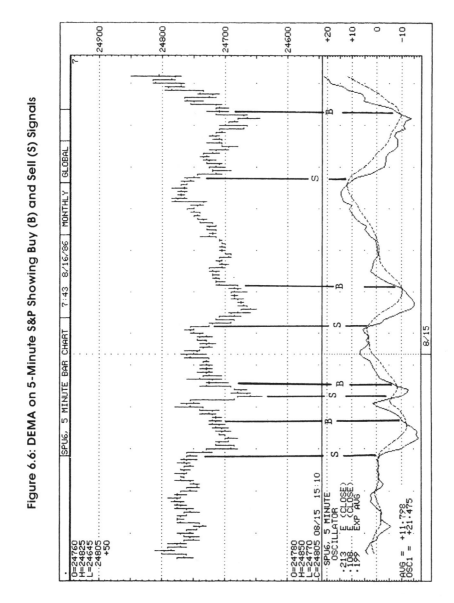

Though DEMA can be used on an intraday chart of five minutes in length, it should be used in conjunction with other indicators.

Figure 6.7: DEMA and SI on Intraday Chart—Combined Signals

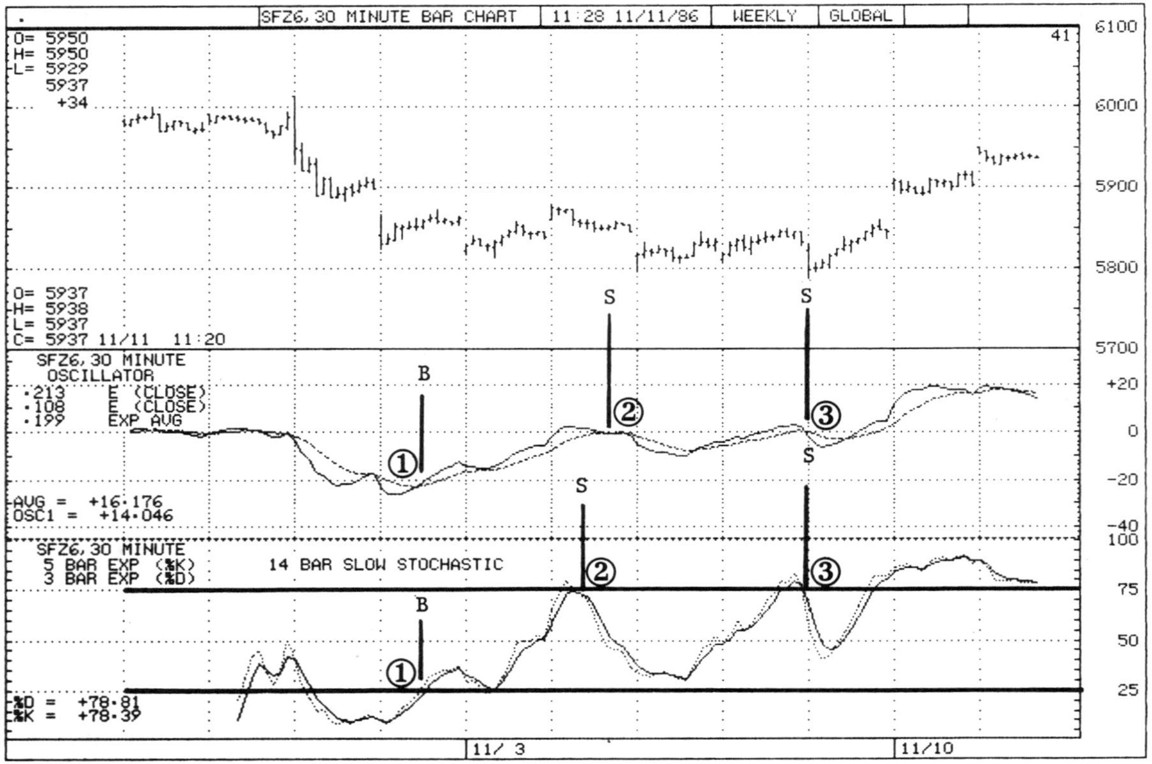

B = Buy, S = Sell

When DEMA and SI are combined, the net result is a more refined approach, one which tends to minimize false signals. Note signals at points 1, 2, and 3, all confirmed by both DEMA and SI.

Figure 6.8: DEMA and SI on Intraday Chart—Combined Signals

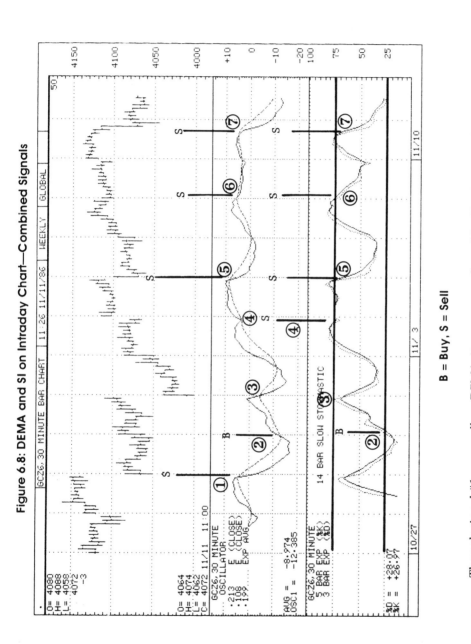

B = Buy, S = Sell

Though signal #1 was a sell on DEMA, it was not confirmed by SI. #2 was confirmed by both, as were #4, #5, #6, and #7. #3 was not a confirmed Sell. Note the strong rally thereafter.

Figure 6.9: DEMA and SI on Intraday Chart—Combined Signals

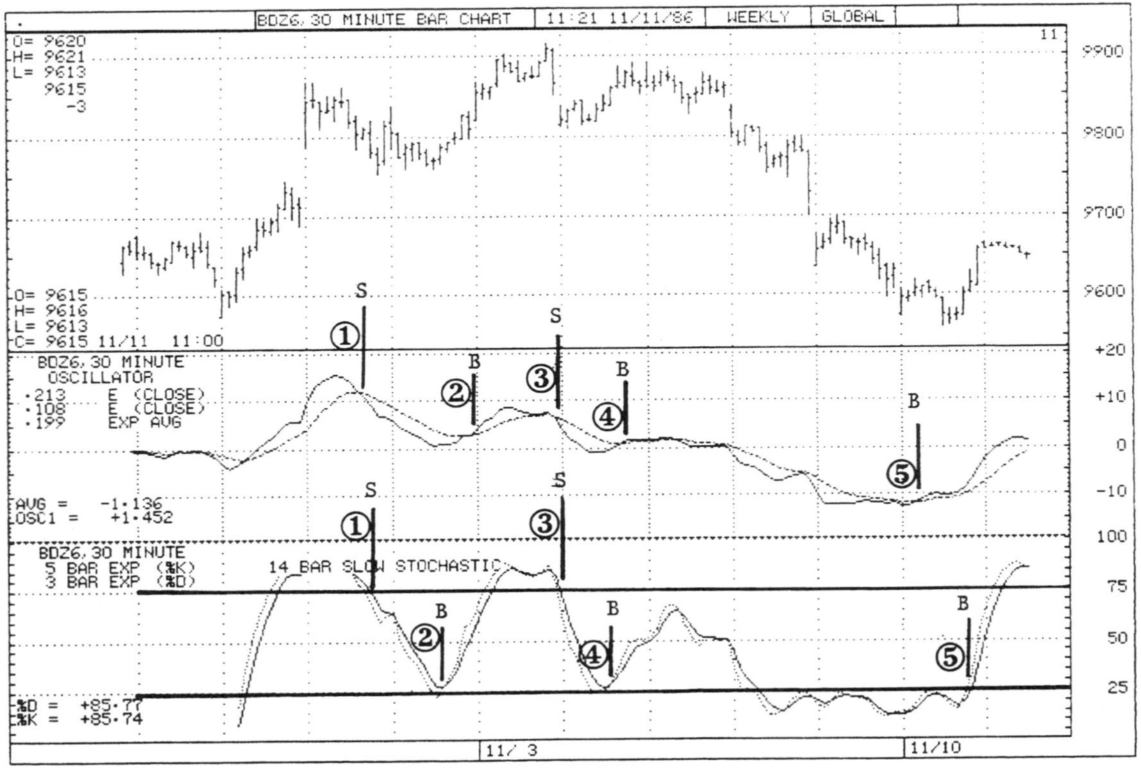

B = Buy, S = Sell

Signals 1-5 all confirmed by both indicators.

Figure 6.10: DEMA and SI on Intraday Chart—Combined Signals

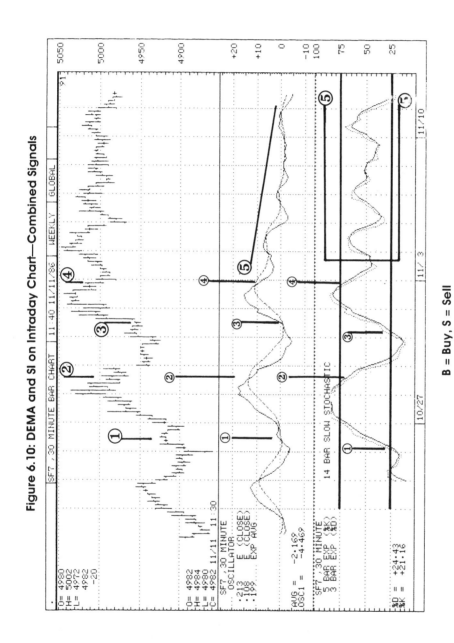

B = Buy, S = Sell

DEMA and SI signals combined. Note that SI tends to turn after DEMA. Note also that while DEMA gave numerous signals from #5 forward, SI did not yield any signals during the same time span (#5), thereby *avoiding* many whipsaws.

Figure 6.11: DEMA and SI on Intraday Chart—Combined Signals

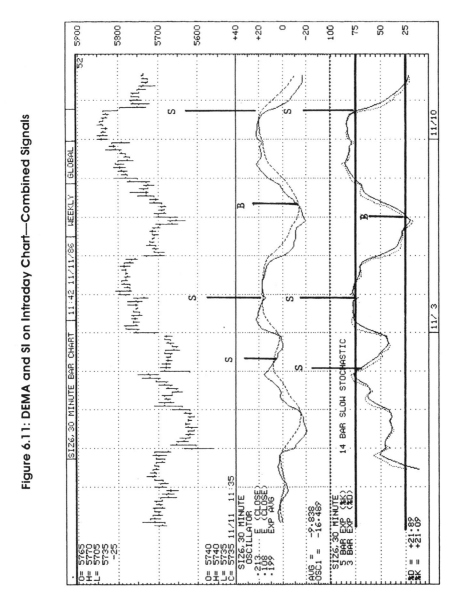

Buy (B) Sell (S)

Figure 6.12: Another Example of DEMA in Short-Term Trading—Combined Indicators

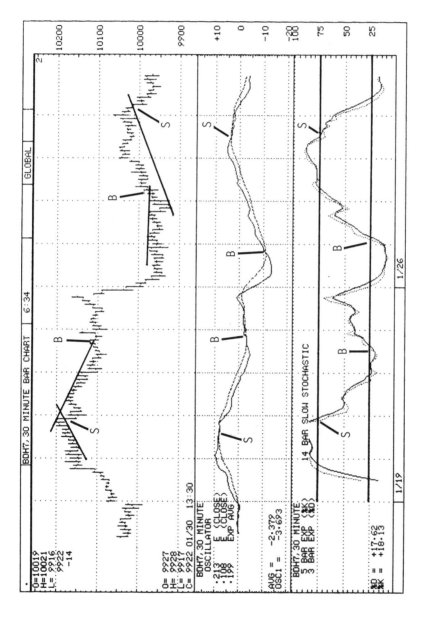

B = Buy, S = Sell

Another interesting combination is to use trendlines in conjunction with SI and DEMA in order to provide additional filtering.

Figure 6.13: Another Example of DEMA in Short-Term Trading—Combined Indicators

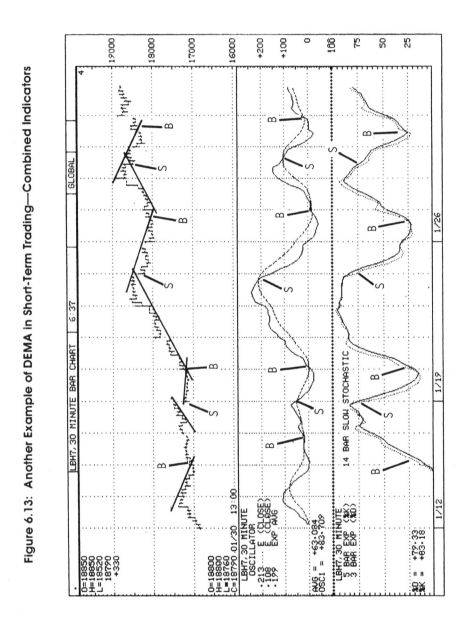

B = Buy, S = Sell

Figure 6.14: Another Example of DEMA in Short-Term Trading—Combined Indicators

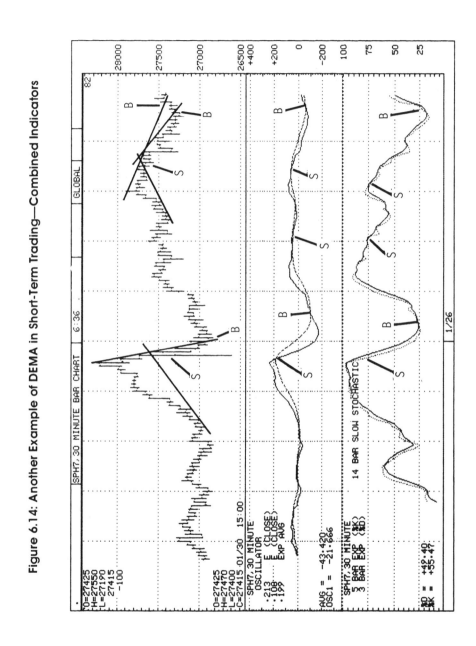

B = Buy, S = Sell

Figure 6.15: Another Example of DEMA in Short-Term Trading—Combined Indicators

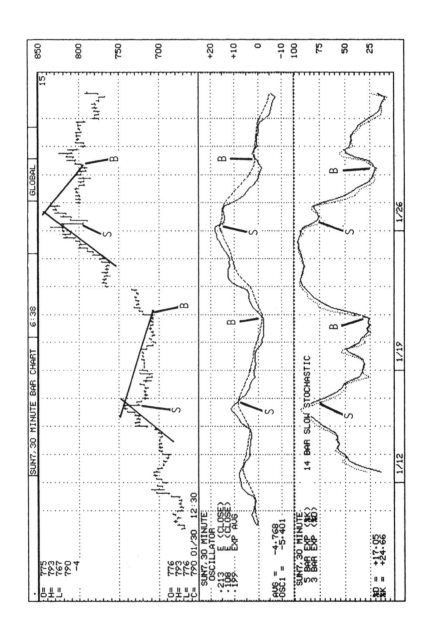

B = Buy, S = Sell

indicators. For those of you who have difficulty computing the DEMA because it requires the use of exponential moving averages, Bruce Babcock points out that the basic DEMA indicators can be duplicatedrather closely without using exponential averages. He suggests using a 12-unit MA of close and 26-unit MA of close for first data point, and a nine-unit moving average of the quantity derived from the calculation above. The signals compare favorably and the plot is smoother than that derived from an exponential average. (See Figure 6.16.)

Although the DEMA has specific values which I've researched, these can change over time and may be adjusted according to the needs of the trader. Furthermore, some values may work better than others. I suggest you do some experimenting on your own until you find the combination which works best for you.

NOTES

[1] Signalert Corporation. 150 Great Neck Road, Great Neck, NY 11021.

[2] Note that many contemporary computer analysis and quotation systems have the facilities to generate exponential MAs; so don't let the mathematics dissuade you. See also values using simple MAs as opposed to exponential.

[3] Babcock, Bruce. *Computer Trading Tutor*. 1731 Howe Avenue, Suite 149, Sacramento, CA 95825.

[4] *MBH Commodity Newsletter*. MBH Commodity Advisors, P.O. Box 353, Winnetka, IL 60093.

Figure 6.16: DEMA Using Exponential Values Compared to DEMA using 12, 26, and 9 MAs

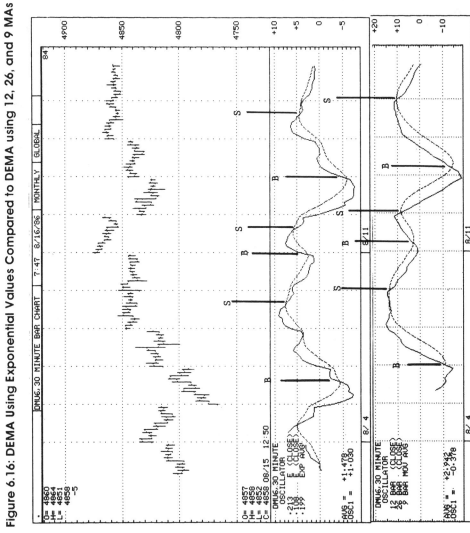

Note that the 12, 26, 9 combination yielded the same number of signals as DEMA; however, the signals came later in every case.

CHAPTER SEVEN

DEMA DIFFERENCE

Chapter 6 examined the Dual Exponential Moving Average oscillator and featured various methods of implementing DEMA with other indicators. The present chapter examines a more advanced application of DEMA, which ultimately may provide a much better indicator for short-term as well as intraday traders. The method of calculating the DEMA difference is, quite simply, to subtract one DEMA value from the other. The rationale behind using the DEMA difference line as a timing indicator exists in the tendency of the DEMA difference to become fairly wide at market turns prior to a convergence, narrowing, and crossing of the DEMA lines (see Figure 7.1). Observe that at point A the indicator lines cross, yielding a buy signal. Shortly afterward, they begin to widen at B, reach their widest point at C, then converge and cross at D, a sell signal. At point E the lines are again at their widest, converging and crossing at F. With one brief narrowing toward the midpoint of their move, they widen again at G, cross at H—yielding a sell signal—widen again at I, cross at J, and so on through N. At point O, the last (or most recent) point on the chart, the lines again converge and a cross to the downside or sell signal is likely. Converging and crossing of the DEMA lines correspond fairly closely to significant market turns.

An easier way to represent the crossings is illustrated by the one-line plot of the DEMA Differences shown in Figure 7.2, with the

Figure 7.1: DEMA Difference Lines Showing Convergence and Crossovers

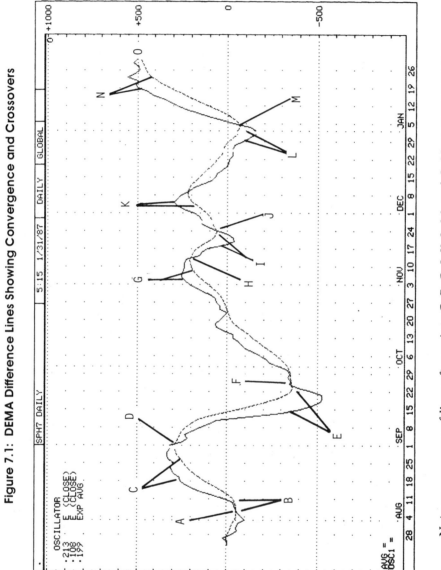

Note convergence of lines after points C, E, G, I, K, L, M, and O. Note crossovers at A, D, F, H, J, and M.

crossings of the DEMA differences being for the same market and time frame as those in Figure 7.1. The only difference is that crossings at the zero lines are marked as buy and sell signals.

Now let's move to Figure 7.3, which shows the DEMA difference line along with the actual price plot for this market. This chart happens to be a daily March S&P, 1987, chart. Examine points A through I and their corresponding price levels to see for yourself why I say that the DEMA difference line is, perhaps, a much simpler indicator on its own than is the DEMA itself.

The calculation of the DEMA difference is most elementary. All you need to do is subtract the two DEMA values from each other. A "+" value indicates a bullish trend, a "–" value indicates a bearish trend, and crosses of the zero line generate signals.

USE ON INTRADAY DATA

Figure 7.4 shows the DEMA difference buy and sell signals on a 60-minute March T Bond chart, and clearly illustrates its validity for determining entry points on the long and short side. I suspect that DEMA Difference has good potential as a reversing approach to the market. Figure 7.5 shows the five-minute S&P chart with the DEMA Difference. In this case, numerous buy and sell signals are generated within the space of a single day. This type of activity may be too much for most traders. It could, in the long run, generate more commission than anything else. However, with different DEMA values to generate fewer signals, and/or with specific price objectives for each of the indicated trades, this technique has excellent promise for intraday trading with 5-, 10-, or 30-minute charts.

SUMMARY

1. The DEMA difference is another way of looking at the DEMA oscillator. Used alone, the DEMA difference has good potential for intraday and short-term trading.

Figure 7.2: DEMA Lines Differenced and Shown as a Single Line Oscillator (see Figure 7.1)

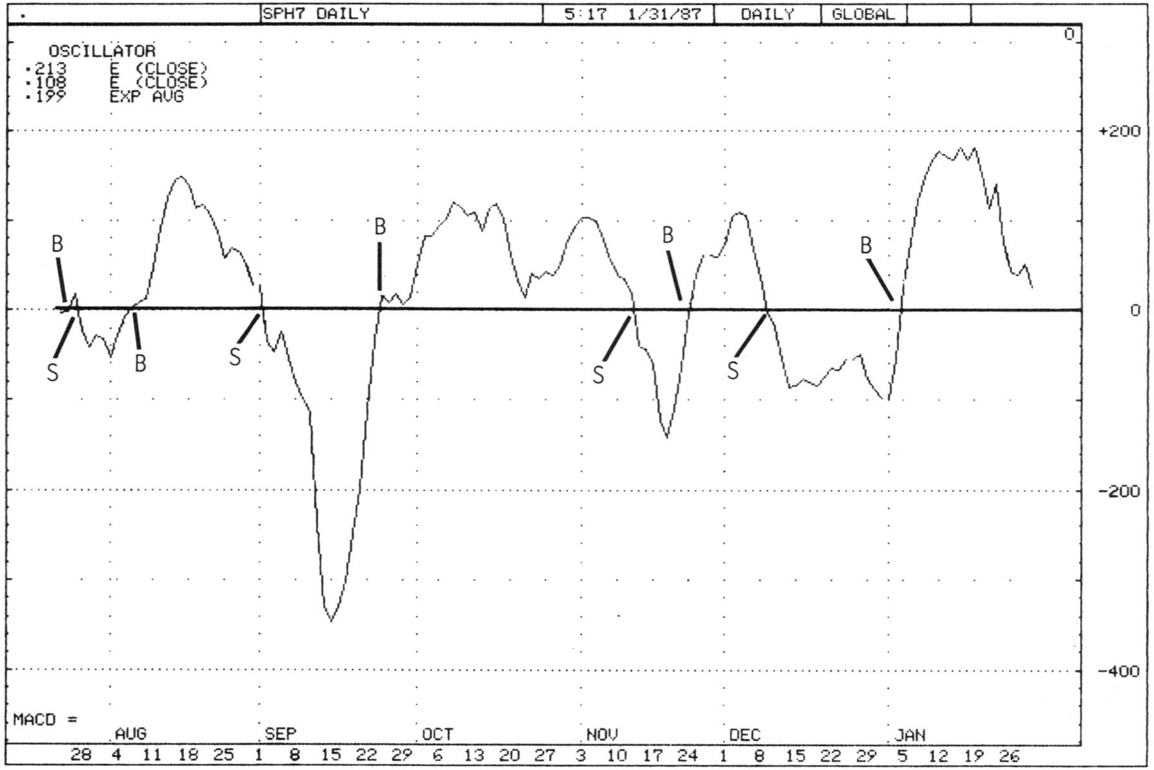

Figure 7.3: DEMA Difference Line Shown in Figure 7.2 Plotted with Price Chart and Buy/Sell Signals A-I

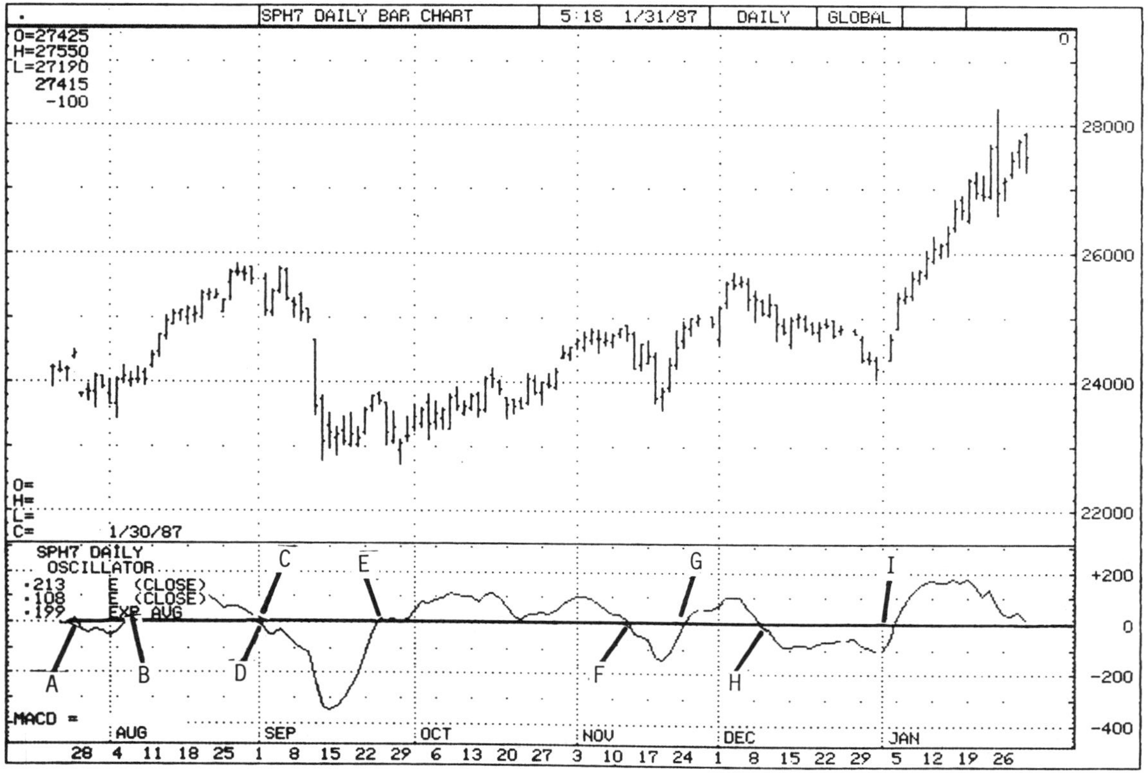

Figure 7.4: 60-Minute T Bond Chart with Buy (B) and Sell (S) Signals on DEMA Difference Oscillator

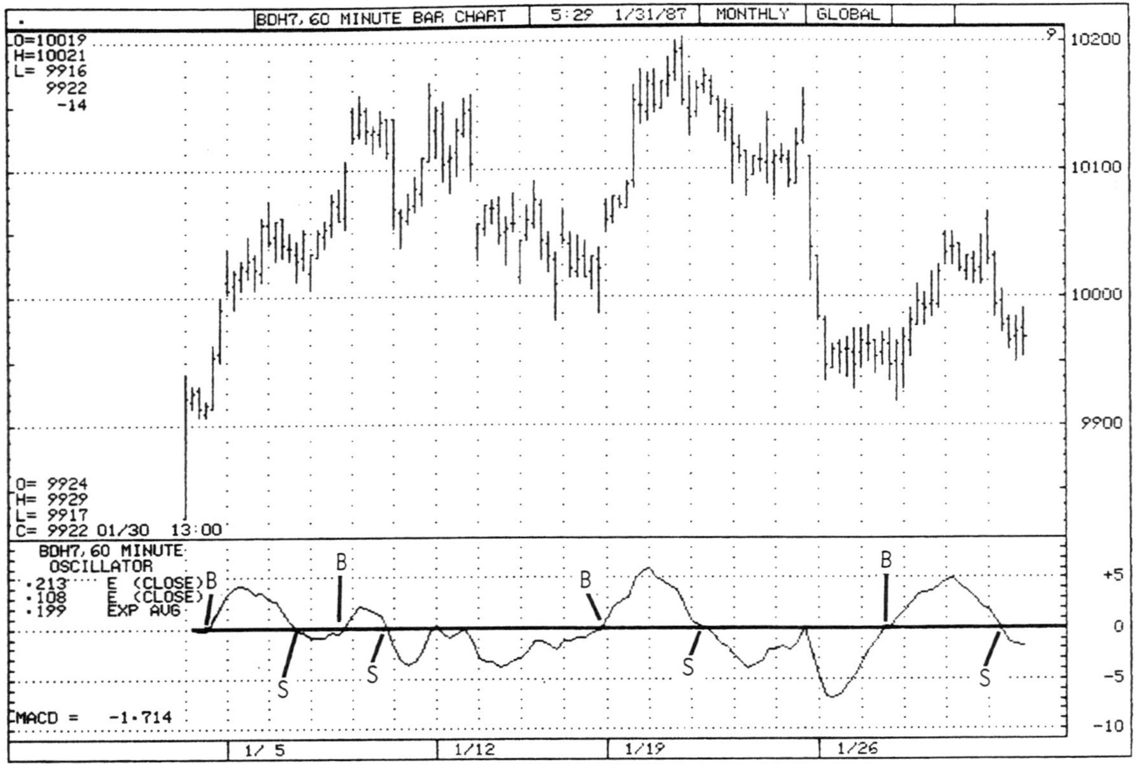

Figure 7.5: DEMA Difference Oscillator on Five-Minute Chart. Note the Frequency of Signals

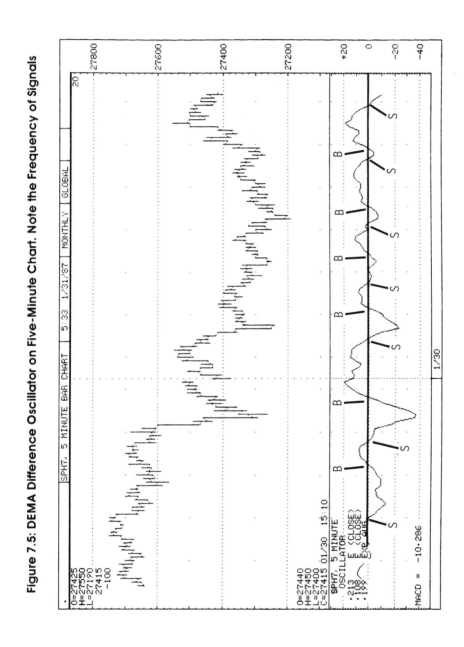

B = Buy, S = Sell

2. The timing approach, simply, is to buy when the DEMA difference crosses from under zero to over zero, and/or to sell when DEMA crosses from over zero to under zero.

3. The DEMA difference appears to be a valid reversing approach (that is, always in the markets).

4. Individuals should undertake studies to determine optimal DEMA values for their own market and/or time frame variables.

CHAPTER EIGHT

USING TIC VOLUME

Markets tend to top and bottom with spikes in trading volume. These volume spikes are caused by an influx of orders by traders acting on news, reports, recommendations by advisors, and/or large buying or selling by commercial interests. Trading volume is important because it often can alert you to market tops and bottoms. The actual final volume of contracts traded at any given price is generally unavailable to the public until after the trading session. Estimates are possible to obtain, but this is a time-consuming process and difficult to maintain on a regular basis. The short-term trader is, therefore, limited in his or her access to, and use of, volume figures. Tic volume provides a good substitute for actual contract volume. Tic volume measures the *number* of price changes rather than the actual number of contracts traded. Tic volume is a cumulative total of price changes over a given period of time. Tic volume moves up and down with increases and decreases in activity.

THE VALUE OF TIC VOLUME

Tic volume is valuable to the short-term trader for several reasons:

131

1. It allows one to determine when and where major activity is taking place.

2. It allows one to gauge whether the activity was primarily selling pressure or buying pressure.

3. It can serve as a technical indicator on its own.

4. It can serve as a confirming indicator when used with other signals.

5. Tic volume can help you spot price levels at which significant activity took place in the past, and is likely to occur again in the future.

SOME BASIC CHARACTERISTICS OF TIC VOLUME

Figure 8.1 is a half-hour T Bond futures chart with tic volume plotted as a histogram below price. The higher the vertical line, the higher the tic volume. Note that the first and last half-hours of each day typically have high tic volume. This is normal. However, note that there are spikes and troughs in Tic volume during the day as well. I have marked the opening volume spikes with Os and the closing volume spikes with Cs. Of much more significance are arrows A, B, and D. You can see that price was near a high at A, and that A also showed the lowest tic volume for the day. This suggests that price was not supported by new buying and that a top should be expected. Point B shows a similar situation. Point D, however, shows a downtrend with low tic volume. This suggests that low prices did not bring in more selling and that a rally was likely due to a lack of participation on the sell side.

Another way to use tic volume is to monitor tic volume trends in relation to price trends. Remember as a rule of thumb that expanding tic volume on the downside is a bearish indication, and contracting tic volume on the downside indicates that the downtrend should soon end. On the upside, expanding tic volume indicates a rally, and contracting tic volume suggests that the rally is likely to end soon. Figure 8.2 illustrates some of these relationships on the 30-minute T

Figure 8.1: Tic Volume with Opening (O) and Closing (C), Intraday Spikes

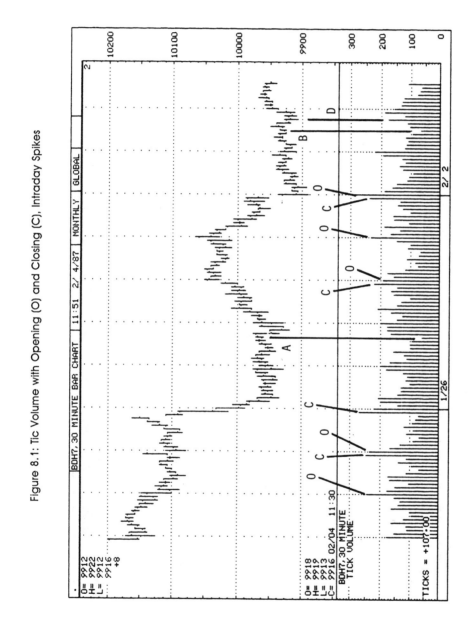

Note also low volume bottom near (A) and top on low volume near (B).

Figure 8.2: Bullish Tic Volume vs. Price Pattern (B) and Bearish Scenario (A)

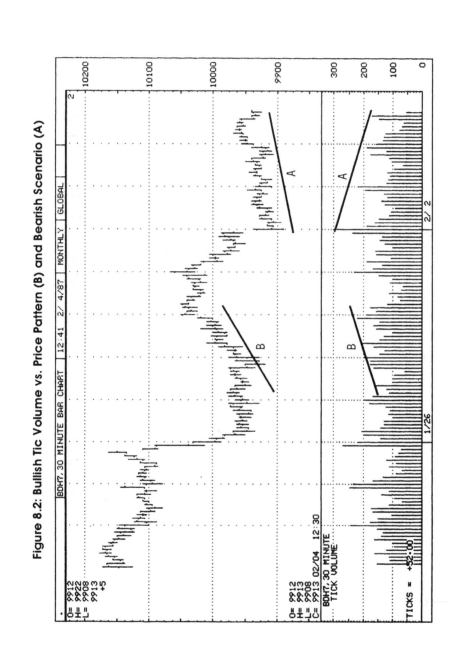

Bond futures chart. A variant of tic volume is the cumulative relative total called On Balance Tic Volume.[1] OBV tic simply presents price in relation to Tic volume. When price is up, tic volume is positive; when price is down, tic volume is negative.

It should be remembered that volume often contracts on price declines because many traders are afraid of the short side. This is why the OBV/price relationships mentioned earlier are not observed easily on the volume and price data. There is, however, another way to look at OBV tic that makes its value more readily discernible—the OBV tic trendline.

OBV Tic Trendline

Another way to look at tic volume in relation to price is to simply monitor trendline penetrations of OBV tic. Figure 8.3 is the 30-minute T Bond chart with an OBV line at the bottom. I have marked buy and sell signals generated by trendline crossings. Note the trendline penetrations as possible buy/sell signals. As you know, trendline penetrations are often subjective. As comical as it may sound, much depends upon how thin or thick the lines are drawn. Yet, there are ways in which trendline analysis can be operationalized, but I must leave this task to those willing to undertake it. Examine the five-minute S&P chart tic trendline analysis (Figure 8.4). As you can see, this market has clearer signals than did the T Bond market by virtue of its larger trading ranges. Though the OBV trendline analysis is a viable method, there are several additional aspects of OBV that can be employed in a short-term trading program.

DIVERGENCE AND TIC VOLUME

"Divergence" is defined as "an indicator and price moving in different directions." Basically, the use of divergence and tic volume takes two forms:

1. When price makes a new high for a given time frame, but the new high is not confirmed by a tic indicator high, divergence is negative, suggesting that a decline in price is likely.

Figure 8.3: OBV Tic Trendline Penetrations and Buy/Sell Signals

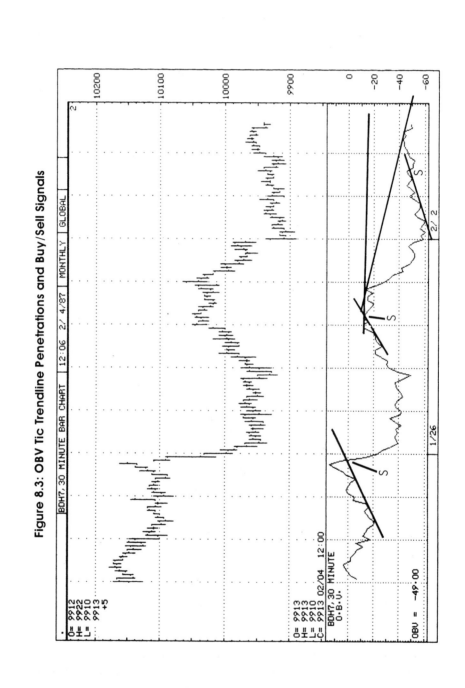

Figure 8.4: OBV Tic Trendline and Five-Minute S&P Signals

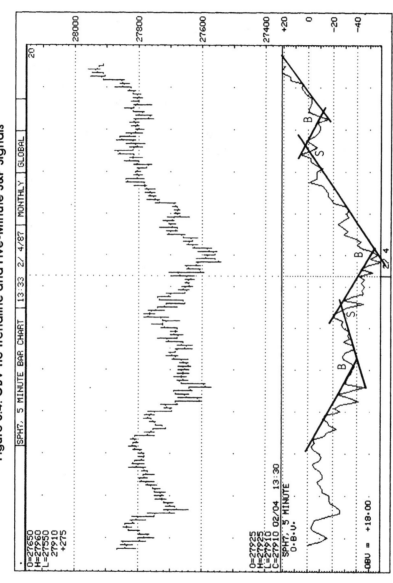

2. When price makes a new low for a given time period but tic indicator fails to make a new low, divergence is positive, suggesting that an upmove in price is likely.

Figures 8.5 and 8.6 demonstrate divergence in a variety of conditions using OBV tic.

OBV is another example of a market technique as opposed to a trading system. On balance volume is an important concept which should be developed further by those inclined to do so. Consider also the possibility of using second order derivatives of OBV. In other words, consider using an RSI indicator of OBV as a second order technical indicator of on balance volume. I have done some preliminary work in this direction which seems to be very promising.

NOTES

[1] On balance volume is a concept originally introduced by Joe Granville in his book *Granville's New Key to Stock Market Profits* (Englewood Cliffs, NJ:Prentice Hall, 1963).

Figure 8.5: Divergence and OBV

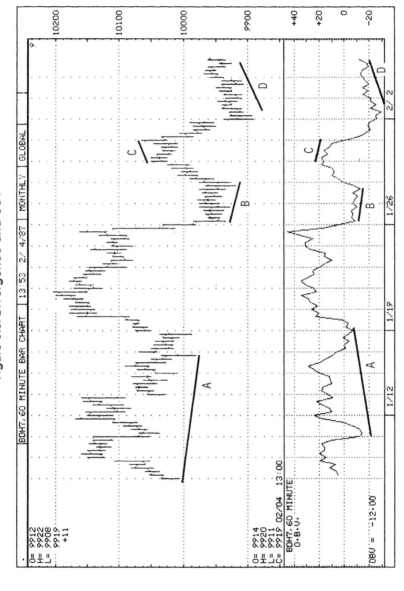

Price makes new low at "A," but OBV does not: Bullish. At "B," price and OBV make new low: not significant. At "C," price makes new high but OBV does not: Bearish. At "D," price and OBV move together: not significant.

Figure 8.6: Divergence and OBV Tic

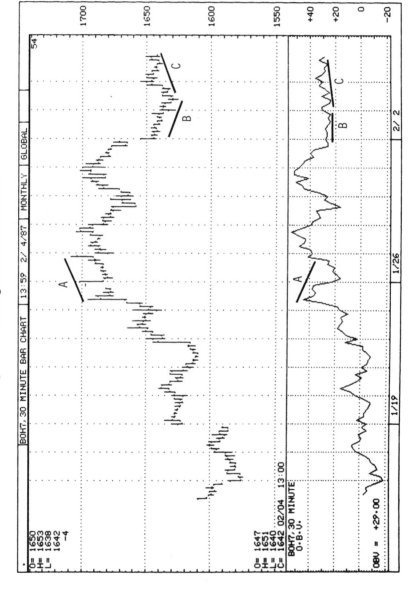

At "A," new price high was not confirmed by new OBV high. At "B," new low was not confirmed by new OBV low. At "C," no signals either way.

CHAPTER NINE

DETRENDING AND DETRENDED OSCILLATOR APPLICATIONS

The moving average is a mainstay among futures traders and technicians. Since the 1950s, when Richard Donchian popularized the use of moving averages in futures trading, the moving average and its literally hundreds of variations have helped sell computers and provided jobs for programmers, research for analysts, programs for money managers, and trading systems for trading-systems merchants. The number of variations, existing and potential, on the moving average never ceases to amaze me. The motivation driving all of this research (mine included) is the desire to "build a better mousetrap," to fine-tune a timing device, and to optimize performance. The truth is that it's doubtful whether futures trading ever can be so fine-tuned as to permit optimal entry. Efforts to tighten up timing signals generated by moving average signals may result in the "broken bolt syndrome"; in other words, efforts to fine-tune moving averages may prove to be destructive, like overtightening a bolt until the bolt breaks. I suspect that the most profitable research with moving averages will not center on efforts to find an optimal moving average or stop loss for each

141

market, but rather on the different ways in which moving averages can be employed and implemented.

This is not the direction that most current moving average research is taking. I see a host of enterprising new traders, equipped with IBM systems (or clones), five years worth of data, tremendous ambition, and the mistaken belief that all they need do is find the "key" combination of moving averages for each market. This fantasy is, in part, a product of computer technology "hype," and it may lead many of these eager traders, feeding their money into the trading jackpot, down the road to ruin. No, I don't think that better answers await those with the fastest computers, optimized moving averages, or the most efficient computer programming. Rather, I suspect that the most productive research will come in the form of new ways of looking at old techniques.

I'd like to illustrate another technique based on moving averages that, based on my experience, has excellent potential, but rarely is used: detrended moving average oscillators.

WHAT IS DETRENDING?

Detrending is a simple mathematical technique for removing the influence of a given trend or cycle from a moving average. In other words, if we want to look at *absolute* price relationships between one time and price point and another time and price point (i.e., without these points being affected by a given underlying trend or trends), we simply remove the trend by a mathematical manipulation. The technique is much simpler than you might imagine. All you need to do is subtract the closing price on any given day from the particular moving average value of that day. Hence, if you wanted to see a seven-day MA detrended oscillator, you would simply compute the seven-day MA of the close and subtract from each of the MA values the closing price for the day. If you wanted a 14-day or a six-hour or a 25-minute detrended oscillator, the approach would be the same, but you would use the specific time length in the calculation.

HOW ARE DETRENDED OSCILLATORS USED?

There are a number of fairly obvious and seemingly straightforward applications of detrended oscillators. Figure 9.1 is a daily price chart with the detrended 18-day MA. Bullish and bearish divergence can be seen at points A through G. When price makes a new high but the oscillator fails to confirm it by making a new high, this is often a sign of weakness and a pending downturn. When price makes a new low but the oscillator does not, this is often a sign of impending strength. See also Figure 9.2 which shows divergence on a 30-minute price chart.

There are many other potential uses of detrending oscillators, some of which are illustrated by the accompanying charts. Descriptions of some of the applications follow.

Timing

The detrended oscillator can be used as a timing indicator, either through trendline analysis or through buy/sell signals generated when the oscillator enters a previous low or high area (see Figures 9.3 and 9.4). Furthermore, the detrended oscillator can be combined with a moving average of the oscillator (similar to the DEMA and/or MACD), in order to provide a more simplified method of generating buy/sell signals.

Divergence

Frequently a market will move to a new high or low for a given time period (or a new contract high, record high, low, etc.). The oscillator, however, will not make a similar move. When this occurs it suggests that a change in trend is likely. If new lows are made, or if a downtrend in price is in progress, and the oscillator fails to make new lows or remains in an uptrend, this suggests a bullish turn in the offing. If a new high is made in price but the oscillator moves lower and/or fails to make a new high, this suggests a potential downside turn. (See Figure 9.2.)

Figure 9.1: Determined Oscillator (Bottom) vs. Price (Top): 1/18 Detrend and Buy/Sell Signals on Crossings of "Zero" Line

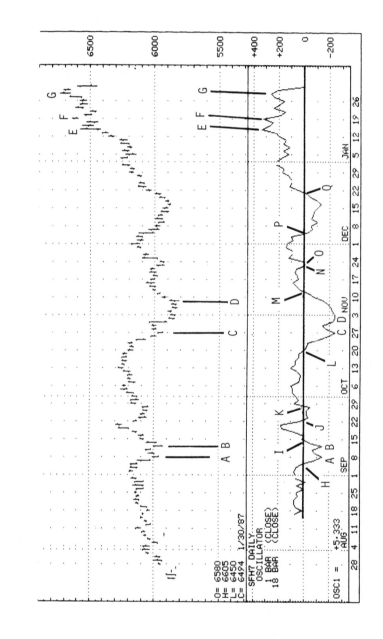

A-G shows divergence; H-Q shows zero line buy/sell signals.

Figure 9.2: Divergence on 30-Minute Chart

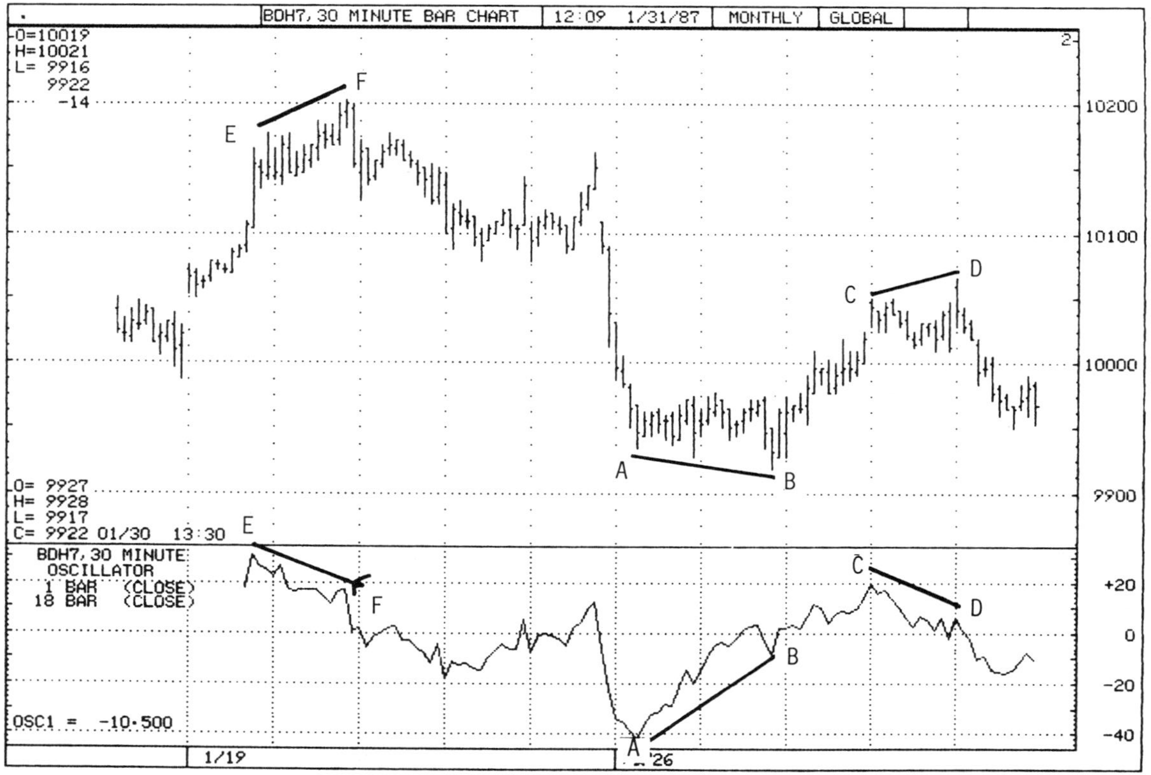

Figure 9.3: 1/18 Detrend Showing Divergence on Five-Minute Chart

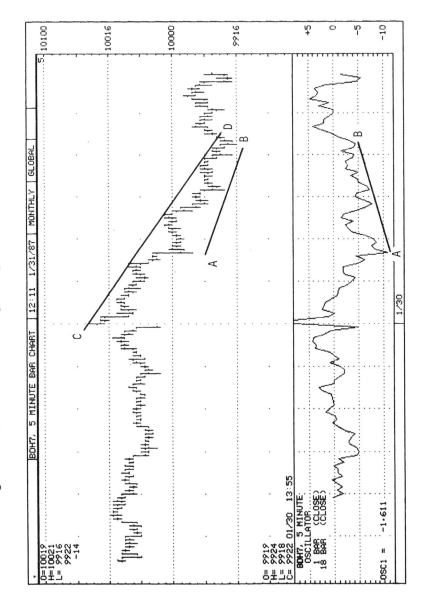

A-B = divergence. C-D shows penetration of resistance trendline after divergent pattern.

Figure 9.4: Divergence on Daily Price Chart with 1/18 Detrend

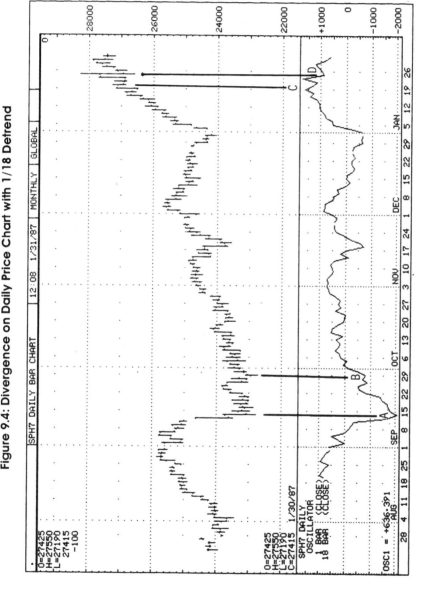

Note new price low at "B" but no confirmation by oscillator. Price high at "D" not confirmed by new oscillator high.

Zero Line Timing

When an oscillator crosses from plus to minus or from minus to plus, it is often a good technical signal to take action. A cross from under zero to over zero often indicates a bullish trend and a cross from over zero to under zero often indicates a bearish trend. (See Figure 9.1.)

Finding Cycles

The detrended oscillator tends to filter out trend effects of various cycles. By running different length detrended MAs, you can filter out the effects of some cycles while looking only at the effects of the cycles you wish to study. This applies primarily to the longer term trader.

Trendline Crossover

Trendline crossovers of the oscillator itself can also be used to generate signals. See Figures 9.5 and 9.6. I am certain that many other applications of the detrended MA exist. In fact, consider this: By knowing the oscillator value of resistance/support and/or previous oscillator highs/lows, you can *predict* what price value corresponds to the oscillator value.

CONSTRUCTING A DETRENDED OSCILLATOR

The method for constructing a detrended oscillator is very simple, either in longhand or by computer spreadsheet. Here are the steps for an 18-period detrended oscillator (for other MA lengths, substitute your value in this procedure):

- Take an 18-period moving average of the closing prices.

- Take the closing price for each time unit. Subtract the 18-period MA for the time unit from the closing price value for that unit.

- ■ The number you get, which can be a positive, negative or zero value, is the detrended oscillator value.

- ■ Plot these values.

If you have a CQG TQ 20/20 machine, simply use the oscillator setup and program the machine for an 18-period MA of the close and a one-period MA of the close (which is the closing price)>

Figure 9.5: Use of Trendline Penetrations and Timing Signals on 30-Minute Charts

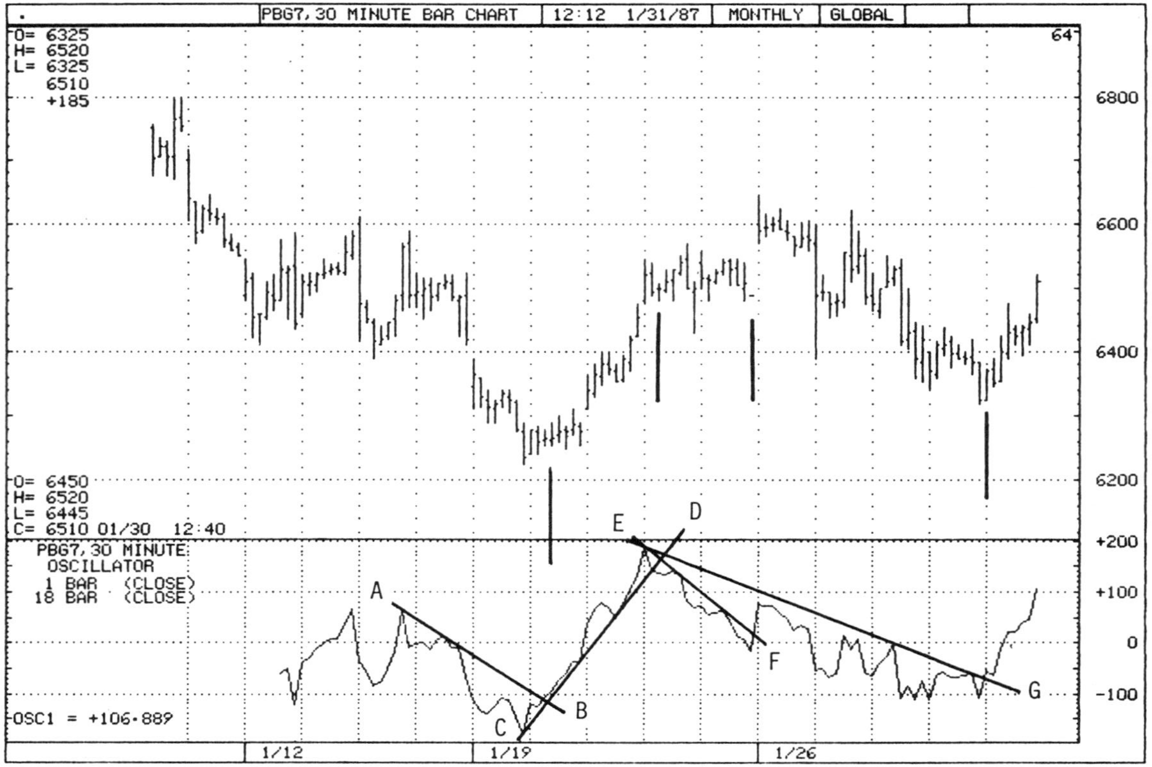

Figure 9.6: 1/18 Oscillator Signals Using Trendline Penetration on 30-Minute Charts

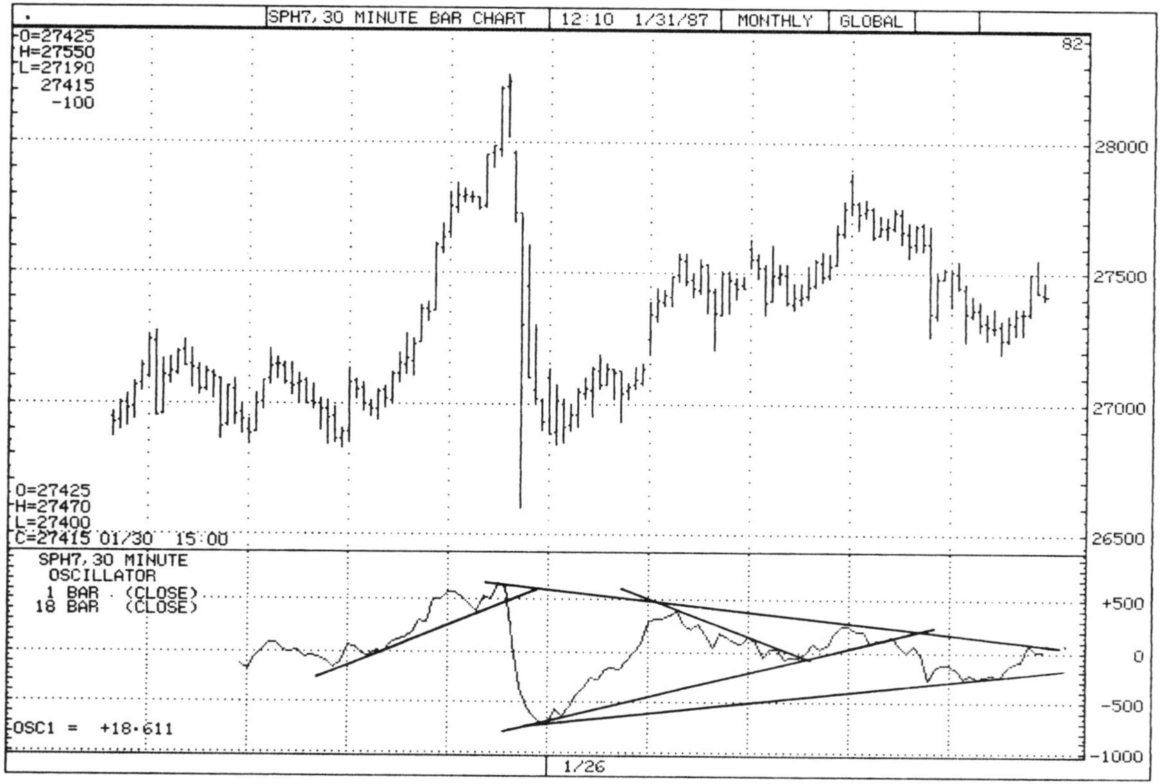

CHAPTER TEN

PRICE SPIKES/PRICE PROBES

Price probes and spikes have received only passing mention in my other writings. Although it is difficult to quantify the effectiveness of price probes and spikes, I suspect that individuals with sufficient time and computer programming know-how can subject this important technique to a thorough testing. My own testing has been primarily observational, but I wish to discuss this approach because I suspect that it may have considerable validity for short-term trading (and for investing as well).

What exactly are probes and spikes? I am certain that if you asked ten traders that question, you would get ten different answers. But, as we need some sort of working definition, we will assume two necessary conditions for a price spike, with a third condition preferable but not necessary. The conditions are:

1. We will assume that a market has been trending, up or down, for at least five time periods. If we are working in the half-hour time frame, for instance, we expect the price spike to the downside to occur no sooner than the sixth unit of a down or uptrend. On a down price spike, the low should be below the lowest low of the last five time segments. Conversely, on an up price spike, the high of the spike should be the highest of

the last five time segments. See Figures 10.1 and 10.2 for models of ideal spikes.

2. The spike should mark a pivot, or turning point, in the market. Though it is not possible to know immediately that a pivot has been made, it is possible to know very soon thereafter.

3. The third condition, though not a necessary one, is relatively high volume in either the actual number of contracts traded or in tic volume. High volume tends to make probes more reliable.

THE IMPORTANCE OF PRICE PROBES

Spikes indicate that a significant event has occurred in the market-place—it could be a reaction to news, a government report, "running" of stops, program buying or selling, or a host of other stimuli. Whatever the circumstances, the spike indicates that traders reacted to an important situation at a given time and, therefore, the price range of the spike becomes important as a support or resistance level, usually within the next 25 time units. However, the importance of spikes is not necessarily limited to the 25-time-unit period.

Intraday price spikes are also significant, but less so than those in daily or weekly time frames. Spikes appear on five-minute charts, 10-minute charts, 15-minute charts, hourly charts, and so on. However, they usually do not become important until some time after their occurrence. The average trader may wish to enter a position on a spike itself, but I find the spike more useful for signaling a trade at a later point in time. After the price spike has been established, a price *probe* into the range of the spike tends to find support or resistance in the spike range. On a probe into a spike low, support is likely. On a probe into a spike high, resistance is likely. See Figures 10.1 through 10.8.

Figure 10.1: Ideal Schematic of Price Probes Up and Outcome

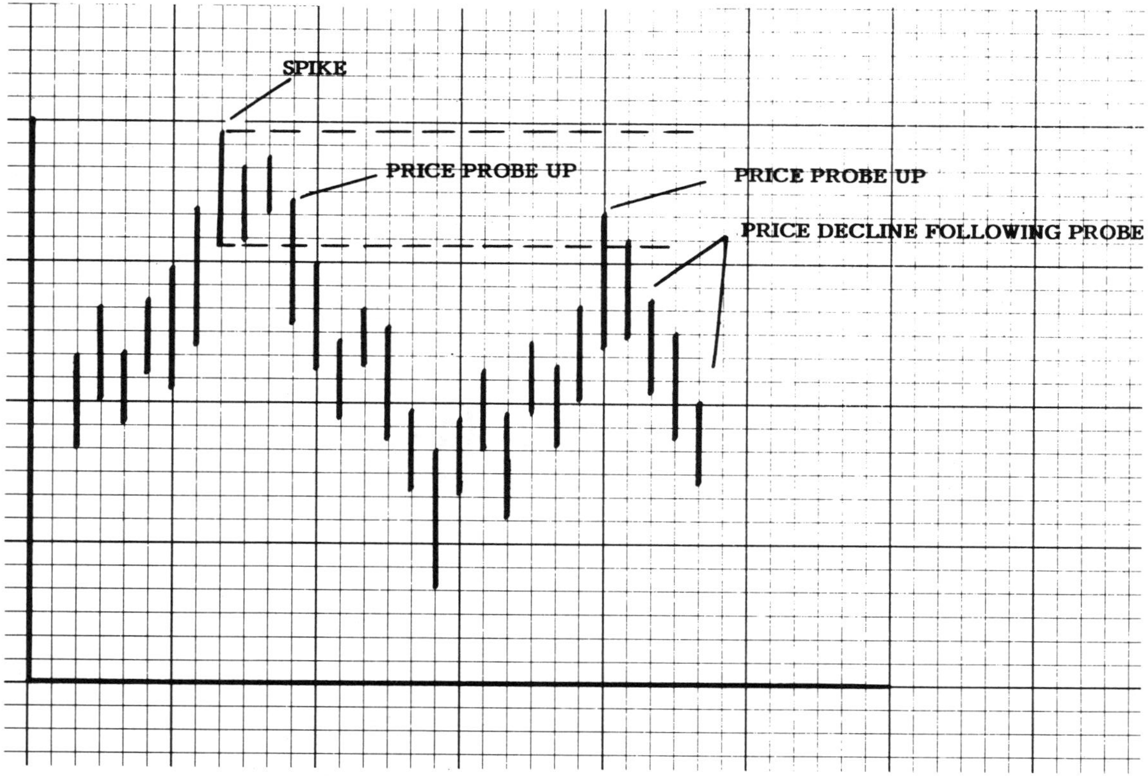

SPIKE

PRICE PROBE UP

PRICE PROBE UP

PRICE DECLINE FOLLOWING PROBE

Figure 10.2: Ideal Schematic of Price Probes and Spikes Down and Outcome

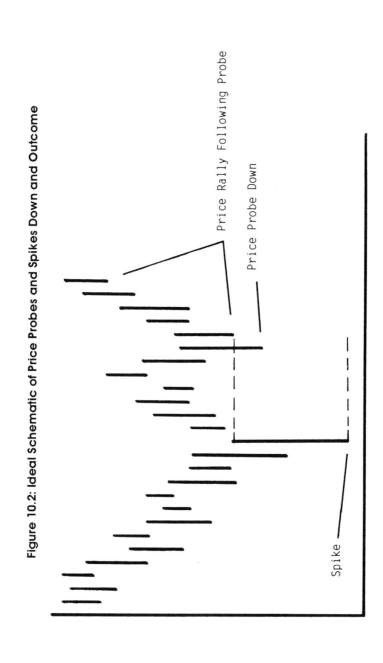

Figure 10.3: Real Time PPU (Price Probe Up) and Outcome

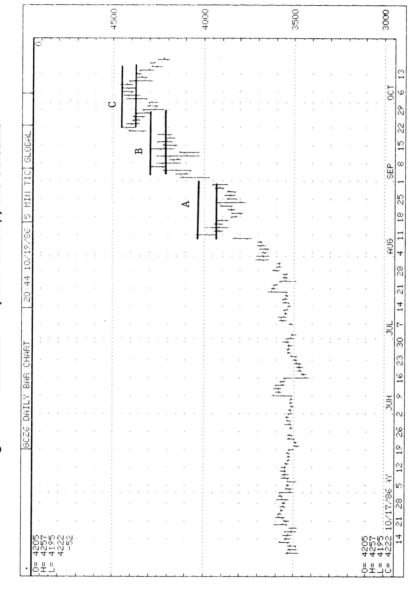

Spikes (A) and (B) both served as support and price rallied. Spike (C) was penetrated on the downside and a decline followed.

Figure 10.4: Real Time PPD (Price Probe Down) and Outcome

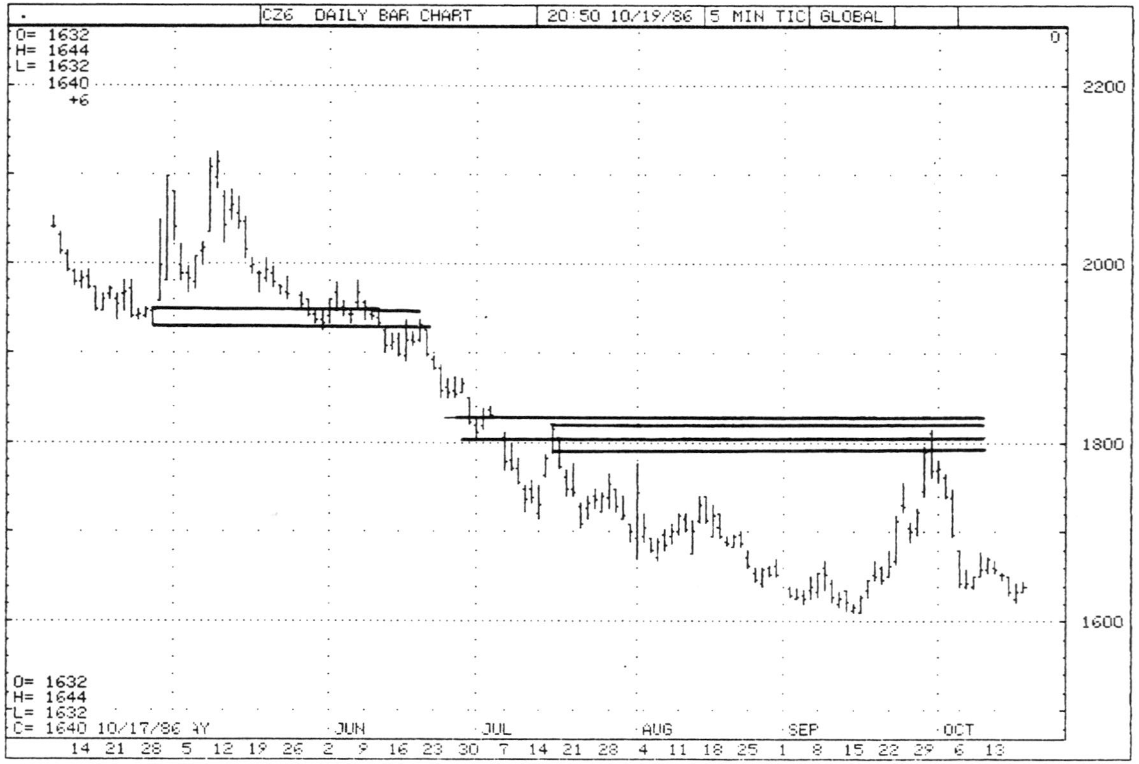

Figure 10.5: Real Time PPU on 30-Minute Chart

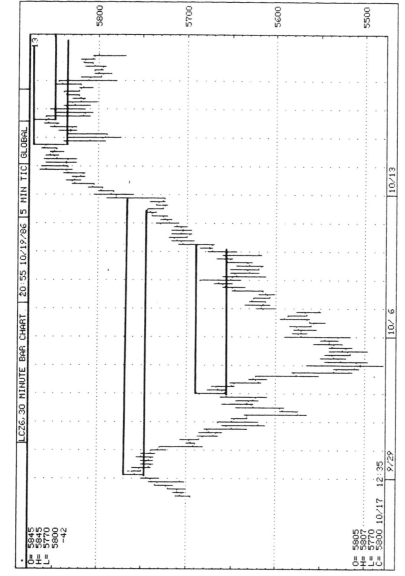

Note the tendency of price probes to halt moves and/or to trigger new moves when probe levels are penetrated.

Figure 10.6: Real Time PPU on Five-Minute Chart

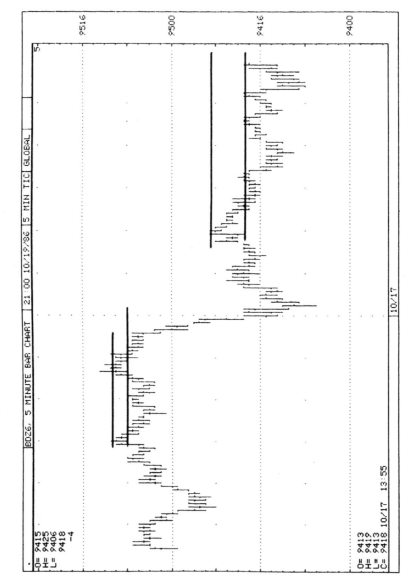

Short-term traders should take note of the many opportunities made possible by price probes and spikes.

Figure 10.7: Real Time PPD on 60-Minute Chart

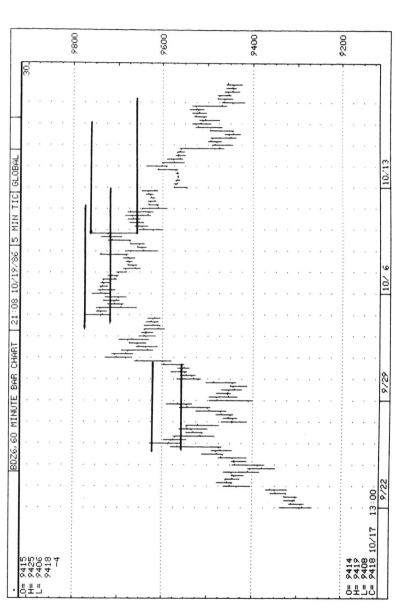

Figure 10.8: Real Time PPD on Daily Chart

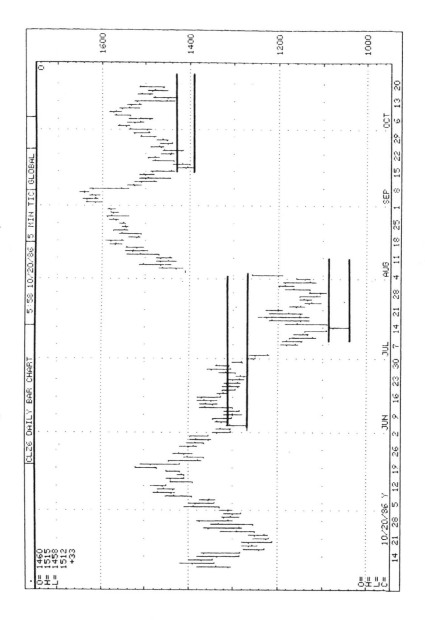

Shows the value of this technique in longer-term trading as well.

Price Spikes and Tic Volume

Figures 10.9 through 10.12 illustrate price spikes and probes in a number of markets and over a number of time frames. Also shown is tic volume to indicate that price turns usually occur on increased tic volume. Higher tic volume—or actual trading volume (i.e., number of contracts)—is important: it suggests that many traders are responding either to a perceived opportunity or to a forced opportunity. Some traders were forced to exit positions while others were forced to enter positions. This makes the spike high and low important at a later point in time.

HOW SPIKES AND PROBES CAN BE USED

Figure 10.13 shows several typical spikes and probes. Observe the interesting relationship between the spikes and the next series of time segments in this market. I have drawn horizontal lines forward in time using the tops of the spikes as my point of origin—note what transpires thereafter. Uncanny? Not at all! I have seen spike projections do some amazing things. Figure 10.14 shows a spike up. I have drawn a horizontal line forward in time with the low of the spike as my point of origin—again, observe what transpires thereafter. Coincidence? I don't think so; I think the spikes, up and down, delineate important price/time occurrences. The market, at some future point, will likely find support or resistance in the price range.

You will notice that the probe does not always project forward precisely. In truth, the market frequently comes to a level *near* or *within* the probe range. Figures 10.15 through 10.20 provide numerous illustrations of probes and their results. I have included probes from all types of markets. In practice, I find that probes are important in virtually all markets, whether they are active or inactive.

Personally, I think probes and spikes should be used for quick trades. You will have to define your own parameters for a "quick trade" and decide whether such trading fits into your own market orientation. With the many short-term trading tools provided in this manual, you can develop various strategies by which to verify the usefulness of probes and by which to exit a trade once you have

Figure 10.9: PPD and Tic Volume Spike

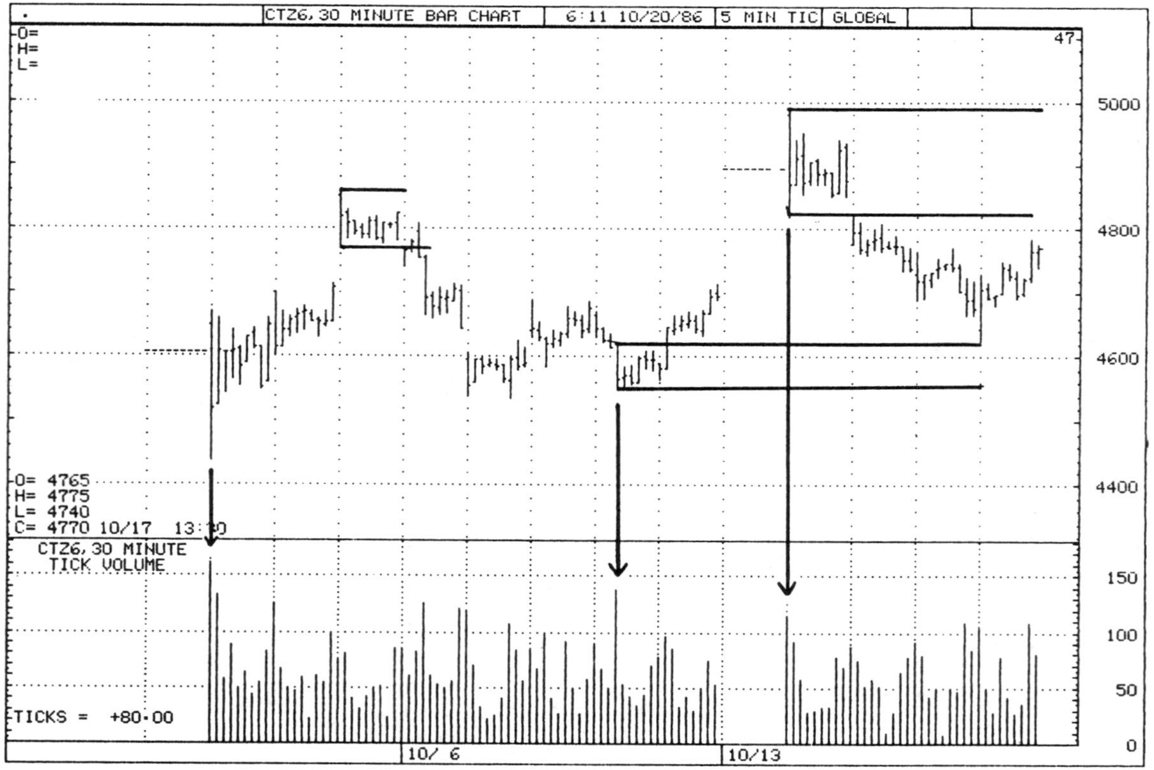

Note that spikes in Tic Volume tend to validate price probes.

Figure 10.10: PPD and Tic Volume Spike

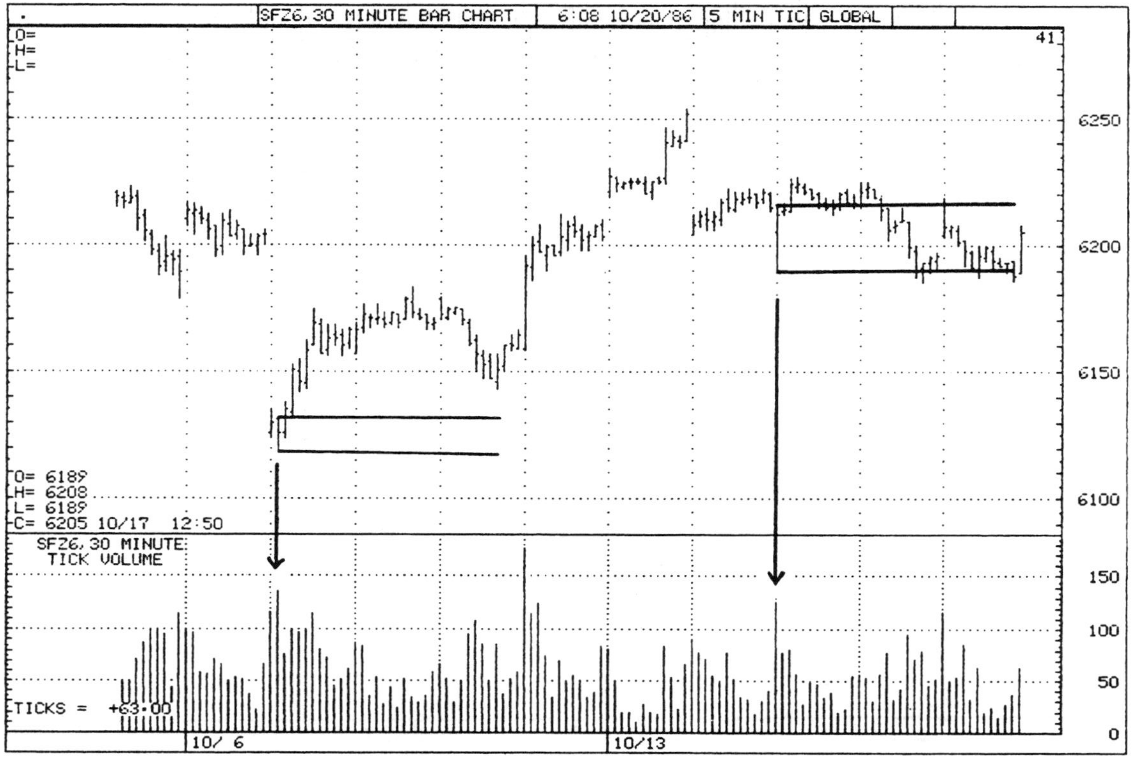

Figure 10.11: PPU and Tic Volume Spike

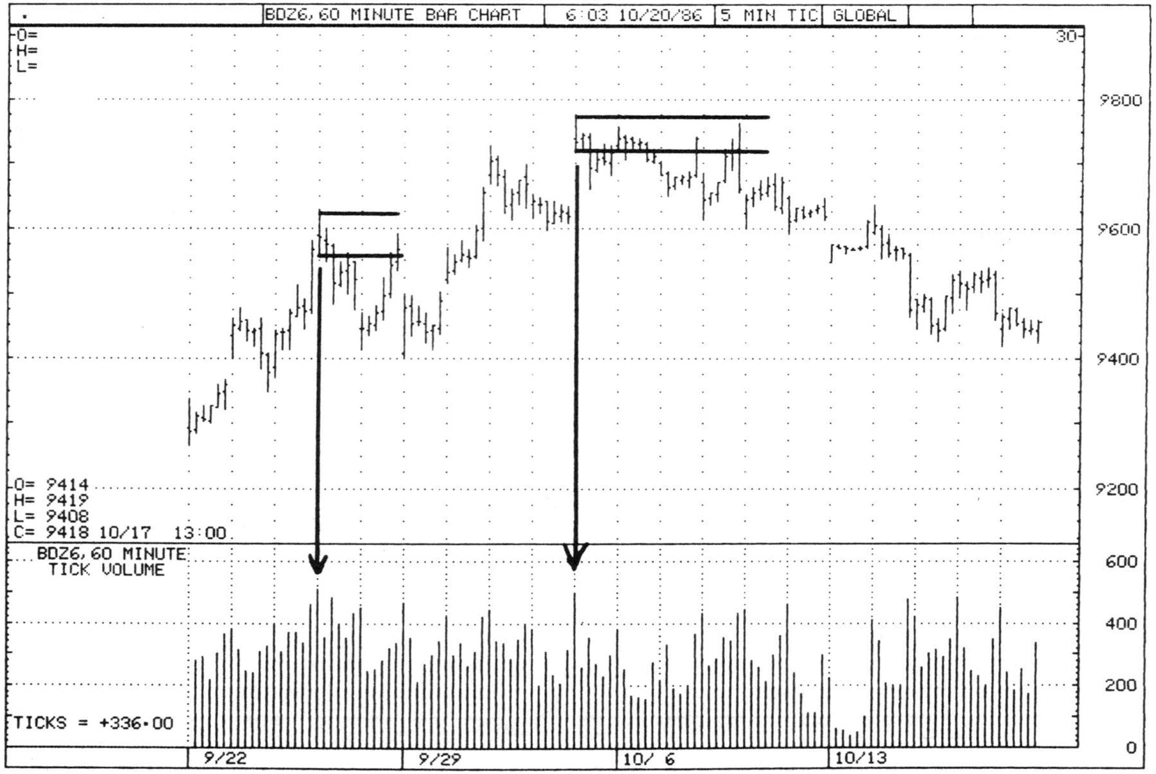

Figure 10.12: PPU and Tic Volume Spike

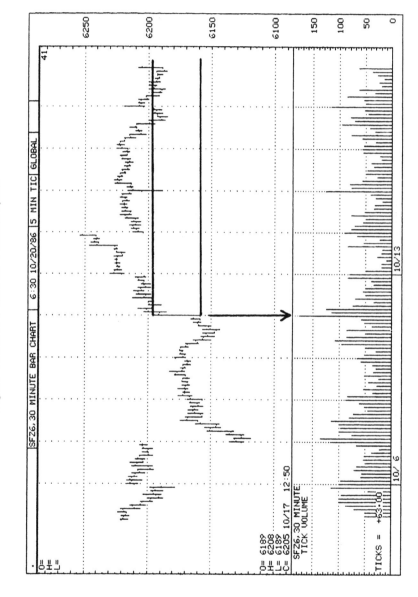

Note how many times this price probe acted as support.

Figure 10.13: PPD Showing Hypothetical Buying in the Support Areas

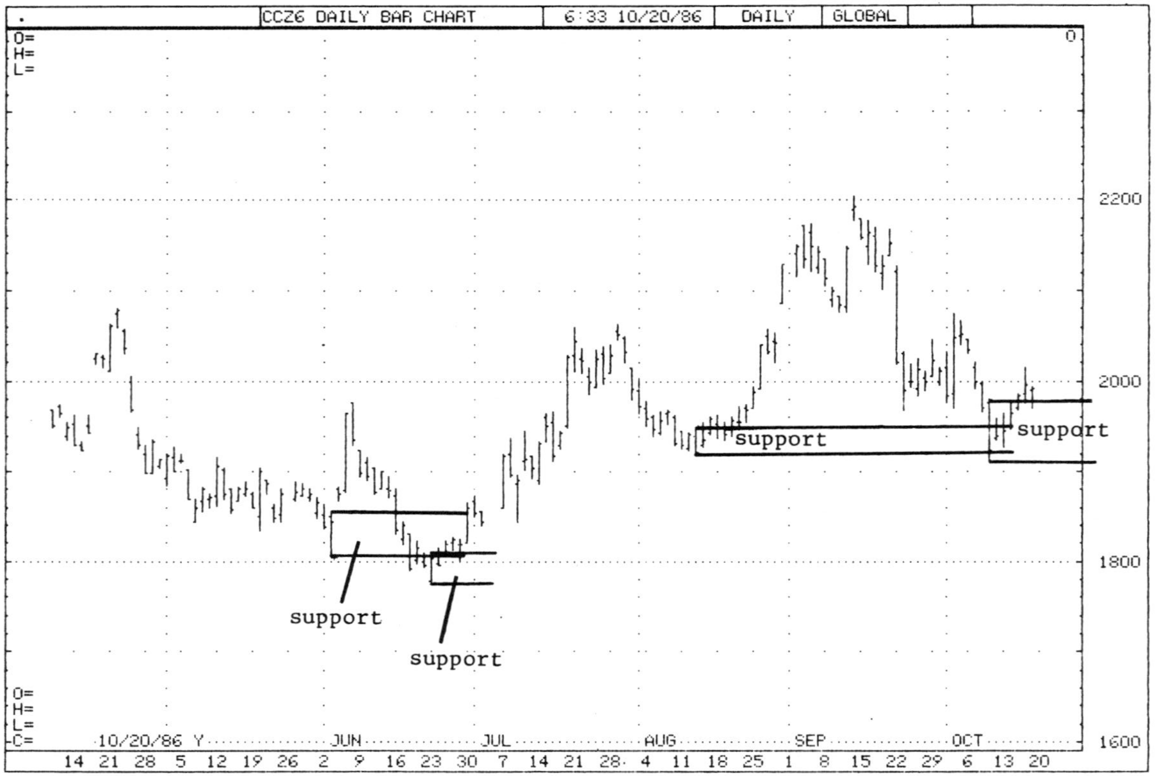

Figure 10.14: PPU and Projected Low Serving as Resistance for Short Sales in the Resistance Areas

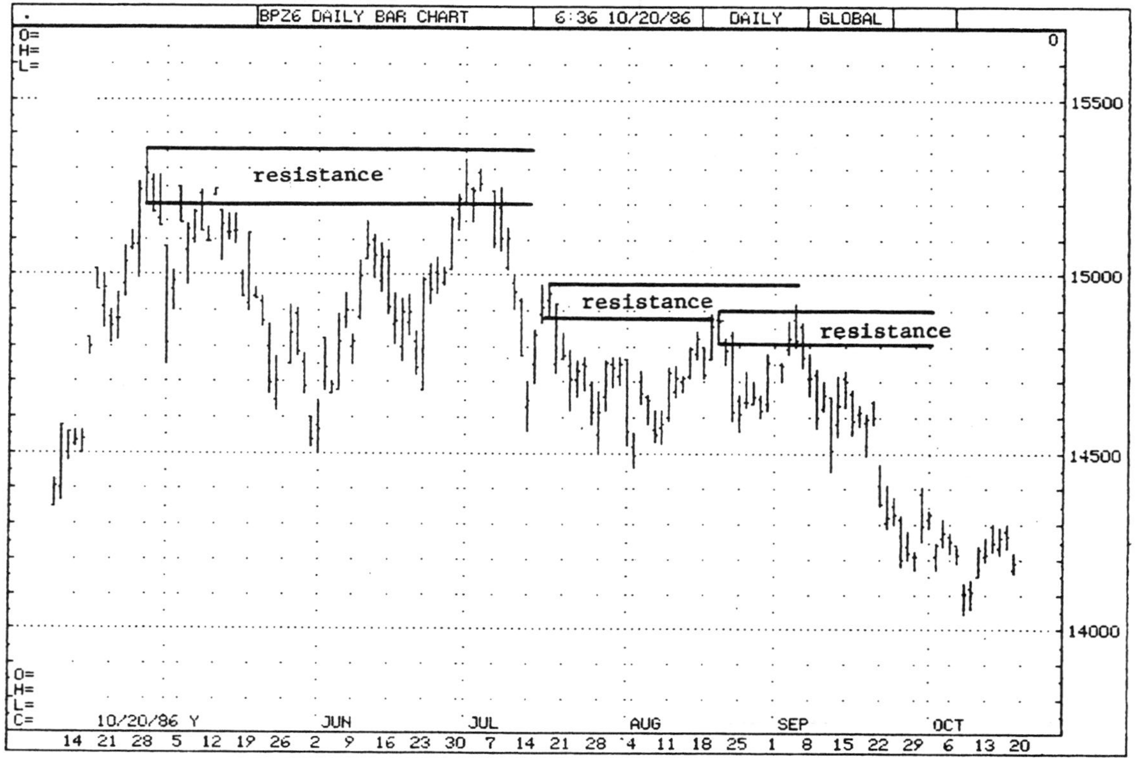

Figure 10.15: Example of Price Probe Application

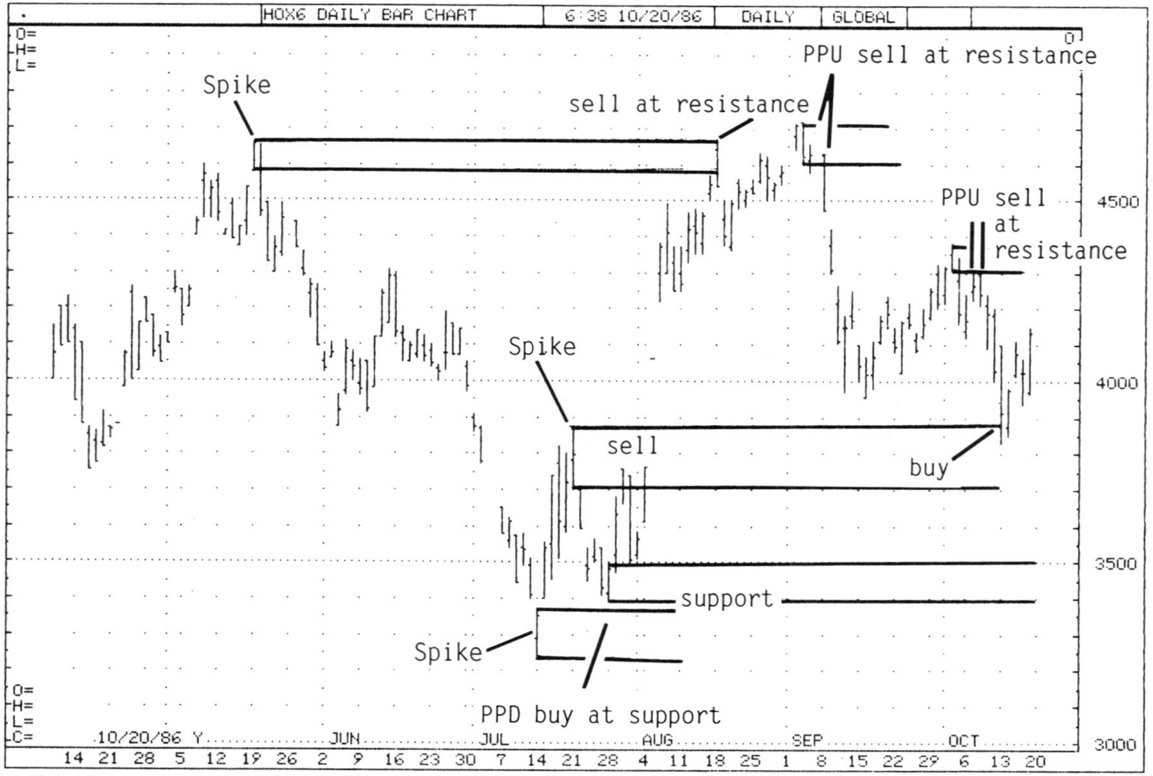

Figure 10.16: Example of Price Probe Application

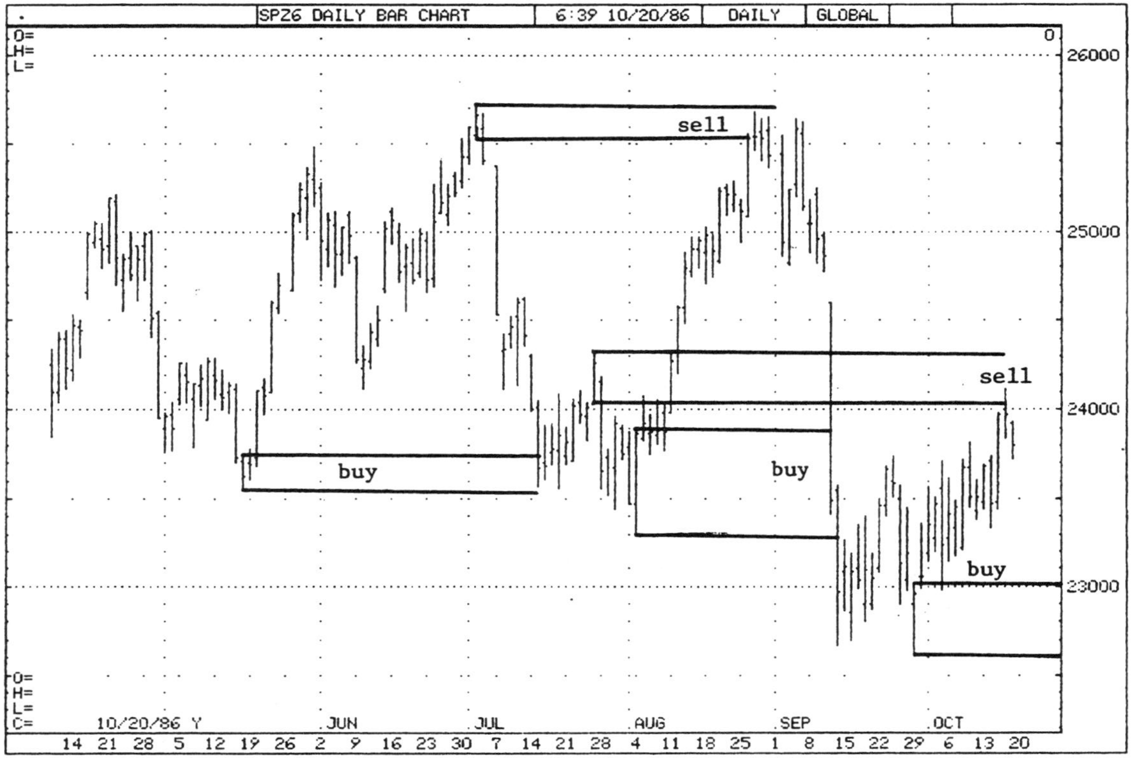

Figure 10.17: Example of Price Probe Application

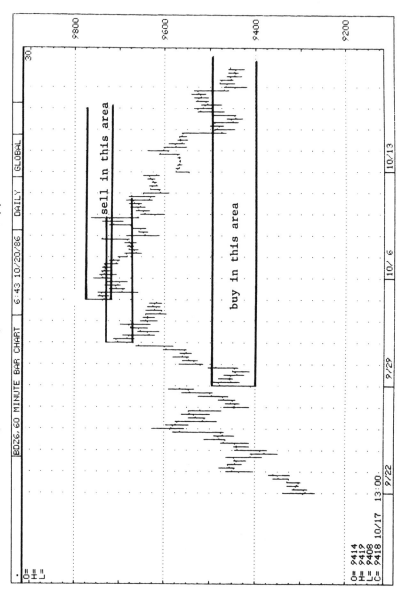

Figure 10.18: Example of Price Probe Application

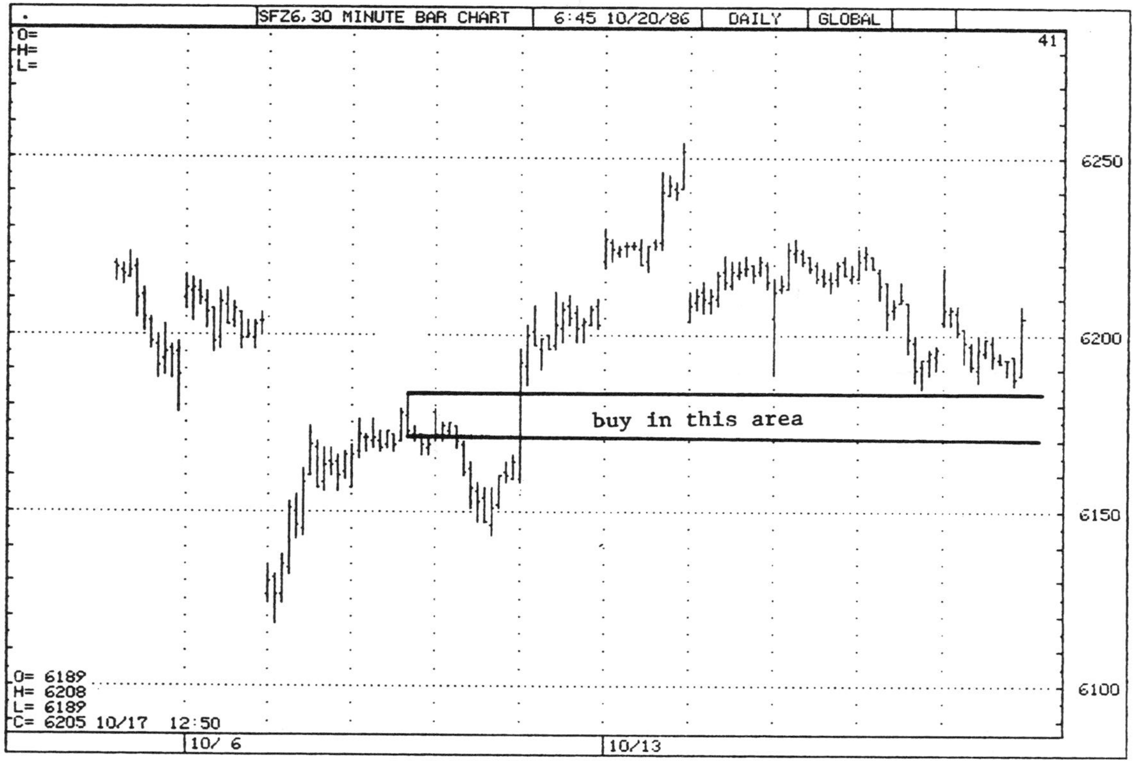

Figure 10.19: Example of Price Probe Application on Intraday Chart

established it. Figures 10.21 through 10.25 are examples of probes, spikes, entries, and exits.

In conclusion I would emphasize that the price probe and spike technique is not a trading method but rather a trading tool which may be used in conjunction with other methods. As I have illustrated in this chapter, price probes can be particularly effective when used with tic volume. Inasmuch as the price probe and spike technique is not operational I the sense of having extremely well defined trading rules, I suggest you watch it closely in conjunction with other indicators. Figures 10.24 and 10.25, for example, illustrate the potential use of the PPD and PPU method in conjunction with the dual exponential moving average technique discussed earlier. This discussion merely scratches the surface of what can be achieved using the probe and spike technique. I leave this research up to the reader.

Figure 10.20: Example of Price Probe Application

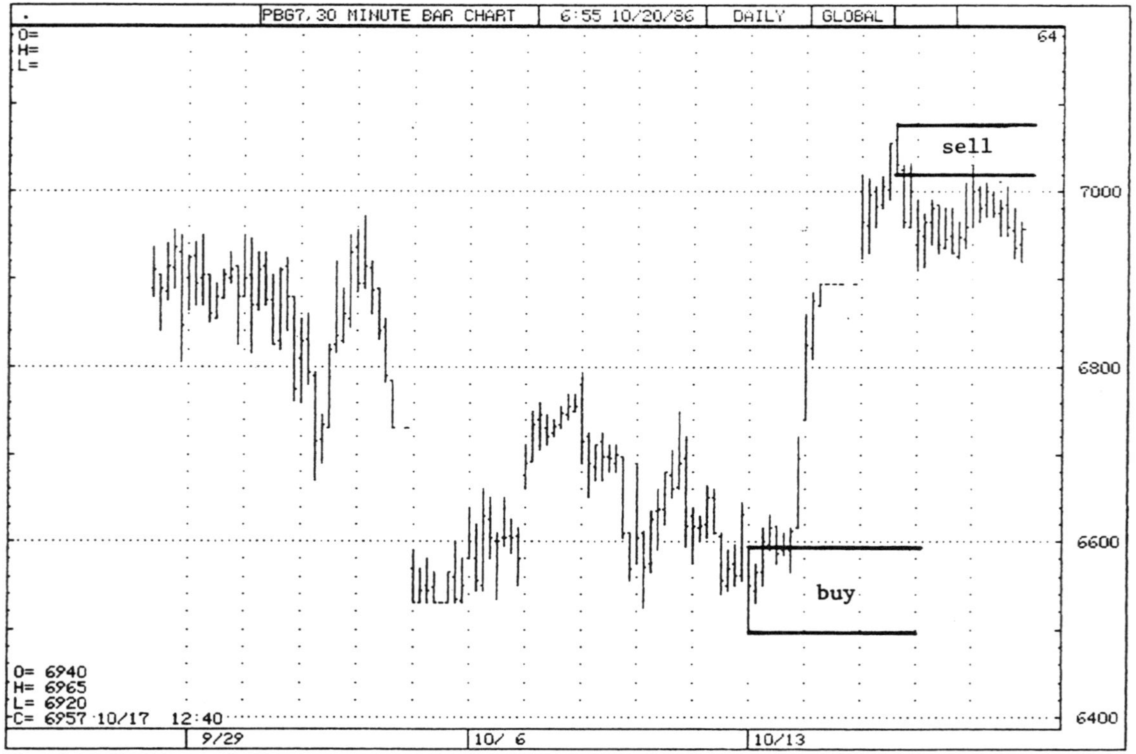

Figure 10.21: Additional Application of the Price Probe Method, in this Case, Using SI for Confirmation

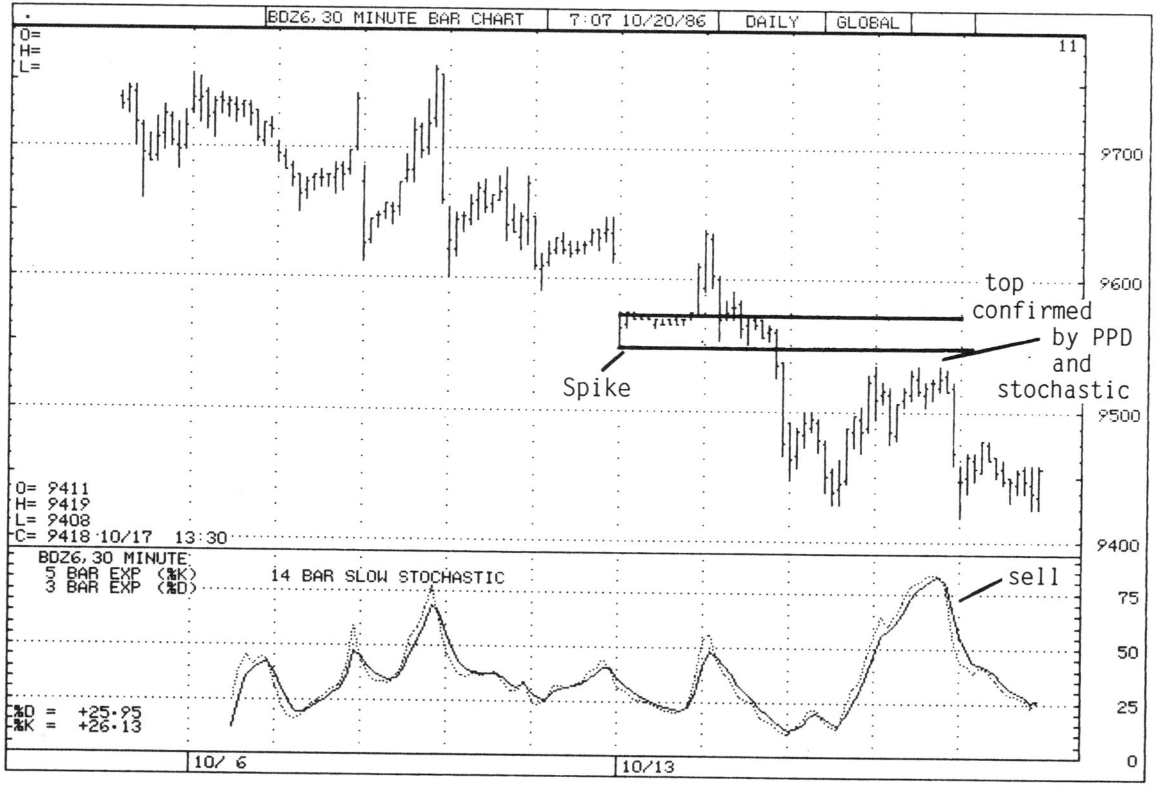

Figure 10.22: Additional Application of the Price Probe Method Using SI for Confirmation

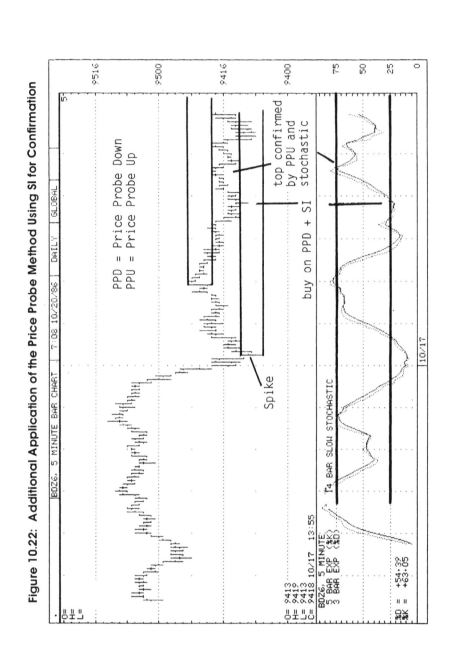

Figure 10.23: Additional Application of the Price Probe Method Using SI for Confirmation

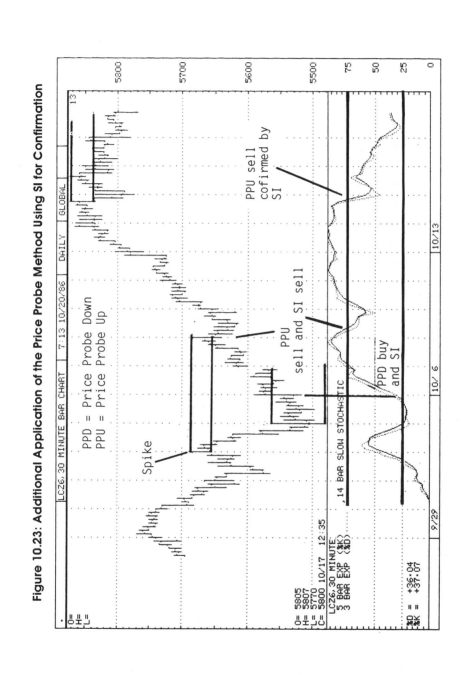

Figure 10.24: Additional Application of the Price Probe Method, in this Case, Using DEMA as Confirmation

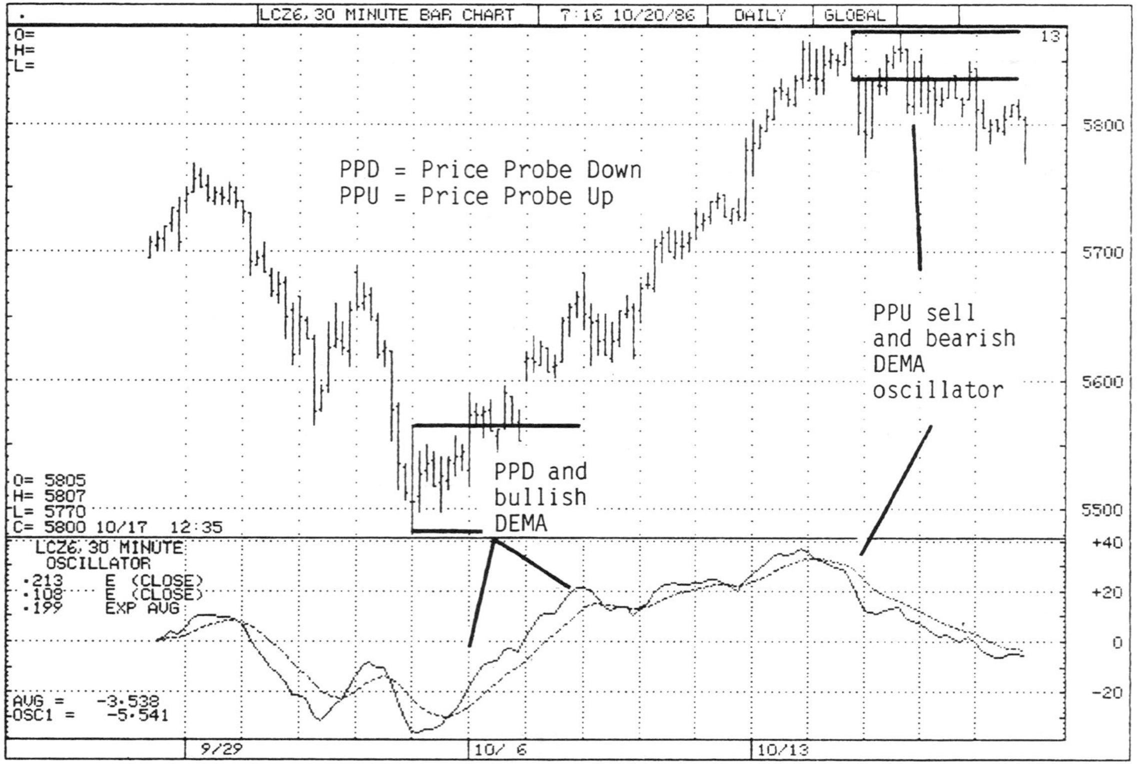

Figure 10.25: Additional Application of the Price Probe Method and DEMA

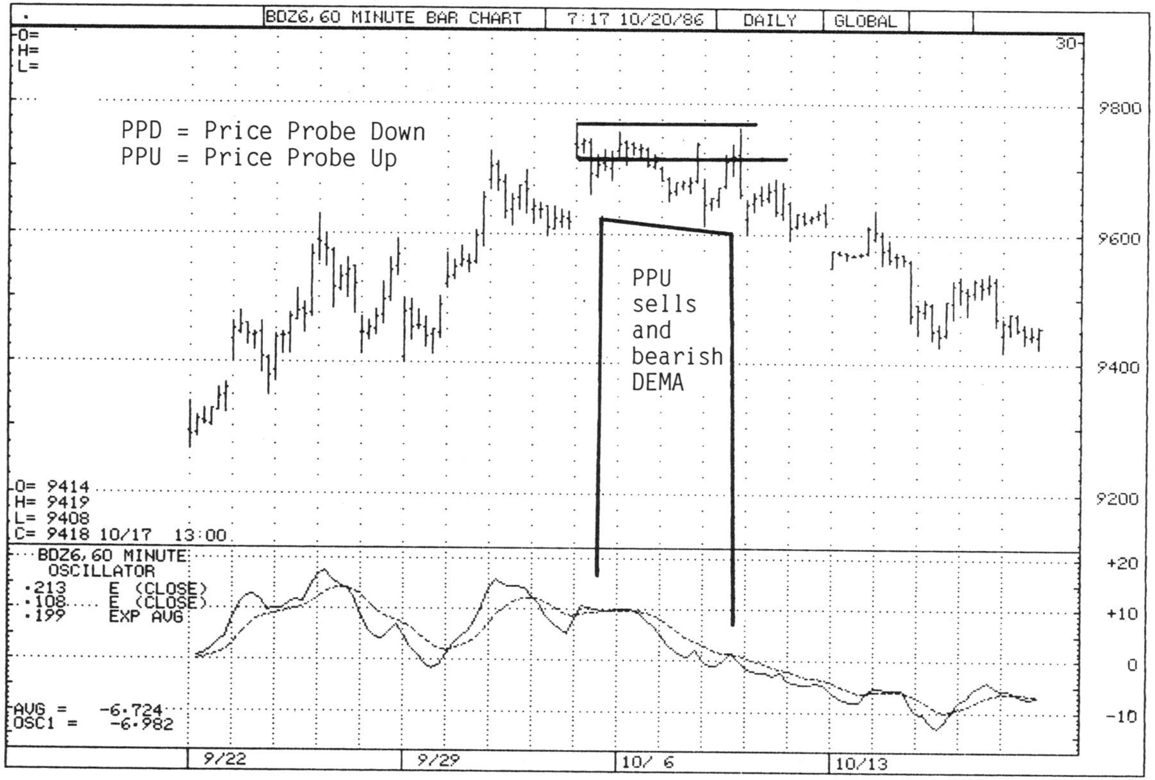

CHAPTER ELEVEN

PUTTING THEORY INTO PRACTICE

This manual has presented you with numerous methods and procedures that can be incorporated into your short-term and/or intraday trading program. Confronted with the many choices, and lacking experience in their applications, some readers may feel overwhelmed, or at least in need of practical, real-life examples of these techniques in action. This chapter provides such examples, in a two -to three-day period of time. I have attempted to structure this chapter chronologically, from before market opening through post-market close, to illustrate the synergy attainable through applications of most techniques discussed in this manual. Note that Critical Time of Day (CTOD), the only technique that is not dependent upon any of the other indicators, is not included in this analysis because the CTOD approach requires either a yes or no (go or don't go) decision each day. Unless you decide to validate the CTOD signals using other indicators, you need not consider CTOD as part of the entire technical picture.

Day One: Thursday October 23, 1986—6:00 A.M.

At 6:00 a.m. Chicago time, the technical structure of Treasury Bond futures was analyzed using the indicators presented in this manual. As of the close of trading on Tuesday, October 21, T Bond futures presented the following technical picture (please refer to Figure 11.1 and the numbers noted thereon for verification of these comments). The price trend represented by bracket A was down. The price oscillator, DEMA, turned bearish at point B and the 14-period exponential stochastic turned bearish at point C. Consequently, the trend as depicted by price, DEMA and stochastic was bearish. Furthermore, at point D, the three-period closing MA fell below the eight-period low MA, triggering a sell signal. This confirmed the general downtrend. The stochastic line at E had crossed below 25 percent and had started to turn higher—this suggested the possibility of a developing low.

Strategy for 10/22/86. (Remember that this analysis would ideally have been made prior to the market opening of 10/22/86, using the data for the closing of 10/21/86.) Based on the indicators, the strategy for 10/22 would be to sell on a rally into the resistance area marked by the top of the 10/8/3 channel. This value can be determined from statistical data provided by the Commodity Quote Graphics TQ 20/20 System.[1]

The value of the 10H line as of the close on 10/21 was 95–25. Arrow G shows where the market would need to rally to on 10/22 in order to trigger a possible short sell. The formation of the possible low indicated by arrow E suggested that unless target G for a short sell was reached early in the trading day, no short side trade would be made since there was a distinct possibility that a bottom might have developed at point F. Accordingly, we move to Figure 11.2, which shows the status of the half-hour chart as of the close of trading on 10/21. I have also included the hourly T Bond chart as of the close of trading on 10/21, along with comments on the major timing indicators. You will note from the comments on Figure 11.3 and Figure 11.2 that a low had, indeed, occurred, and that with the potential development of the low on the daily chart (Figure 11.1, indicator E) the short side was not the side of choice for 10/22/86. In fact, you will note that both the hour and half-hour charts gave buy signals early in the day on 10/21.

All indicators on both charts were bullish as of the close of trading on 10/21, and had turned in excellent performance during the day.

Figure 11.1: Daily T Bonds Dec. 1986, With Indicators as of Close on 10/21/86

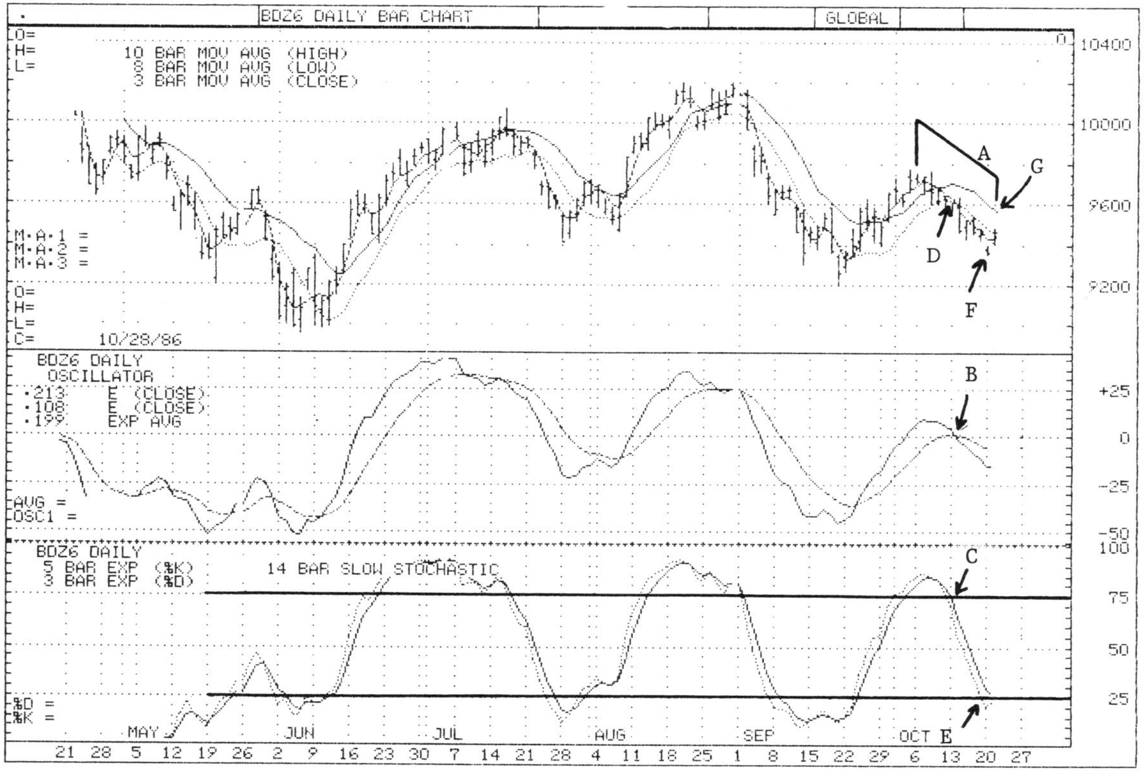

Figure 11.2: 1/2-Hour T Bonds Dec. 86, with Timing Indicators as of 10/21/86 Close

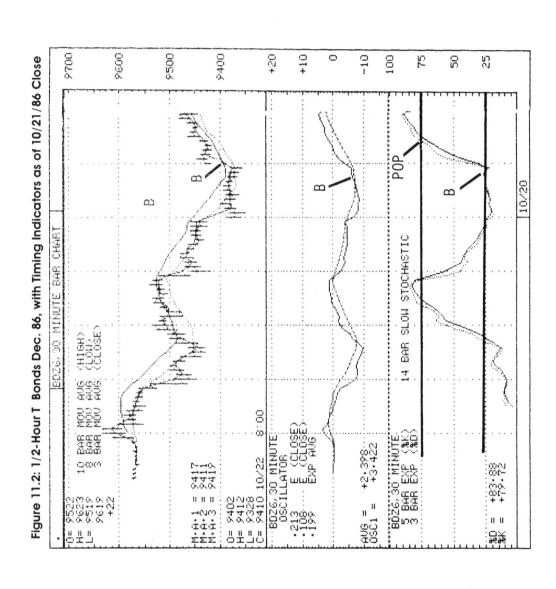

The short-term trader should have reached this conclusion based upon the weight of the data and the evidence that the daily trend was likely bottoming.

The path of least resistance is to sell into the market on rallies to resistance. It should be noted from Figure 11.2 that the indicators actually turned bullish on 10/20 regarding DEMA and Stochastics plus bullish early in the day on 10/21 using the 10/8/3 channel. The half-hour chart also gives a buy pop signal using the 14-period stochastic as indicated on the chart.

Assume, however, that you have reached a conclusion entirely different from mine regarding the trading for 10/22. Assume that you would have wanted to sell short at point G on Figure 11.1, on a possible rally to resistance, since the trend was still down. The high of the day for 10/22 was 95.23. The channel high reading at point G going into the day of 10/22/86 was 95.25. If you had decided to sell short at point G or slightly below it, you may actually have been filled on your short sell. Had you entered your order at point G, you would not have been filled. Had you entered your order several tics below point G, you may have been filled. In any event, after examining the chart structure of the half-hour and hourly charts on an intraday basis, you should have changed your mind about holding the short position overnight, since the indicators were clearly turning bullish on a broad front. Friday's (10/24) indicators were available on the daily charts (which in the case of Quote Graphics would have been late in the session, since the indicators update on a tic-by-tic basis) and were a clear sign that a bottom was forming and that the path of least resistance for short-term traders would now be the long side.

Figure 11.4 shows the daily T Bond chart December 1986 as of the close of 10/22/86. A number of things have developed as a function of the day's trading. The DEMA lines at point A have converged after having widened, suggesting the possibility that a low has formed. The stochastic at point B has turned bullish. One sees now that the decision to not trade from the short side was a wise one, and that if one had traded from the short side, the loss could have been minimized even if the trade had been filled on 10/22/86. We now have a distinctly different situation for the short-term trader and a distinctly different decision to be made for trading on 10/23/86.

We turn now to the analyses of the hourly and half-hourly charts for 10/22/86. I find that the half-hour chart is more useful for the short-term trader than is the hourly chart; however, it is often helpful

Figure 11.3: Hourly T Bond Chart Dec. 86, With Timing Indicators as of Close 10/21/86

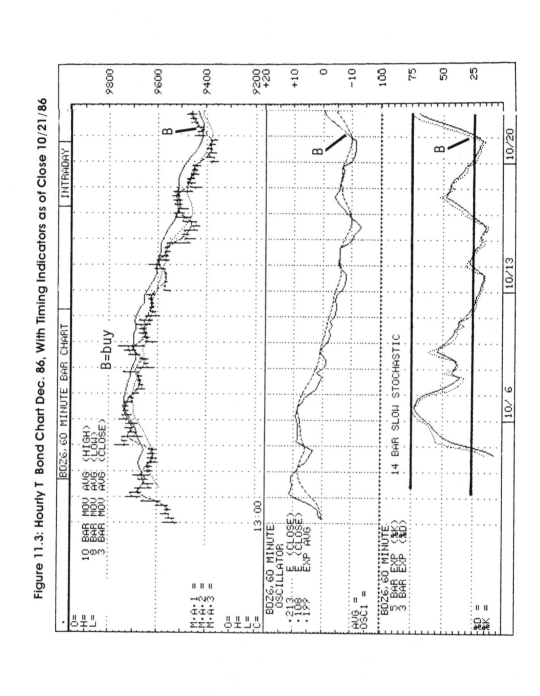

Figure 11.4: Daily T Bonds Dec. 86, and Technical Indicators as of 10/22/86

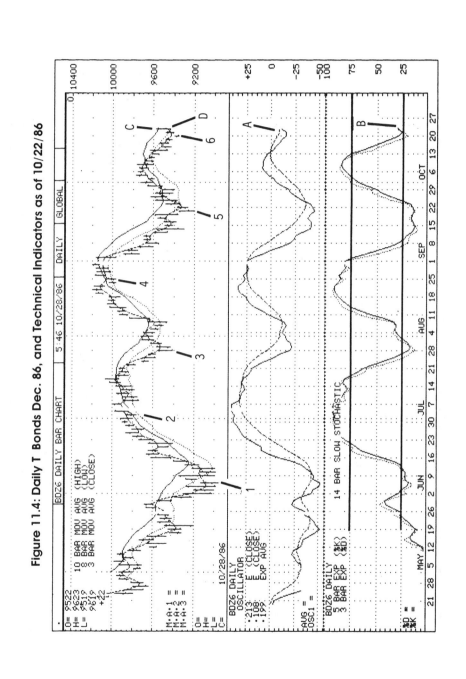

Figure 11.5: Hourly Dec. 86, T Bonds and Indicators as of Close Trading 10/21/86

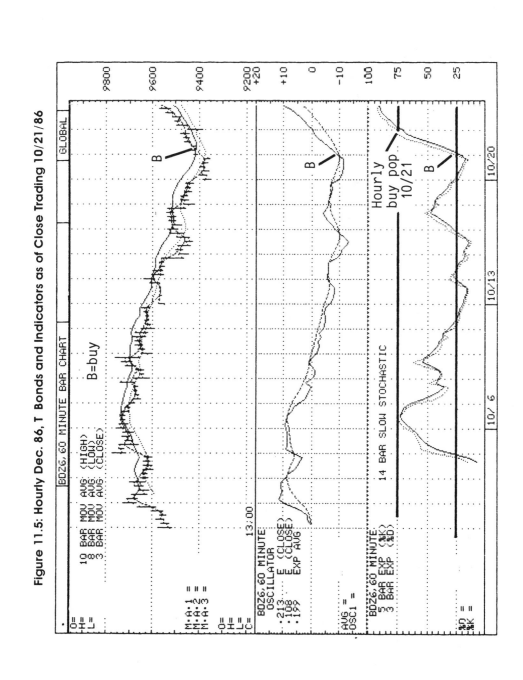

to examine the hourly chart as a confirming indicator or for additional technical input. Figure 11.5 shows the hourly T Bond chart as of the close of trading on 10/22. All indicators were bullish. The hourly buy pop that had occurred on 10/21 was, perhaps, close to being closed out since the two stochastic lines were very close in value and might cross early the next day. Note also that the DEMA lines were quite wide, with the stochastic above 75 percent, suggesting the possibility that a top might be reached on 10/23.

But before going into the work of 10/22 let's take a step back and examine what transpired during the day on 10/22. Figures 11.2 and 11.5 both show that the indicators on the intraday charts had turned bullish previous to 10/22. The short-term trader therefore would have adopted a bullish strategy and traded primarily from the long side on 10/22. Figure 11.6 shows that day's trading on the half-hour chart. You can see that buying into reactions would have been very profitable on the half-hour chart during the day. Reactions into the 10/8/3 channel or to the top of the 10/8/3 channel are marked A through F as buying opportunities. The day trader would have been out on the close at G. The position trader looking for a two- to three-day move could have carried the trade into the next day, 10/23. Note also that the half-hour pop trade as marked on Figure 11.6 exited the trade early in the day on 10/22 as the first half-hour closing price came in. This represented a very small profit, and later in the day there was another pop buy signal to re-enter on the long side.

As of the close of trading on 10/22, the stochastic indicator was overbought and the DEMA indicator was still in the bull trend with no indication of a top having, as yet, been made. All other indicators, channels, stochastics, and the underlying trends were bullish.

Returning to Figure 11.4, the daily T Bond chart, December 1986, we can see that this market should be approached primarily from the long side because an upturn is likely. Cycles traders will note the development of a possible cycle low at point 6, indicated by a pattern showing the lows on Figure 11.4 at 1, 2, 3, 4, 5, and potentially at 6, based on a short-term cycle of approximately 17 to 19 days low-to-low. This gives further evidence of a potential low in the present time-frame, and there's a distinct possibility that point 6 was, indeed, such a low. The strategy, therefore, for 10/23 would be bullish—trade from the long side, but cautiously, because the stochastic indicator was considerably overbought as of the close of 10/22, and an uptrend had been in existence now for approximately three days.

Figure 11.6: 1.2-Hour Dec. 86, T Bonds as of Close 10/21/86 and Various Indicators

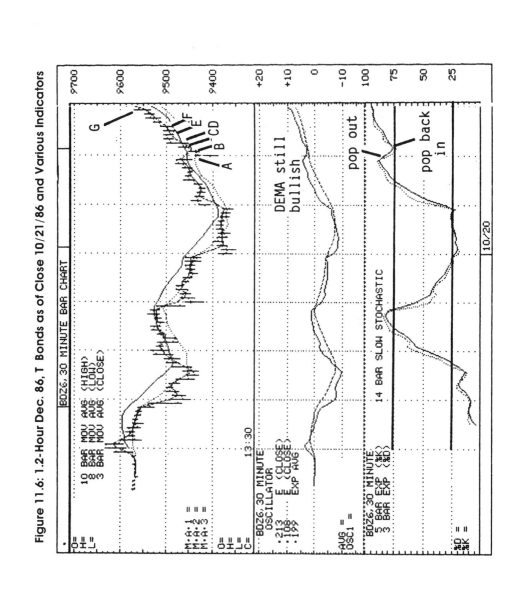

In terms of buy and sell levels for trading on 10/23, one need only go to the closing statistics of 10/22 on the daily chart in order to arrive at the broad parameters or entries. Refer again to Figure 11.4. Working from point D, the lower support level of the 10H channel, the number derived as the 8-low MA was 94.11. In order to buy at 94.11, or slightly higher, it had been entered for the trading on 10/23. Of course, this price was not hit during the day, and the short-term or day trader would have resorted to the strategy of buying into support as determined by the charts for 10/23, Figures 11.7 and 11.8. (These charts are accompanied by my notes as to what actions might have been taken by the short-term trader on an intraday basis during 10/23/86.)

Figure 11.7 shows that all indicators continue bullish throughout the day; however, the trend was sideways for the day and only late in the session did the price range for a given hour come close to the top of the 10H. The DEMA oscillator lines had widened and were beginning to narrow, suggesting a possible crossover and a potential minor top. A rally was in its fourth day, suggesting the possibility for a minor correction, and stochastic was overbought and had turned lower, also suggesting the possibility of a top. However, as of the close of trading on 10/23, no sell signals had appeared, and other than a small correction no major change in trend should have been expected. Furthermore, the daily charts for 10/22 indicated more important trends bottoming rather than a possible top forming.

Figure 11.8, the half-hour chart, reveals some interesting activity based on the technical indicators. Early in the day at point A, and later on for the next three half-hour segments (marked 1, 2, 3), prices did touch and bounce up from the top of the 10H channel. The nimble intraday trader would have had several opportunities to enter the market for short-term upside moves. At point B, the DEMA turned bearish; however, the stochastic had not dropped below 75 yet, indicating that an uptrend was still in effect. The 10/8/3 channel remained bullish, as the three-period of the close had not closed below the 8-period of the low; therefore, additional opportunities to trade the market intraday from the long side appeared at points 4, 5, 6, and 7. During the day of 10/23/86, the very short-term trader (i.e., intraday) had at least seven opportunities to trade from the long side on setback to the 10H channel support, all potentially profitable.

Through 20/20 hindsight, it becomes clear that entering trading on 10/23/86 with a bullish but cautious orientation (as determined

Figure 11.7 Hourly Dec. 86, T Bonds and Indicators as of Close 10/23/86

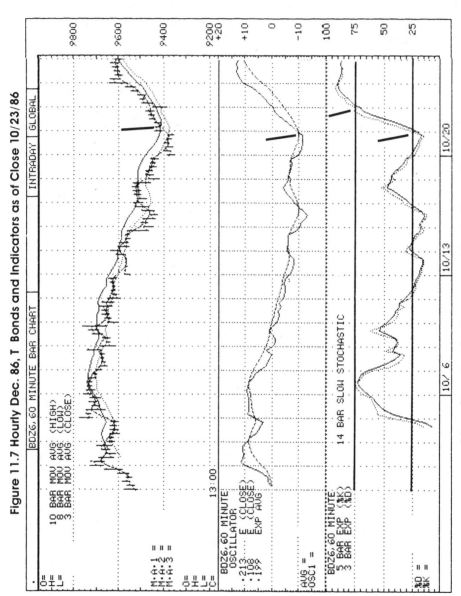

Lines show signals. Can you spot the indicators?

Figure 11.8: 1/2-Hour June 87, T Bonds and Indicators

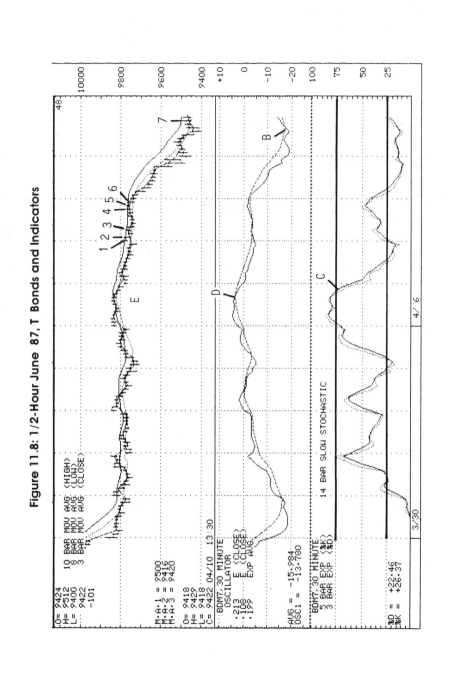

from the daily chart as of the close on 10/22) should have been a very productive and profitable approach for the intraday trader. In the meantime, the two- to three-day position trader would have held positions, closing them out at a profit.

SUMMARY

The foregoing chapter has attempted to provide you with a step-by-step description of applications of the methods and techniques discussed in this manual. The analyses, presented in diary form and in chronological sequence over a period of three trading days, represents real-time applications of the techniques and indicators. Although the analyses were written with the benefit of hindsight, the procedures, methods, and applications described should not differ significantly in actual application. Of course, each individual will develop a unique style of analysis and application. Such individual creativity, although an intangible factor in terms of objective measurement, can have a significant impact, either positive or negative, upon the results of technical trading systems. J. Peter Steidlmayer,[2] a man for whom I have great respect, has repeatedly said that as a trader you must "think for yourself." I wholeheartedly subscribe to this simple but powerful statement.

NOTES

[1] Note that my indicators also can be programmed on other quote systems as well.

[2] J. Steidlmayer and Kevin Roy, *Markets and Market Logic* (Chicago: Pelican Press, 1987).

CHAPTER TWELVE

SOME RULES FOR THE SHORT-TERM TRADER

The strategy of the short-term trader is distinctly different from that of the intermediate or long-term trader. The long-term trader seeks to establish a position at or near major turning points, in expectation of a fairly long ride in the expected direction; the day trader and the short-term trader rarely consider such endeavors. Rather, the short-term trader looks primarily for opportunities within the existing trend. I compare the behavior of the short-term trader and the long-term trader to the hunting strategies of the lion and the vulture. My comparisons are certainly not intended to insult any trader; I employ these analogies because there is much to be learned from them.

Unless exceptionally hungry, the lion hunts big game. Days and days may pass before the opportunity for a big kill presents itself, but when it does, the lion moves in stealthily, carefully, with forethought and cunning. Once the lion has its teeth in its prey, it will not relent: it will fight, risking self-injury in its efforts to win the large prize. If the prey escapes, the lion has invested no more than effort and, perhaps, a bit of its hide. If it is cautious, the lion will not suffer much pain in executing its strikes, which, though few and far between, are handsomely rewarding. And so it is with the long-term trader.

The vulture seeks opportunities created by the misfortune of others. Rather than going after living, large prey—which requires a tremendous amount of effort and considerable risk—the vulture looks only for many small opportunities that are relatively free of danger; its only competition comes from other vultures seeking the same opportunities. As base as this analogy may seem, I think it strikes home. The short-term trader must be a vulture, looking for opportunities that present limited risk as well as the potential for a quick reward. Because of his or her very nature, the short-term trader is not concerned with big prey, or with what the competition (i.e., the long-term trader) is doing at any given point in time. It is entirely possible for both kinds of traders to exist without competing with each other, as do the lion and the vulture. An opportunity for the lion may also prove ultimately to be an opportunity for the vulture. By reacting to living prey the vulture can alert the lion to a possible opportunity. The lion may take the big risk and fell the prey, leaving the remains for the vulture.

Since the short-term trader and long-term trader seek different types of opportunities, they can work well in the same environment. A long-term trader may sell to a short-term trader, and vice versa. Each creates opportunities for the other. At times, both may compete for the same opportunity, but with different expectations.

In order to take effective advantage of short-term opportunities, the trader must keep in mind a number of general rules and principles about short-term trading. The suggestions that follow deserve the consideration of anyone and everyone who wishes to trade in short-term time frames.

Decide on Your Time Frame

Determine whether you plan to be a day trader or whether you are willing to carry positions for up to five days. By knowing your time orientation in advance you will know how to act within the time frame. A day trader will be out of all positions by the end of each day. This means that he or she will need to respond more quickly to market opportunities during the day. I don't believe it is a good idea to enter the market in one time frame with certain expectations and then to change those expectations in order to exit the market from another time frame. It is important to determine whether you will be a day trader or another type of short-term trader. Although the techniques of entry may be similar, techniques and expectations for exit are not.

As a Short-Term Trader Your Approach Primarily Will Be Technical

Reports, fundamentals, announcements, and news will provide temporary shifts in market trends that, with effective technical tools, you will be able to take advantage of for the purpose of entry and exit on your short-term trades. A majority of your trading should be on technical signals.

Commissions

Commissions and losses combined form the cost of trading. Few traders realize the extent to which commissions can affect their bottom line. It is important, therefore, to pay the lowest commissions possible without sacrificing service and safety. When I speak of safety I mean, specifically, the financial condition of the brokerage firm with whom you are doing business. *Take these factors into consideration at all times. The broker with the cheapest commissions may not be the best, just as the broker with the most expensive commissions may not be the best.* Prompt order execution and reporting back of fills are paramount to the short-term trader.

Types of Orders

Many of your orders will be market orders. Learn to use market orders. Don't hesitate to enter or exit at the market, particularly if you are a day trader. Although some of the methods in this book require price orders, do not be afraid to enter or exit at the market when necessary.

Don't Ride Losses

Don't ride losses beyond your originally intended point. Make certain that you enter and exit according to your system as often as you can, sticking to your rules as much as possible.

Mechanical Trading vs. "Artistic" Trading

While there is much to be said in favor of a totally mechanical system, there are times when science must give way to art. Try to establish the validity of your market intuition; determine when it can be trusted. Being overly rigid is not always in your best interest.

Don't Be Afraid to Enter on Reactions within an Existing Trend

Many of the techniques described in this book are based on trend reactions. When reactions within the trend occur, traders often believe that the trend has ended and that further trades can't be justified. In a good uptrend or downtrend, though, reactions are usually quite reliable for entry purposes. You must learn to overcome the fear of entering the market, and you must avoid second-guessing the system. The odds are clearly in your favor when you enter on trend reactions.

Think for Yourself

Don't rely too much on information from outside sources. Take the systems, methods, and ideas to which you have been exposed and integrate them into an approach that makes sense to you and gives you results. Develop your own style, methods, and rules.

Don't Attempt to Trade by Long Distance

As a short-term trader, you must be in touch with the markets quite frequently. It is unwise to trade with insufficient information or while you are out of touch with the market. I know many a trader who has attempted this and has paid a dear price indeed.

Do Your Homework

Whatever combination of techniques or system you ultimately arrive at, make certain that you keep your work up to date. If your work is not up to date, don't trade.

Trade Frequently, but Not Just for the Sake of Trading

The best way to maximize capital from day trading or short-term trading is to trade frequently. This keeps your capital working. But you must be careful not to create trades or signals where none exist. To trade simply for the sake of trading is ultimately a losing proposition.

Be Aggressive

After you have traded with a particular system or method for a while you'll develop a sense for it that will alert you to the best opportunities—when you see these you'll recognize them, and your response should be an aggressive one. Follow the major trend of the market, adding to positions when you can, thereby maximizing your profit from such moves.

Understand Market Behavior

There are many different theories about the marketplace, each with its own rules and explanations. Understand how your system works: what it is saying about the marketplace and what it is saying about each trade you make. Understanding how a system works can tell you a great deal about the nature of the market at any given point in time.

Trade Active Markets Only

Short-term and day traders have minimal price and time advantage in inactive markets. They need good volume for entry and exit, and good prices swings to make entry and exit worthwhile.

CONCLUSIONS

There are many other things that the short-term trader will need to know. They can be learned only from experience. The guidelines I have offered here are gathered from my study of and experiences with the markets since 1968. Because the character of the market changes with time, it is impossible to declare without reservation that all of these suggestions will continue to serve you many years hence. As an individual speculator, the most important thing that you can do is understand the concepts of the market and the nature of your relationship to the market. Then you will be able to change with the market, instead of fighting change in the market.

CHAPTER THIRTEEN

WHEN TO TRADE

The depth of information contained in this manual may seem excessive to some, insufficient to others. Certain individuals are overwhelmed by too much information; others are constantly striving for more information. Even with the assistance of computers it is difficult for the human mind to process all of the inputs affecting the marketplace at any given point in time. But once you understand the purpose of market information you begin to realize that *not all information is important at any given point in time. In fact, some information is more important than other information.* What's truly amazing is that information that may be important in one type of market at a given time may not be important at all at another time, even in a similar market.

The purpose of information is to create opportunities for the trader. The trader should view such things as government reports, rumors, news (expected and unexpected)—in short, all factors that affect the markets—as opportunities upon which to trade. More often than not such opportunities will be consistent with the existing market trend. However, when this is not the case, the news or other influence is likely to provide an opportunity to establish a trade. Although most traders evaluate the content of the news, it is market response to the news that is of primary importance. The market is at any time a balance (whether fair or unfair) of buyers and sellers. These two groups are always looking for reasons to establish or abandon their positions. Furthermore, bulls will be looking for bullish news, and bears will be looking for bearish news. Astute bulls will be looking for bearish news so that they may buy into downside reactions. Astute bears will be looking for bullish news so that they may sell into upside reactions. The market ultimately rules all, and news in and of itself, taken out of context to market trends, is virtually meaningless.

Since our orientation considers the purpose of news as being to create opportunities for traders, the market can be evaluated in terms of the opportunities created by the news. A very bullish piece of news in a bull market that results in liquidation (i.e., a selloff) *is not bullish news at all*. It is news that has been taken advantage of by astute traders to mask considerable selling. Bearish news in a bear market that ultimately has a bullish effect is bullish news. Astute buyers have been using the news to establish long positions, masking their buying under the smokescreen of bearish fundamentals. In a bull trend, bearish news that has a brief impact on the market is a bullish indication and vice versa in a bearish trend. As a consequence, the short-term trader, whether technically inclined or not, should be aware of market response to information even though the processing of such information is not his or her primary consideration. Unfortunately, I cannot provide a mechanical framework by which such evaluations may be performed: this must be based ultimately on experience and personal skill. Some traders are better off never knowing the news; others make very good use of it, fitting it adeptly into the framework of their technical trading system. This is part of the art of trading. I maintain that it cannot be taught. Individuals must develop it through experience in the marketplace.

THE LANGUAGE OF THE MARKETPLACE

Markets do not function like machines. As I've indicated, all technical trading approaches or theoretical constructs of the market seek to impose a framework upon the marketplace in order to understand the message of its behavior. In other words, technical analysis or fundamental analysis are methods of interpreting the language of the marketplace. In some cases, traders are content to watch the behavior of the marketplace and to predict, based on past experience, what its next action is likely to be. Other traders, however, are interested in a much more detailed understanding of the marketplace. They wish to understand both the language and the behavior. A grasp of market language tends to increase your performance by improving your timing and flexibility in the marketplace.

Consider the following analogy. A stranger who does not speak my language approaches me. If I understand his language I would know what to expect if he says "I am about to knock you in the head," or "I am going to give you a hundred dollars in five minutes." I would be prepared to duck when the stranger struck out in an attempt to injure me, or to have my hand open when the hundred dollars was given out. If I do not know the language, then I must await the behavior. When the behavior begins to develop, I may not be quick enough either to avoid punishment or to accept reward.

Some trading approaches attempt to help you understand the language of the marketplace. Others cannot, and do not seek to do so, but this does not mean that they cannot help you make money. It does, however, mean that your market understanding will be limited, and that you must therefore be quick to exit when you are wrong and quick to enter when you are right. In other words, *a mechanical response to the behavior of the marketplace tends to be slower than a response that is prompted by an understanding of market language.* The purely mechanical approach to market analysis is certainly valid, but it leaves you in many situations that will be unclear to you, both before and after a trade. You will need to act very quickly in order to take advantage of market opportunities. Ultimately, a true understanding of the market must be acquired in order to increase your percentage odds of making a profit on any given trade.

What I have been teaching you in this manual *does not interpret the language of the marketplace for you.* It is merely designed to show you some behavioral characteristics of the marketplace.

Unclear Situations

Since we must assume that our understanding of the market at any point in time will be far from complete, we must also assume that this condition will lead to situations that are unclear. The lack of clarity will often result in losses. Since it is important for the short-term trader to reduce losses, it must follow that losses can be minimized if the trader avoids unclear situations (i.e., instances that are characterized by a lack of agreement in your technical indicators). As paradoxical as it may sound, unclear situations are rather clear. Though the result of these situations may be a profit, they can just as easily yield a loss. *Traders are better off doing nothing in such instances than they are in forcing a trade.*

Quick Response

There are many technical traders in today's markets. In fact, I would say that an overwhelming majority of traders are technical. Many technical trading systems that have been developed on the same general concepts will trigger a trade simultaneously or in very close proximity to each other. Therefore, your response time must be as brief as possible. You will need to (a) collect the data as fast as possible; (b) analyze the data promptly; and (c) respond immediately once conditions "a" and "b" signal a trade. This holds true for entry as well as exit. Experienced traders will understand precisely what I am saying. Newcomers may not yet understand this but they will understand quickly—I only hope their education does not cost them dearly.

PRE-HOLIDAY MARKETS

Over the years, many traders have come to avoid trading in pre-holiday or post-holiday markets. This aversion has been reinforced by the fact that pre-holiday markets tend to have less trading volume, as many traders leave early and do not participate in trading while they are gone. Some traders feel that the thin volume of the pre-holiday market should exclude their participation because their particular trading indicators may not work as effectively in such conditions as they ordinarily would. Though this may have been true in the past, I suspect that it is no longer the case. The overall increase in market activity, and the need of many market participants, particularly commercial interests, banks, and other financial institutions, to be involved in the markets at virtually all times, have made pre-holiday markets more conducive to trading. I find, in fact, that many significant price movements occur in pre-holiday periods and, furthermore, that important seasonal price tendencies have clustered around holiday periods. This is particularly true in the case of stock market averages and indices. I recommend *The Behavior of Prices on Wall Street*, by Art Merrill, as a good book on this topic.[1]

THIN MARKETS

Thin markets are characterized by very limited trading volume for extended periods of time. Though there are some perennially thin markets (such as orange juice), these do change at times, and traders should monitor them periodically in order to assess their liquidity and/or volume in light of their own particular purposes.

DAY OF WEEK

Some traders have strong feelings about which days of the week are best suited for short-term trading. Some claim that their findings are based on statistical research. Others know that their expectations or conclusions are based upon intuition or rumor. My limited research indicates that Tuesdays, Wednesdays, and Fridays appear to be the best days for short-term trading. These conclusions are based strictly upon observation and experience and most certainly are not written in stone. I imagine that the ultimate truth of the matter will be that virtually any day of the week is as good as any other day of the week for intraday or short-term trading.

IN CLOSING

This chapter offers some general guidelines about when to trade and when not to trade. How valuable they prove is eventually very much an individual matter. Though all may not necessarily be entirely sensible to you, I trust that a few will strike home. In closing, I would like to add a caution to traders to avoid trading when they are ill or otherwise incapable of giving the markets their full attention. I must add, however, that I have encountered arguments against even this conventional wisdom; in fact, some traders may actually trade better in such circumstances, because their tendency to overtrade or over-analyze is diminished.

NOTES

[1] Art Merrill, *The Behavior of Prices on Wall Street* (Chappaqua, N.Y.: Analysis Press, 1984).

CHAPTER FOURTEEN

ODDS AND ENDS

This chapter contains some random observations, in no particular order of importance, which I think will help you improve your understanding of, attitude toward, and interpretation of the markets.

THE CONDITIONED RESPONSE TO TRADE

Many of the maladies that tend to affect short-term traders are conditioned responses (unconsciously learned) to market behavior. Because traders have engaged in trading for such a long time, the stimulus of the marketplace elicits the response of wanting to trade. This response can occur even in the absence of trading signals. The mere act of watching the market is often enough to arouse the trading response in many traders. Such behavior provides a textbook case of operant conditioning and stimulus generalization, concepts defined and discussed by B. F. Skinner in his classic works on the conditioning of organisms. Essentially, Skinner's work demonstrated that much of our behavior is learned, or conditioned, voluntarily and subtly, by those around us, from our environment, and from our experiences.[1]

   An understanding of the work of such psychological learning theorists as Skinner, Hull, Tolman, Pavlov, and others, will help you understand how we are conditioned by the stimulus of the marketplace to respond in a certain way. Although much of their work was done with laboratory animals, many findings of the learning theorists have been clearly and unequivocally demonstrated to apply to humans as well. It is entirely possible that rats and pigeons are better learners than humans, but I am not interested in debating the applicability of results from animal studies to the behavior of human beings—I know that they are applicable in one sense or another. Conditioning (otherwise known as learning) can result in the development of faulty behavior patterns. The need to trade is a conditioned response that occurs as a function of the unconscious learning process. Knowing you are susceptible to such behavior, and being able to recognize it, will allow you to stop it before it starts, or at least stop it shortly after its onset.

These theories of conditioning have been previously presented in my books, *The Investor's Quotient*[2] and *Beyond the Investor's Quotient*.[3] I won't go into a major discussion of them here, but I do think you should understand the basics of the conditioned need to trade (or, for that matter, any conditioned response that has negative results), before you take the plunge into short-term and day trading.

THE INABILITY TO STICK TO YOUR PLANS

The most common trading error commited by those involved in short-term trading is the inability to stay with a plan, program, system or method. This is so common a problem, in fact, that an entire book could be written about it. Many of the chapters in *The Investor's Quotient* and *Beyond the Investor's Quotient* deal with these issues. Without entering into a lengthy explanation of this issue, here are a few things to consider if you are having difficulty staying with your method or system:

Do You Really Have Confidence in Yourself?

If you lack the conviction that you can do well in the markets, you will be prone to inconsistency in your trading decisions. Such inconsistencies will not only limit your ability to stay with a given system or method—they will also manifest themselves in a constant need to second-guess or modify the specific dictates of your trading system. Another manifestation will be the inability to ride winners and close out losers. All in all, the entire potential of your trading approach could be considerably diminished if you fail to have a positive attitude about your abilities.

Do You Have Confidence in Your Trading System?

Some trading systems naturally inspire confidence, either in oneself or in one's system. But if you lack confidence in your system or method, you will be susceptible to the same inconsistent and unprofitable behaviors described earlier. Furthermore, you also will be vulnerable to the error of mixing your system with the input of other systems, and market behaviors that are not systematic. The result will be no system at all. One way to build confidence in your system or method is to study its performance over a fairly lengthy period of time. Learn how your system works in good times and in bad. Learn how the system has behaved in bull markets, bear markets, and sideways markets. *Although it is certainly true that the historical performance of any trading approach does not guarantee its present or future performance, there is some confidence to be gained from its record, particularly if it has a long history.* If you can't have confidence in the system and if the system can't instill confidence in you, drop it and find something new.

Too Much Information

Many traders are influenced by a steady influx of information from outside sources such as associates, brokers, newspapers, newsletters, relatives, and so on. Some traders are unable to minimize the influence of external information and frequently react to it by misinterpreting or mishandling their trading approach. The best way for most traders to deal with this type of input is to shut it off. If you find, upon review, that a good many of your losses are due to unwarranted reliance upon external information, then by all means take steps to prevent your exposure to it.

NOTES

[1] B. F. Skinner, *Science and Human Behavior* (New York: Free Press, 1953).

[2] J. Bernstein, *The Investor's Quotient* (New York: John Wiley & Sons, 1980).

[3] J. Bernstein, *Beyond the Investor's Quotient* (New York: John Wiley & Sons, 1986).

CHAPTER FIFTEEN

ON RISK MANAGEMENT

Throughout the years, we've all been exposed to various perspectives on money management and its most effective implementation. Most professional traders advocate a strict approach to money management in order to facilitate success, especially for short-term trading.

What, exactly, is money management? Consider the following general aspects:

Preservation of Capital

Simply stated, you must preserve your capital by cutting your losses if you wish to survive in the futures game. This may seem an obvious enough rule, but I assure you it is easier said than done. Many short-term and day traders find it virtually impossible to manage their money. The many reasons will be explained later on.

Proponents of capital preservation have advanced the concepts of maximization of return on each profitable trade and minimization of loss on each losing trade. Having a maximum amount you are willing to risk when you enter a trade, or setting a risk limit based on technical indicators, will, it is said, help you achieve these goals. This is seemingly sound reasoning. Yet, upon closer examination, it may well be found to be incorrect and even presumptuous. I continue to find that the practice of using stop loss placement as a function

213

of predetermined dollar risk is misguided. It is not necessarily consistent with the objectives of a technical system. It is a requirement imposed by psychological and financial needs as opposed to technical indicators. Even if one optimizes stop loss procedures by basing them on market history, the logic may not necessarily be any more solid. Money management stop losses are artificial. They manage by money and not by market behavior. Yet the notion of a maximum dollar risk is appealing. Its value is in imposing a limit on losses. It helps circumvent a speculator's major weakness—riding losses too long. In other words, a rigid limit of dollar risk, if adhered to, will force the speculator out of his or her position if the technical system fails to do so or if signals from the system are ignored. The issue of capital preservation is, therefore, difficult to resolve by predetermined dollar risk on each trade. As always, a truly workable solution is an individual matter.

A reasonable alternative is to let each trade take its natural course and allow the indicators to get you in and out, but with a "fail-safe" level established for each trade that will get you out if the indicators fail. Each speculator must find his or her particular solution to this dilemma.

Maximization of Capital

The second function of successful money management is maximization of capital. Some traders feel that they must be in the market at all times or that they must trade every day if they are to maximize their capital. I suspect that operating on this basis alone is a good way to *minimize* capital. Capital maximization, as I understand it, involves (a) preserving trading capital for only the most promising situations; (b) allotting capital on the basis of performance and potential; and (c) trading only the *required* amount of capital, with the excess employed in other areas of speculation and or investment.

Dispersal of Profits

Believe it or not, this is a frequent problem: many traders often make profits quickly and give them back even more quickly because they don't have a well-prepared plan for distributing their profits. I view the marketplace as a treasure chest—when it is open, one must grab all one can get before the heavy lid slams shut. The idea is to take it quickly and to keep it out of the treasure chest. At times, you may have to force the lid open; this will take time, energy and money (for the proper tools). Yet, the goal is always the same: to take out more than you put in. Therefore, I urge all traders to *regularly remove some profits from the market,* placing them in investments that guarantee a slow but steady rate of return. Routinely removing profits from the market will help you in two ways: first, you'll have funds to put back into the market in the event that you need to refinance your account, and second, you'll have funds for other purposes.

Double Up or Cut Back

It is not uncommon for traders to double up after one or two losing trades. This practice was, perhaps, originally adapted from the Black-jack card game. The mere fact that this practice may be derived from gambling puts it in a bad light among traders; however, I suggest that *under the right circumstances it might not be bad to double up*. If, for example, you have a system that rarely takes more than three successive losses, you can double your position after the third successive loss. But if you do so you must remember that you are taking more risk and that you will not necessarily be guaranteed a profit. Ultimately, a trading system with a high number of winning trades will benefit from such a procedure, though it takes stamina and fortitude to implement.

On the other side of the coin we find the practice of cutting back when things are not going well. There's nothing wrong with this procedure. In fact, it's not a bad way to preserve capital while you try to figure out what's going wrong.

Loss Management By Market Behavior

As discussed earlier, there are two basic approaches to loss management. One method limits losses by setting a predetermined dollar amount per trade. One decides, *a priori*, that one will risk only a certain amount on each trade or on each market. This approach, however, imposes an artificial limit on the market and on your trading, and therefore seems impractical to me. It makes more sense to manage losses by market behavior. After all, is it not ultimately the market that must be followed? Before you decide to go with a strict maximum dollar-per-trade risk approach, consider loss management by market behavior as an alternative.

Before deciding which approach best suits you, consider the following:

1. Loss management by market behavior (that is, using timing signals and trading objectives only) may require you to take more risk per trade.

2. A maximum dollar-per-trade risk may limit your loss on each trade, but it may also remove you from situations that could ultimately turn out profitable.

3. A maximum dollar-per-trade risk may allow you to trade more markets at once, thereby allowing you to diversify your trading.

DIVERSIFICATION

I won't spend too much time on this aspect of money management. The fact is that many traders fail to diversify. Your success or failure should not depend entirely upon the performance of your trading approach in only one or two markets. I suggest that you monitor and trade in a variety of markets. Avoid the thin markets, but monitor at least 14 to18 markets regularly and diversify your trading accordingly.

CONSIDER MULTIPLE POSITIONS

I find that a particularly valuable strategy is to trade in multiple contracts (if you can afford to do so) *but in a manner distinctly different from the old pyramiding approach*. In the typical pyramiding approach, the initial entry consists of the smallest number of contracts. As the market moves in your direction more and more contracts are added, leading eventually to an upside-down pyramid with the largest number of contracts at the highest price. This leaves the trader vulnerable—a small reversal can bring the house down. This is not, to my way of thinking, the way to trade. I advocate building a real pyramid instead: begin with your largest position and add successively smaller units along the way.

Another procedure particularly suitable for the day trader is to begin with multiple contracts. As the market moves in your favor you can take a profit quickly on half of your contracts, keeping the remaining contracts for a more optimistic target. I prefer this approach because it allows one to take some profits and to let some profits ride.

BE WELL CAPITALIZED BEFORE YOU BEGIN

I strongly urge you to avoid any type of trading until you are well capitalized. Though this should be an obvious caveat to all traders, it is, indeed, one that tends to be ignored by the overly zealous. Let's face it: By today's standards, any account of less than $10,000 has little chance of success. Increase your initial trading capital and you'll have more staying power. Don't begin trading with an amount so small that you are beaten before you start!

ADVISORY SERVICES

Some traders do well by following a particular service or newsletter that specializes in short-term trading. There's nothing wrong with this approach. In fact, traders who lack discipline can often better their results by subscribing to a service that will help them with specific entry and exit points. The failure of many traders to practice appropriate discipline is due to a lack of specificity in their trading approach. If this happens to be your problem, then you should seriously consider such services and newsletters.

However, remember that subscribing to too many services or newsletters leads to confusion. Also, once you've taken a particular service or newsletter, don't second guess it. Trade as it instructs. Don't pick and choose.

BEWARE OF WHAT YOU READ

Since the 1980s the price of computer hardware and market development software has declined substantially. It is now possible for individuals to develop trading systems which, although back tested over a fairly lengthy period of time, may also be optimized or curve fitted to reflect the best possible results. Although these results will certainly look very attractive on paper, when you attempt to implement them in actual trading you will find them ineffective in many cases. Earlier in this book I referred to a statement taken from the Jack Schwager interview by Bruce Babcock. Let me reiterate Jack Schwager's words: "The easiest thing in the world is to develop a system which makes 200 hundred percent or 400 hundred percent a year in the past. It doesn't mean anything except that you fitted the rules to exploit past price action. When you trade such a system in the future expect a drastic reduction in performance." I caution you to be particularly mindful of such trading methods. In particular, be especially rigorous in examining the methods by which they manage risk. While some systems may promise outstanding results they do not provide sufficient information on such important parameters as maximum consectuive losing trades and drawdown. As short-term trading becomes more prevalent, more short-term and day trading systems will be made available to the public. Many systems developers will seek to capitalize on an otherwise ignorant or uninformed trading public. I suggest you avoid being one of the uninformed masses.

CHAPTER SIXTEEN

DEVELOPING YOUR OWN INDICATORS

It seems to me, after many years of experience in the futures industry, that almost everyone who trades in futures has a need to develop his or her own trading approach, regardless of what has been done or presented by others. This is a strong statement about human individuality. It is also a strong statement about the individuality of futures traders in particular. Though down deep many of us are attracted by simple cookbook-type methods, we seek somehow to improve upon what we've learned. The results are not always for the better, but the effort continues. Actually, it is a fact that most traders will not profit from their various methodologies that are at fault, but rather the psychologies of the traders, which often prove to be the undoing of otherwise effective or promising techniques. I suspect that no matter how advanced the field of futures research becomes, the need to improve available systems will always predominate in the marketplace.

Individual personalities and trading styles seem to manifest themselves in individual strategies, leading to a multitude of opinions and actions, all within the same time frame. It is this very multiplicity of action that *creates* a marketplace. It provides opportunities for buyers and sellers. It allows the liquidity that makes the marketplace a

219

significant economic institution. In other words, the more systems and methods there are, and the more variations there are upon these systems and methods, the more efficient and liquid will be the marketplace.

Because I feel there is something to be learned from the experiences of all traders, I think it would be helpful for me to share with you some thoughts and experiences regarding my efforts at developing trading methods. (There are many excellent books that can guide you, with great detail, through trading systems research.) Here, then, not necessarily in order of importance, are some general items to consider when you conduct your own short-term trading research.

1. *Determine whether the length of your data history is sufficient.* Many systems are tested on very limited data. Though it is not necessary to test a system on too many years worth of data, you should make every effort to test a system in different kinds of markets (bull markets, bear markets, sideways markets). More specific information on this will follow.

2. *Do you intend to test a true system, or merely a set of indicators?* There is a big difference. Some traders work better with a set of indicators that is not entirely systematic; others need the discipline of a strictly mechanical system. Decide what's right or best for you, and then test.

3, *Attempt to innovate.* Don't get stuck in the rut of doing what everyone else is doing. Take new directions. Seek out unique indicators that make sense to you and that work best for your particular needs and markets.

These general guidelines are discussed more thoroughly in what follows. Certainly, I have not covered all the relevant topics, but I suspect that I have highlighted the major issues. Remember, above all else, that your indicators should be designed with your best interests in mind. So many current trading systems are based upon the same traditional concepts. I myself have been guilty of this, though I think you can see by my presentation that I have added many unique features. I find that there is much to be said in favor of new concepts and approaches. I do not necessarily mean that the actual parameters you study must be different; rather, your methods of application and interpretation should be unique. Don't worry about what anyone else will think about their logic or sense—if they work for you, that's all you need!

TESTING A SYSTEM

Perhaps the most common frustration shared by traders who seek to develop their own systems and methods is that of developing a technique that appears to have great promise when subjected to testing, but fails to make profits in actual application. I have seen many excellent ideas and very logical concepts fail to generate profits in real time trading. There are numerous reasons for this, but unless they help you improve your performance, they'll be meaningless. Some possible explanations are suggested below.

Slippage on Entry and Exit

Most systems testing routinely assumes ideal entry and exit. Even in cases where a certain amount of slippage (i.e., deterioration from hypothetical results) is permitted for poor entry and exit, it is more often than not insufficient to account for actual losses due to slippage. In real-time experience, slippage can account for significant differential in bottom-line performance. The day trader, in particular, should be very concerned about this since 50 percent or more of his or her potential profits can be eaten up by slippage. Therefore, I suggest that when you test a system, you allow a specific amount of slippage per trade above and beyond what seems reasonable to you. Tests for performance in the marketplace should be designed to give you the *worst-case result rather than the best-case result*. Traders are naturally inclined to test for maximum performance or best results, but in real time experience such results are rarely duplicated.

Commissions

Although a relatively minor consideration, particularly to active traders who pay significantly low "discount" commissions, this cost of doing business is important. It is a simple matter to include the cost of commissions in analyzing bottom-line performance, but it is often overlooked.

Time Delay

Computer-testing of systems is usually based upon immediate market entry on a timing signal. Frequently, traders forget to account for possible time lag in generating signals. This holds true for both entry and exit signals. The deduction for slippage, mentioned above, should help compensate for such delays.

Insufficient Data Base

In recent years a plethora of trading systems have been developed upon limited data. I find no problem with the use of a limited time span in systems testing; however, the time spans that are tested should be representative of many different types of markets. See the next section for suggestions regarding this topic.

CREATE A RANDOM REPRESENTATIVE TEST FILE

Contemporary statistical methodology is based upon the valid assumption that data drawn from a limited, random but representative sample are sufficient for testing a given market indicator. Such data are gathered according to the principles of random representative testing. The same principle is used in compiling television and radio ratings. The idea here is a very logical and simple one, indeed. In order to appraise a system, method, indicator—or assess public opinion—one compiles a test file consisting of data taken from a random, representative sample. Such a sample ensures that bias or preselection will not color the statistics (because it is random) and that the data will reflect the market as a whole (because it is representative). Therefore, if you have a random representative test file for your indicators or systems, you won't have to test literally thousands of days or weeks worth of data.

CONSTRUCTING A TEST FILE

Obtain a historical chart book that surveys many different types of markets over a significant span of years. Or obtain weekly charts that cover a ten-year time span—they will ultimately serve the same purpose. Examine charts for all of the markets. When you do so, be sure to classify each market as one of the following types:

- **Major Bull Market**. Generally defined as a market that moves higher for most of its contract life, with few interruptions in trend. (See Figure 16.1.)

- **Minor Bull Market.** A bull market that moves generally higher for most of the contract life but that has significant downside corrections along the way. (See Figure 16.2.)

If you are using weekly charts, first select the periods of time that show up as bull markets or bear markets; then go to the specific daily charts. Your final selection should be based on daily price charts. If you are testing indicators on an intraday basis, you must also be specific as to your time frame. For example, if you intend to trade in the day or in a one to three-day time frame, you must use intraday data for your analyses and testing. If your needs are very specific—for example, if all of your trading will be based on five-minute data—then you must select five-minute bull or bear markets for your testing. In short, your test file must replicate the length of the time-frame you are using, otherwise the file may not be truly representative.

- **Major Bear Market.** A market that tends to head lower for the majority of its run, with very few and only minor corrections to the upside. (See Figure 16.3.)

- **Minor Bear Market.** A bear market that also heads lower but that has significant rallies and upside corrections during the course of its run. (See Figure 16.4.)

- **Sideways Market.** A market that tends to move sideways for the majority of its move without really going anywhere. The moves up or down are not major within the sideways trend and are relatively brief (i.e., ranging from a half-hour to five or six days). (See Figure 16.5.) Note that sideways markets are distinguished from whipsaw markets, discussed below.

Whipsaw Market. A market that has sharp back and forth moves, up and down, but that tends to end up in the same place or near the same place at which it started. At the end of this chapter I have provided a few examples of the different kinds of markets I have described here. (See Figure 16.6.)

Your random representative test file should consist ideally of approximately ten samples of each type of market. Once it's assembled, you're ready to test your indicators, systems, or methods in a logical fashion, based on a sound sampling of data. Of course, you must be careful not to assume that the test result will be 100 percent accurate; nevertheless, I think you will find that such testing yields fairly representative results, which should provide a close approximation of market realities.

IN CLOSING

When you develop your own indicators and/or systems, remember above all else that the ultimate value of a trading system or indicator is not measured by its apparent logic or lack thereof. It is measured in terms of its results and, in particular, its effectiveness in your trading program. I often have observed that what works for one individual does not necessarily work for another. Perhaps this is so partly because of traders' differing abilities to implement the same programs. Intuition and art are clearly influential. In fact, they frequently can play an important role in the success or failure of systems and methods.

Figure 16.1: Major Bull Market

Figure 16.2: Minor Bull Market

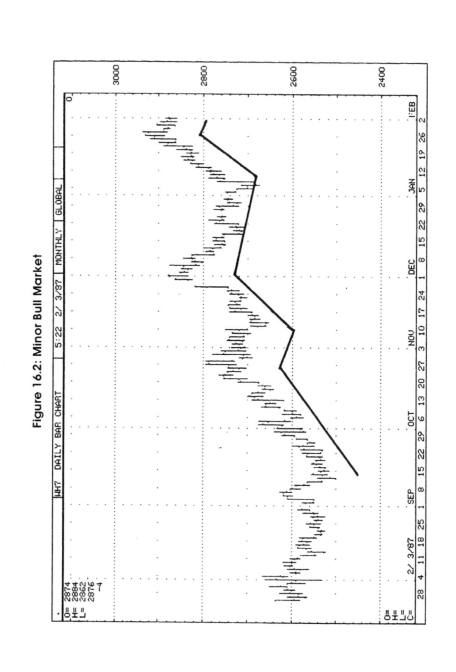

Figure 16.3: Major Bear Market

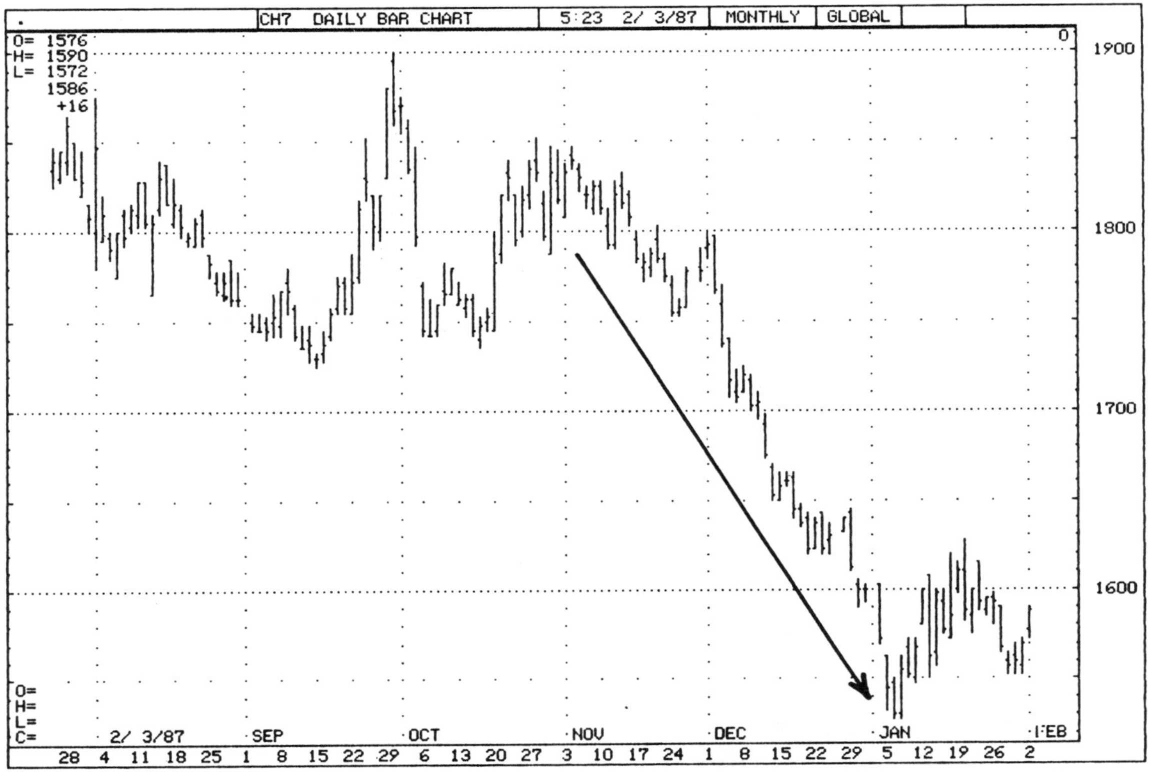

Figure 16.4: Minor Bear Market

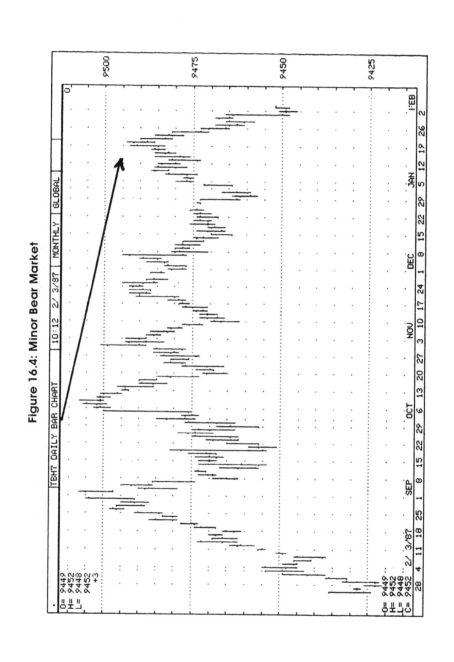

Figure 16.5: Sideways/Choppy Market

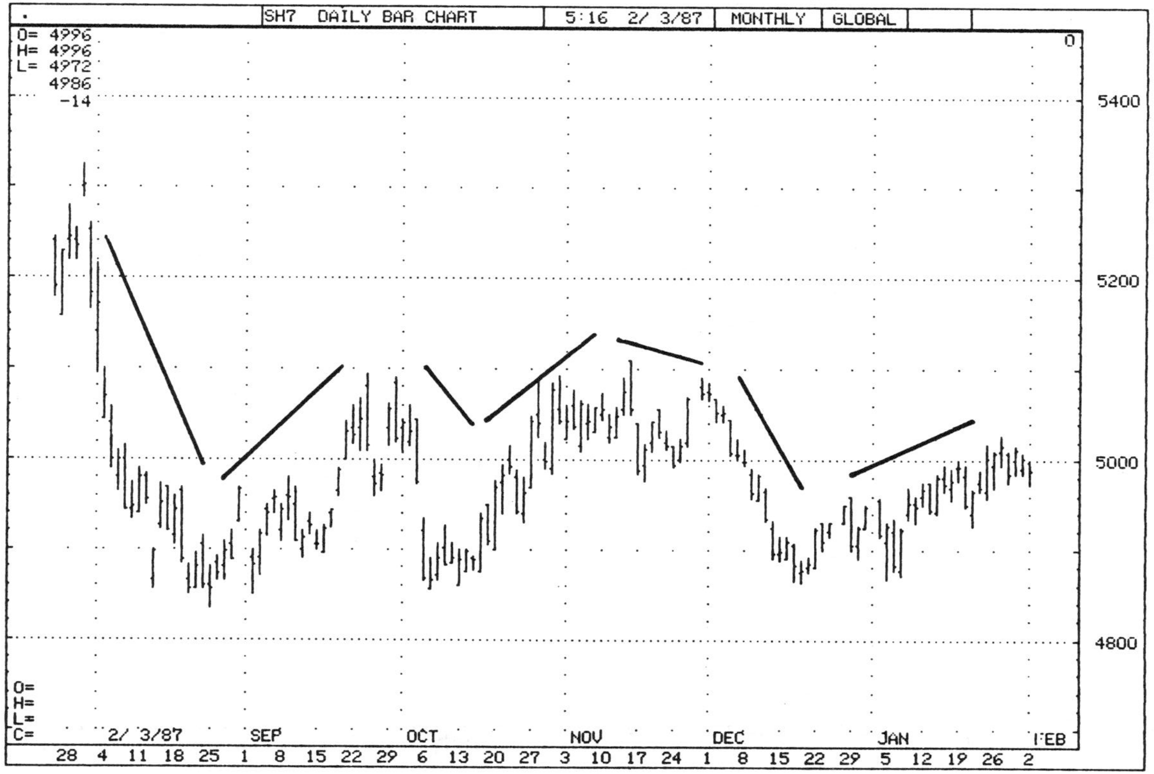

Figure 16.6: Whipsaw Market

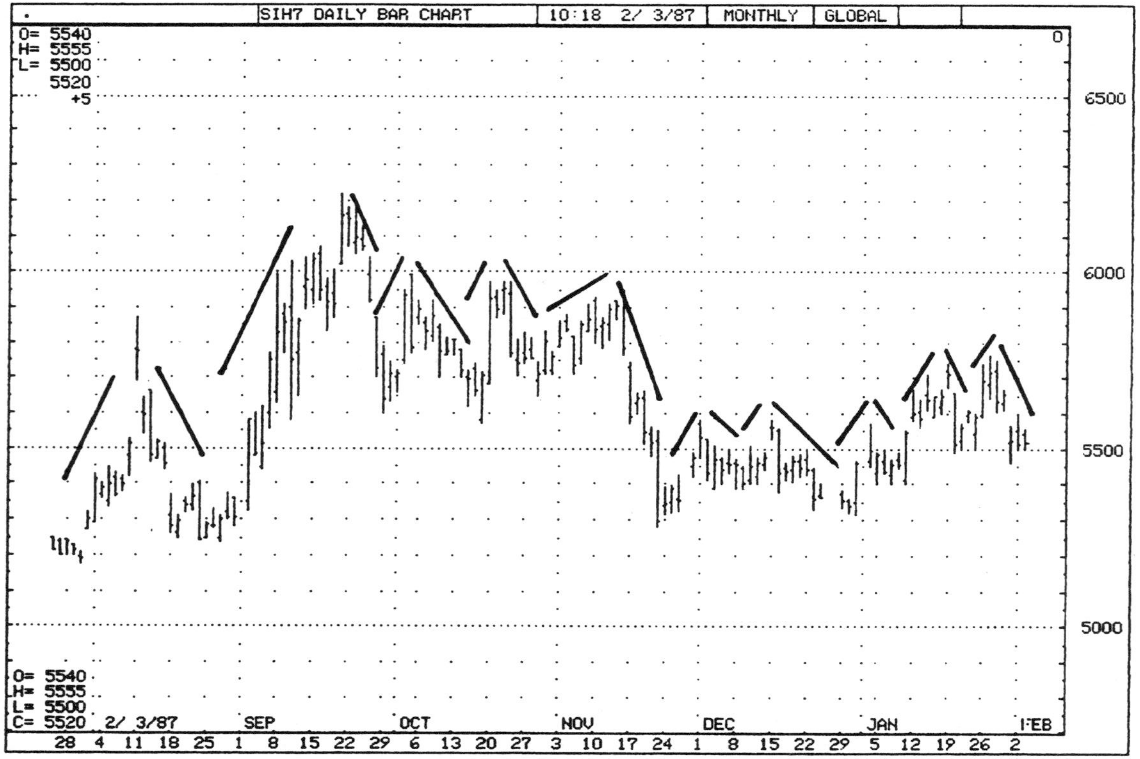

CHAPTER SEVENTEEN

DAILY SENTIMENT INDICATOR

Since the first edition of this book was published in 1987 I've completed a considerable amount of research into short-term timing indicators. It has become increasingly clear to me that many of the indicators which traders have been using for quite a few years are either ineffective, inefficient, or not appl,icable to today's volatile markets. Since I first started trading in the late 1960's the idea of market sentiment as a timing indicator has always intrigued me. The only reliable market sentiment data available at the time was compiled weekly by R. Earle Hadady. Unfortunately, there was a time delay in the release of Hadady's data inasmuch as the process of collecting data (frequently by mail) and then disseminating the data to subscribers did not lend itself to use by short-term traders. Consequently, in 1987, along with several associates, I initiated the DSI, Daily Sentiment Index. The DSI is intended for use strictly by short-term traders. It is compiled daily by telephone and is available by 4:00 P.M. Chicago time in order to permit application to either the overnight markets and/or the next day's trading. The Daily Sentiment Index is strictly a short-term sentiment indicator which can change dramatically from one day to the next since trader sentiment is frequently affected substantially by market developments and news. Although

231

such dramatic changes from one day to the next may be considered a drawback for the position trader, they are ideally suited for the purposes of short-term trading. Before giving you some suggestions on how short-term trading may be enhanced by the use of daily market sentiment, I'll give you a few definitions and working rules.

DEFINITIONS

Market sentiment is defined as the collective opinion of traders regarding their bullish or bearish expectations for a given market or markets. When market sentiment is highly bullish, a vast majority of traders who are assessed in our daily sample expect higher prices. We therefore consider their sentiment to be bullish and high. Operationally, high bullish sentiment is defined as 80 percent or more of the total sample expecting higher prices. Conversely, bearish market sentiment is defined as 20 percent of the total sample expecting higher prices. For the sake of convenience we express market sentiment as a percentage ranging from 0–100. Sentiment of 50 percent and under indicates a bearish tone while sentiment of greater than 50 percent indicates a bullish tone.

For more thorough information on how the Daily Sentiment Index is compiled and interpreted I suggest you read my book, *Why Traders Lose ,How Traders Win* , published by Probus in Chicago. For the purposes of this discussion the present brief summary will suffice. Market sentiment is an indication of how strongly traders are committed to one side of the market or the other. We find through empirical research that the more bullish market sentiment is, the more likely prices are to be at or near a short-term top. On the other hand, the lower the Daily Sentiment Index (the more bearish our sample) the more likely prices are to be at or near a bottom. When we study extremes in daily sentiment, for example, readings of 80 percent and higher as well as 20 percent or lower, we find that the majority of the sample is generally wrong at or near significant short-term turning points in virtually every market.

We also find that some markets have distinct sentiment characteristics which distinguish them from others. Stock index futures for example have established tops within days virtually every time sentiment has risen to 90 percent or higher. Furthermore, daily sentiment tends to remain at fairly low levels for extended periods of time when markets are bottoming; however it tends to remain at high levels only briefly when markets are topping. Hence, timing must be very precise in expecting market tops whereas there is more time to make decisions regarding market bottoms, and timing indicators must be adjusted accordingly.

CHARACTERISTICS OF DAILY SENTIMENT INDEX

The Daily Sentiment Index characteristically precedes or closely correlates with market tops and bottoms. It is therefore one of the few leading indicators of market trends that are available to futures traders.

Because market sentiment is based on the response of traders, it is, by its very nature and design, an index of the emotion. Typically market sentiment tends to rise as prices rise and decline as prices fall. Figure 17.1 illustrates the relationship between market sentiment and price trend. Although this figure illustrates an ideal situation this is in fact very similar to what actually occurs in the real world of market sentiment versus price. Figures 17.2 through 17.4 show recent price versus raw market sentiment charts.

VARIATIONS ON THE THEME OF MARKET SENTIMENT

In my work with the Daily Sentiment Index I found that the raw sentiment figures may at times be too variable for the purpose of short-term trading. Whereas they may be ideal in their raw form for day trading for the purposes of short-term trading the sentiment data must be slowed by the use of moving averages. I have employed three-, nine-, and five-day moving averages for this purpose. Figure 17.4 shows a comparison of raw sentiment versus a nine-day sentiment on the same market. As you can see, the nine-day moving average of raw sentiment is much more workable for the purpose of short-term trading.

Figure 17.1: Ideal Relationship between Market Sentiment and Price

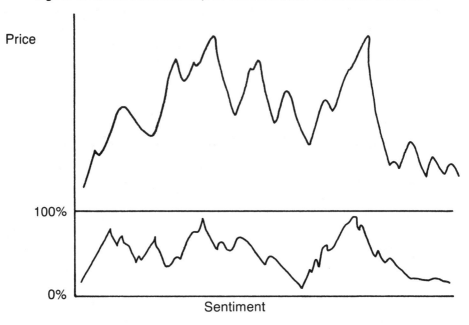

As price increases, bullish sentiment increases; as price falls, sentiment falls.

Figure 17.2: Price versus DSI

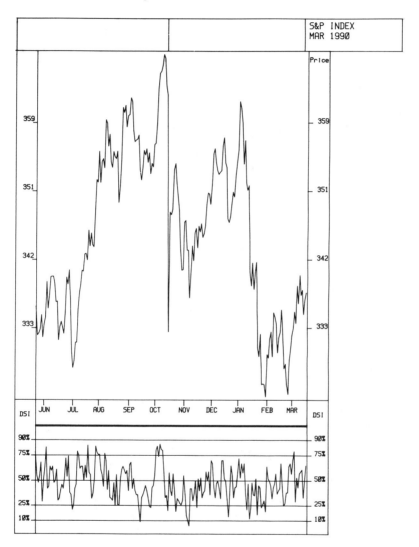

Figure 17.3: Price versus DSI

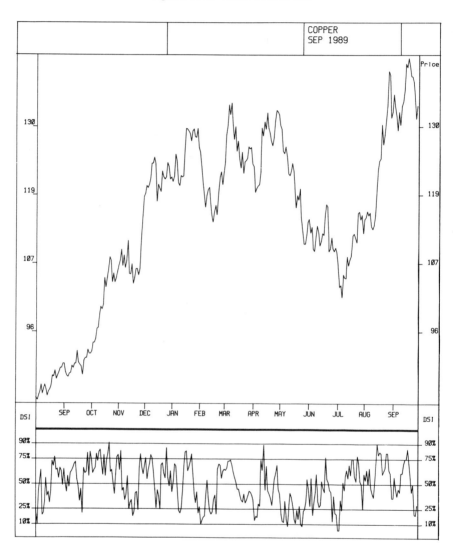

Figure 17.4: Price versus DSI

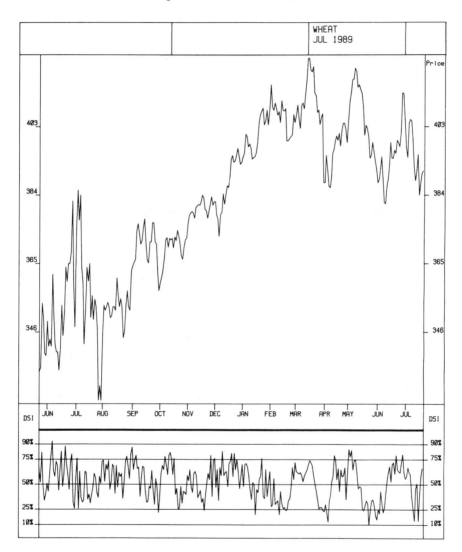

GENERAL GUIDELINES FOR THE APPLICATION OF DAILY SENTIMENT TO SHORT -TERM AND DAY TRADING

In order to apply market sentiment effectively you must be aware of the following general theoretical considerations regarding market sentiment.

1. Most futures traders lose money most of the time.

2. Most futures traders make incorrect decisions at major and minor turning points.

3. When futures traders are in general agreement that a given market is bullish or bearish they will usually be incorrect.

4. The larger the degree of agreement the more likely it is that the strongly held opinion will be incorrect. And this holds true both at market tops and market bottoms.

5. Since most futures traders are buyers rather than sellers they are most likely to be wrong when they are in strong agreement that a market will move higher.

6. It is more important to determine the opinions of average traders as opposed to professional traders since professional traders are professionals by virtue of their skills and, therefore, more knowledgeable about the markets and about their own behavior in the markets.

Strong bullish sentiment as determined by an assessment of opinions is closely correlated with changes in market trend and with market turning points. Consider the following scenario by which bullish sentiment develops.

1. Prices have been in a declining mode and most traders are negative. Fundamentals also tend to be bearish. There usually seems to be no apparent reason to buy the market since there is no apparent reason to expect higher prices. Sentiment is

therefore declining and tends to continue to decline for an extended period of time.

2.   A move to higher prices tends to begin seemingly for no reason whatsoever and is generally unrelated to any specific event or events. The move to higher prices is usually not accompanied by any significant degree of increase in bullish sentiment although bullish sentiment will rise somewhat in conjunction with the new uptrend.

3.   The move tends to continue with reasonable and normal corrections during its course and perhaps the market will even witness a temporary test or penetration of the recent low. Bullish sentiment does not grow appreciably as long as price movement is relatively slow while volatility and trading volume continue relatively low. The only factors which tend to increase bullish sentiment are moves to higher prices or exceedingly bullish news.

4.   There are peaks in bullish sentiment when prices move sharply higher for one or two days or for a series of days. Sentiment tends to decline and move lower when prices begin to move lower again.

5.   As fundamental factors supporting a given move begin to develop so will public interest, and bullish sentiment will increase. While the day-to-day changes in bullish sentiment may vary considerably, a weekly or even monthly average sentiment will show more trending behavior and will correlate well with price movement, rising in an uptrend and declining in a downtrend.

6.   As price moves gain momentum to the upside, as bullish fundamentals become more widely known among traders, and as buyers begin to control prices bullish sentiment begins to increase more rapidly and eventually reaches high levels.

7.   The news backdrop continues bullish and eventually becomes very positive at least in terms of trader perception.

8. Eventually, the news backdrop becomes so very constructive that all roads seem to lead to higher price expectations. The more bullish the market sentiment the more likely the current bullish trend is apt to be nearing its end and, in this case, as the news back drop becomes so very constructive, it is likely that bullish sentiment will rise to 80 percent or higher.

9.   Finally, the market surges higher, and bullish sentiment increases to its highest levels in many days or weeks—perhaps even to its highest level in months. This is often a telltale sign that the top is being made. The greater your inclination to buy and the closer your inclination is in agreement with the consensus of opinion, the greater the probability that you are incorrect.

10. Then, as if for no reason and often in response to very bullish news, the market tops and those who are long are caught with large positions usually at an important price peak. Frequently, the market can decline sharply once sentiment has reached very high levels.

Although not all bull markets develop precisely in this fashion the general trend and characteristics frequently are similar to those I have described. Psychological correlates of bull markets are anticipation, wish fulfillment, and hope. These emotions are counterproductive: they cloud judgment and all traders can see is higher prices. Their opinions reflect their greatest hopes, wishes, expectations, and ambitions. Unfortunately, their judgment at such important market junctures is usually incorrect.   Conversely, the psychological and behavioral correlates of market sentiment in bear markets is a function of negative opinions. Consider the following general scenario:

1. Prices have been in a rising trend. Most analysts are quite bullish. The fundamental situation is very constructive there seems to be no apparent reason to sell the market since there is no apparent reason to expect lower prices. The uptrend is alive and healthy.

2. A decline tends to begin seemingly for no reason whatsoever and is often unrelated to any specific event or events. The

decline is usually not accompanied by any significant degree of increase in negative market sentiment.

3. The decline tends to continue with reasonable and normal corrections along the way. Negative sentiment does not increase appreciably as long as price movement is slow while volatility and trading volume are relatively low.

4. From time to time there will be peaks in bearish sentiment when prices move sharply lower for a given day or series of days and bearish sentiment will become higher when prices move lower. Please note that bearish sentiment as assessed for our purposes is defined as sentiment which approaches zero as a limit. In other words, as traders become more bearish their bullish sentiment declines. In order to keep our terminology consistent, increased bearish sentiment for our purposes is synonymous with decreased bullish sentiment. Therefore, when I refer to bullish sentiment becoming low, this is the same as saying bearish sentiment becomes high.

5. Even as the fundamental factors supporting the decline begin to develop, public interest will frequently not increase appreciably since bear markets attract little public attention. Day-to-day changes in the negative sentiment or decreases in bullish sentiment will vary considerably and will correlate well with price movement as bullish sentiment declines in a falling market and as bullish sentiment rises in a rising market.

6. As the price moves lower gaining momentum on the downside and as the bearish fundamentals become more widely known, sellers begin to control prices, and the feeling that the prices will move even lower becomes more pervasive. As this process continues bullish sentiment will decline (bearish sentiment increases).

7. Eventually the news backdrop will become very negative. All indications will be that the trend is apt to continue lower for an extended period of time. The lower prices move the more negative the sentiment becomes.

8. Eventually the backdrop of news becomes so negative that the market reaches a bottom and aggressive traders begin to ac-cummulate new long positions. Rising daily market sentiment in conjunction with the timing indicators presented in this book can be a very profitable combination.

CHAPTER EIGHTEEN

SUMMING IT ALL UP

Hundreds of hours of research and trading went into the preparation of this work. Yet no manual, book, or course possibly can take the place of actual participation and experience. In fact, the best application of the principles presented in this manual may be their synthesis with your individual trading approach and techniques. As I have said earlier, every trader ultimately must develop his or her own style. If you can take the work I have presented here and combine it synergistically with your own work, then my efforts will have been fruitful. The merit of my work can only be measured by its ability to stimulate your creativity and, in turn, your self-discovery as a trader. This process of personal growth will facilitate your success in the marketplace and prompt a greater probability of profitable trading.

This manual advocates no single approach or indicator as being "the best." Instead, I have presented several approaches, some easily implemented manually, others facilitated by, or impossible without, the assistance of a computer. I've opted to provide you with a selection of methods to study and from which to choose. Yet, the methodologies I have elucidated represent just a part of the total picture. Any effective technique is made so by the creativity and discipline of the individual trader who employs it.

I have, to the best of my ability, provided you with trading guidelines and explanations of many intangible aspects of short-term trading. You must integrate them into your overall approach. *Don't blindly follow any single technique or haphazardly pick and choose among all the techniques.* Study them seriously and develop them further according to your needs. I'll close with a number of suggestions designed to help you achieve these ends.

1. Review the techniques I have presented. Select those that appeal to you.

2. Dedicate at least one month to the study of their behavior or performance in the marketplace. Several months would be even better, but one month at the minimum is what I recommend.

3. Keep a diary for each trade (whether "real" or "hypothetical"). Record what you did, why you did it, the outcome, and, most importantly, what you did right and what you did wrong.

4. Before you accept or reject an approach, determine from your diary whether you maintained discipline or whether you made too many emotional or non-system decisions.

5. If the method performed well but required a great deal of extraneous input and spontaneous decision making, continue to test it. More importantly, attempt to identify the specific type of additional decisions you'll have to make, and integrate them into the technique as part of your trading rules.

6. If your method did not work well and you find that it behaved unpredictably, you may not have tested it properly—the method may still have good potential. You may wish to return to the test with better discipline.

7. After all of this is done, begin a real time test. If you are pleased with the results of this test, then begin trading larger positions, being certain to monitor performance as you go.

8. Don't change systems repeatedly. Once you've found something that works for you, don't be tempted to change it too often. As long as it's working, leave well enough alone. Your

research may continue, but change the system only when the research and real time tests are definitive.

9. Don't form too many opinions or expectations. Naturally, when you enter a position, you do so with the expectation that it will produce a profit. But that's as far as your expectations should go. As I've demonstrated, and as you should know, expectations can and do shape perceptions. Expectations can lead you to take profits too soon and losses too late.

10. Avoid too much input—especially from other short-term traders. As you know, the input of others can be destructive. If the opinions of others agree with your position, then you may be lulled into a false sense of security. If, however, their opinions are opposed to your position, you may be prone to liquidate too soon.

There are many other things to learn, but most of them will come to you as a result of direct experience. It is my sincere hope that the suggestions in this manual, both technical and otherwise, will help you avoid the most costly errors. However, to expect both to learn the market and escape its vengeance unscathed is a fantasy.

A CLOSING WORD ABOUT EXPECTATIONS

Traders are not machines. They are human. While each trader must maintain an exterior visage of discipline and fortitude, the heart of each trader is filled with hope, fear, greed, and insecurity. The degree to which these basic emotions and needs express themselves externally in each trader varies as a function of many variables which are all, primarily, functions of learning experiences. Yet, there are many needs which are basic for survival. These are not learned, but innate. Such necessary needs as food and shelter combine with learned emotional needs to form the complex personalities of all humans.

In order to satisfy our many needs, we are driven to action. The specific actions vary with the needs they are designed to fulfill. When needs are not immediately filled the human mind strives to find solutions. Alternatives are developed, analyzed, rejected, or embellished. A by-product of this creative problem solving is expectation. Expectation often leads to disappointment. Traders are more subject to expectation and disappointment than, perhaps, any other human beings. Disappointment leads to frustration and anger, both with self and others. Anger tends to obscure logic and rational behavior. The end result is, most often, destructive to the trader.

In order to avoid the chain reaction of expectation-frustration-anger-error, I urge all readers to remember that the present manual is designed to achieve *only* the following results:

1. To introduce various methods and approaches to short-term trading.

2. To prompt possible development of these ideas into trading systems and to further research into these ideas.

3. To provide an overview of the various risk and money management concepts important to the short-term and intraday trader.

4. To stimulate avenues of new research.

This manual is clearly not one of the many "sure-fire," "can't lose," "riches beyond imagination" systems so commonly advertised these days. My ideas should be used to stimulate creative problem solving approaches to futures trading. Avoid unrealistic expectations and you will avoid disappointment. You must think and create for yourself!

CHAPTER NINETEEN

PRACTICE CHARTS

To some of you, the techniques and methods presented in this manual are totally new. Others of you may have had experience with the indicators and their application. In either case, the importance of practice, both "on paper" and in "real time," cannot be overemphasized. To this end, I have provided a number of practice charts designed to assist you in assimilating the information presented in the preceding chapters. Many different futures markets are represented by these charts, as well as markets in uptrends, downtrends, and relatively sideways trends. Thus, you will be exposed to different types of conditions.

Some of the charts which follow contain my notes (the symbol key of which appears on the following page). Other charts contain no notes whatsoever. In all instances the charts are provided for your specific practice and I strongly suggest you work with them accordingly. Should you have any questions please don't hesitate to contact me. I can be reached either at (708) 291-1870, or you can fax me at (708) 291-9435. While I can't guarantee I'll have the time to answer all your questions, I'll certainly try and help you to the best of my ability.

I recommend the following procedure for optimum benefit for our practice:

1. Cover the entire chart with a large thick index card or a heavy opaque sheet of paper.

2. Beginning at the left of the chart, work forward in time, one price bar at a time, uncovering the chart.

3. Stop after each price bar and its corresponding indicators have been uncovered.

4. Make a technical evaluation of the market based on the indicators. Make some buy, sell, or hold decisions.

5. Lightly mark your signals in pencil (as I have done on charts throughout this manual).

6. Keep a written log of your decisions and their outcome.

7. Refer to the Practice Chart "Symbol Key" provided at the end of this section.

Naturally, nothing can replace real time experience with the markets. Ultimately you will want to take my indicators, combine them with other work you have studied, or with your own trading style, and implement them in the fashion which best suits your needs, abilities, and temperament.

SYMBOL KEY TO PRACTICE CHARTS

S = INITIATE SHORT POSITION
B = INITIATE LONG POSITION
CS = COVER SHORT POSITION(S)
SL = SELL OUT LONG POSITION(S)

s = stochastic signal (as opposed to "POP" signal)
p = stochastic "pop" signal
d = DEMA signal
c = 10/8/3 channel signal
t = CTOD signal

Please note that capital letters refer to the action taken and that lower case letters refer to the type of signal or method used for market entry. For example, "St" means "CTOD sell signal."

Also note that I have attempted to show all of the signals during the given chart history within the limits of chart clarity. Actual buy and sell prices would need to be determined using the data printouts for the given charts. Such a printout would give the most accurate representation of the indicators.

For trading purposes, not all signals would be followed. Remember that the trader can choose to follow all signals from one or two particular methods, or better yet, to act only on the confluence of several signals and/or indicators. *These charts do not show any filtering or actual trades: they merely show signals on various indicators. It is the trader's job to integrate the signals into meaningful trades.*

Figure 19.1: Practice Chart

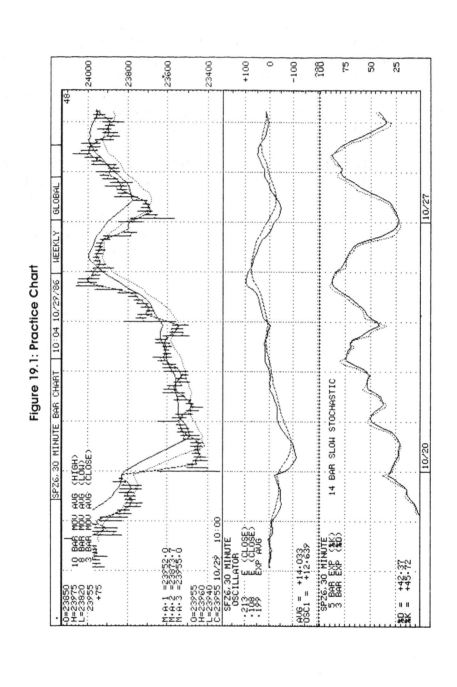

Figure 19.2: Practice Chart

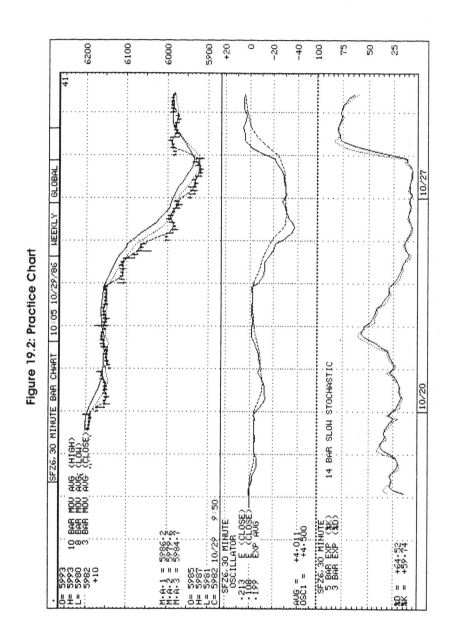

Figure 19.3: Practice Chart

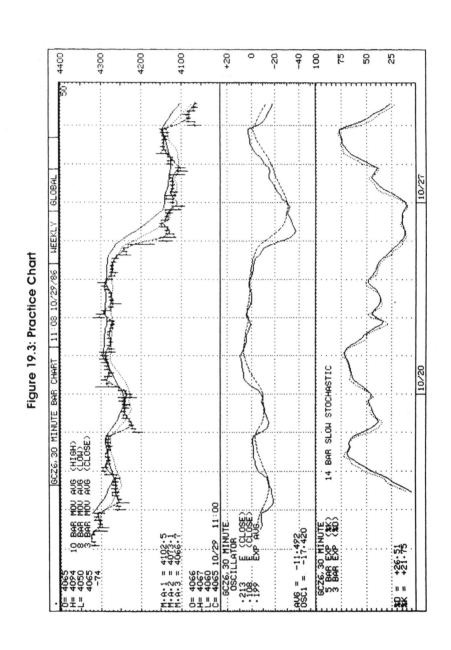

Figure 19.4: Practice Chart

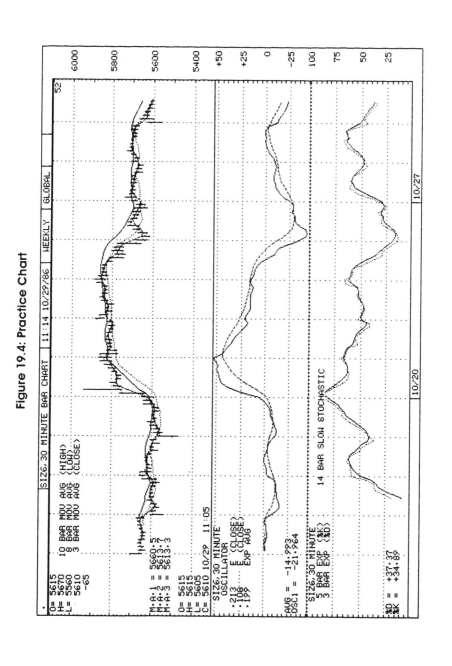

Figure 19.5: Practice Chart

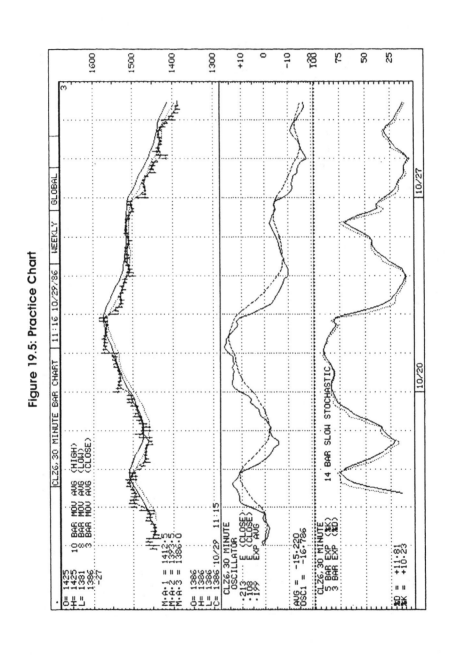

Figure 19.6: Practice Chart

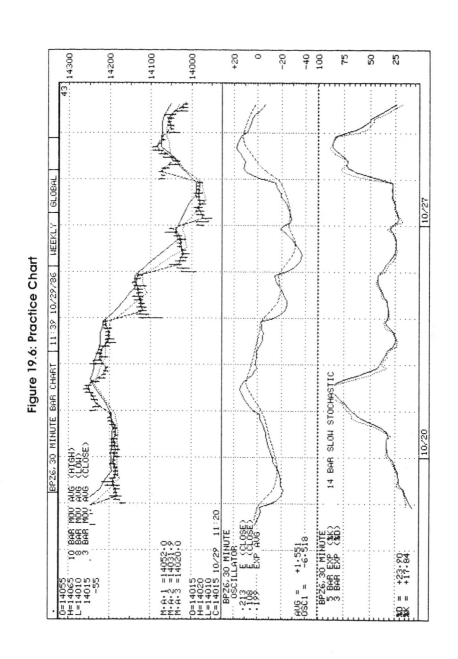

Figure 19.7: Practice Chart

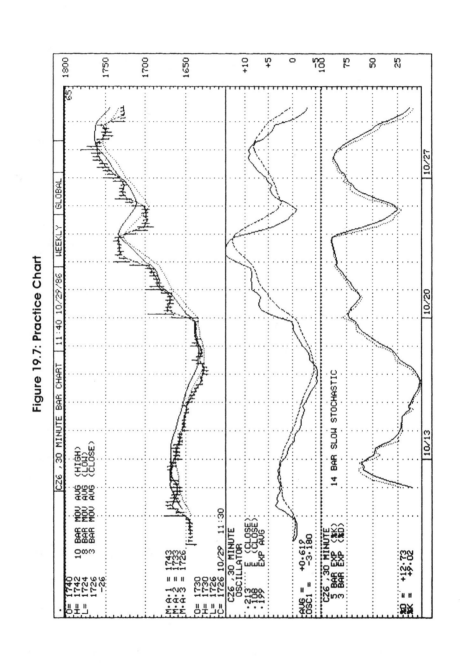

Figure 19.8: Practice Chart

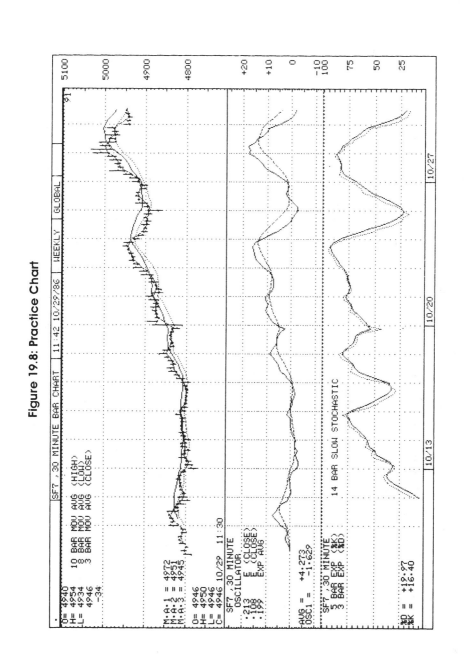

Figure 19.9: Practice Chart

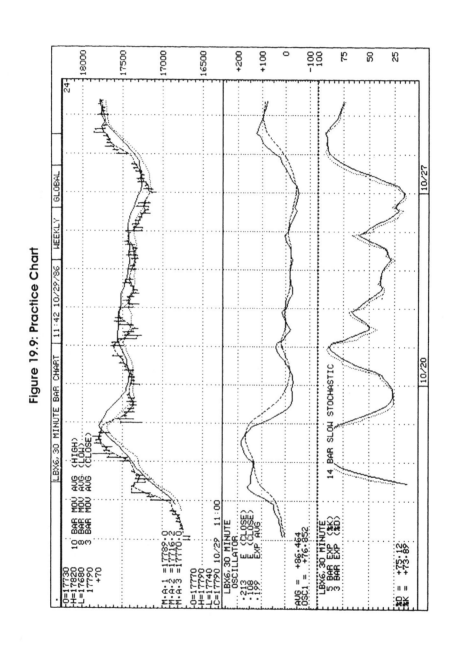

Figure 19.10: Practice Chart

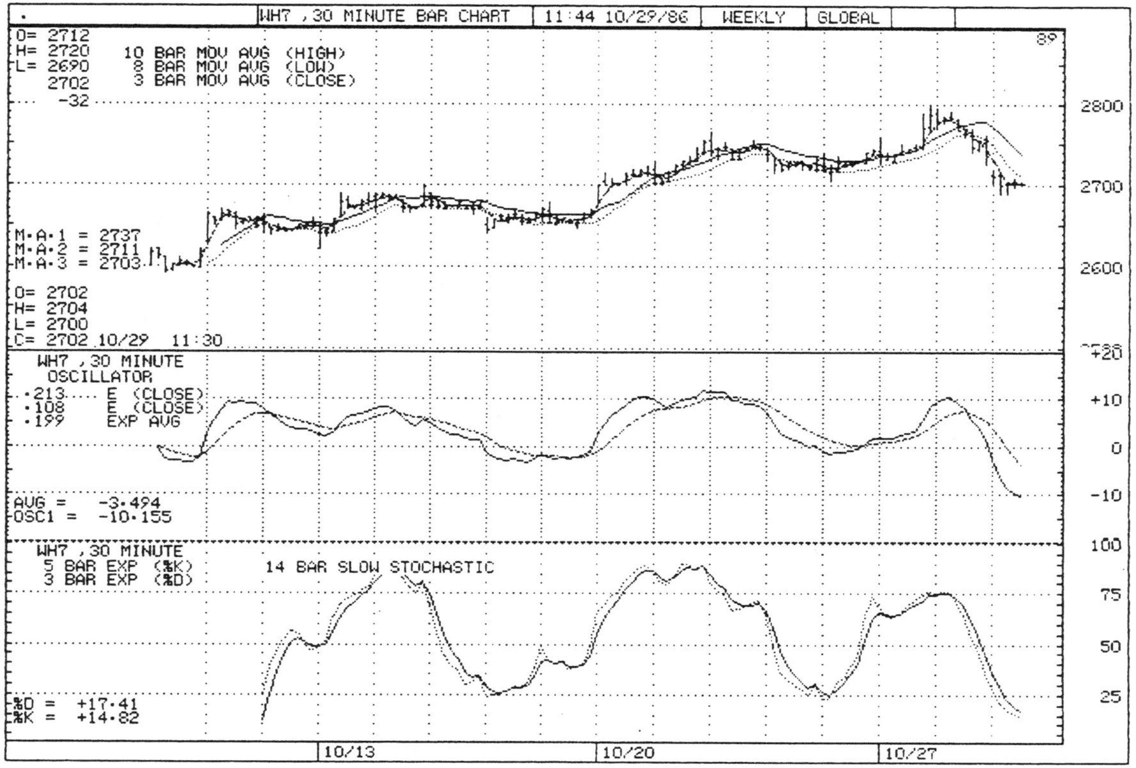

Figure 19.11: Practice Chart

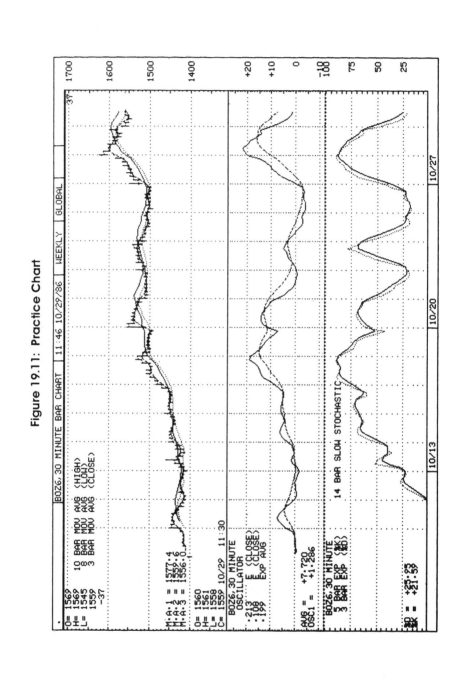

Figure 19.12: Practice Chart

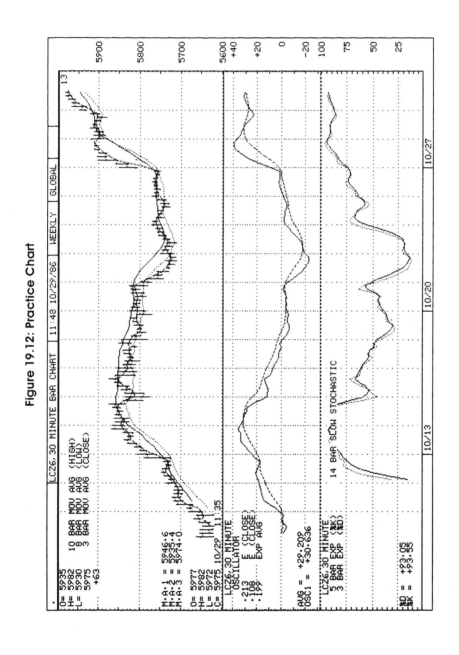

Figure 19.13: Practice Chart

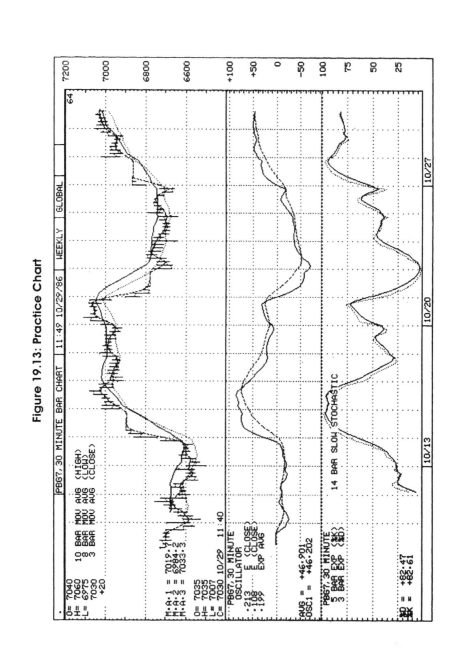

Figure 19.14: Practice Chart

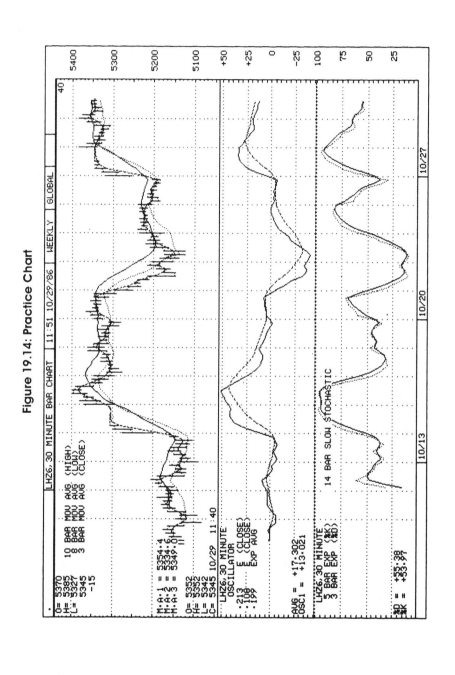

Figure 19.15: Practice Chart

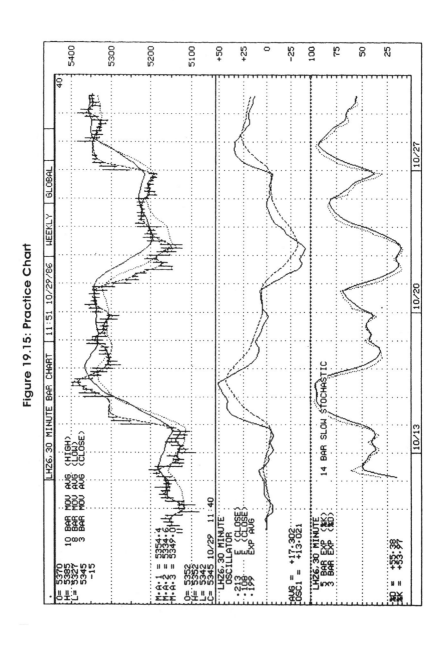

Figure 19.16: CTOD Practice

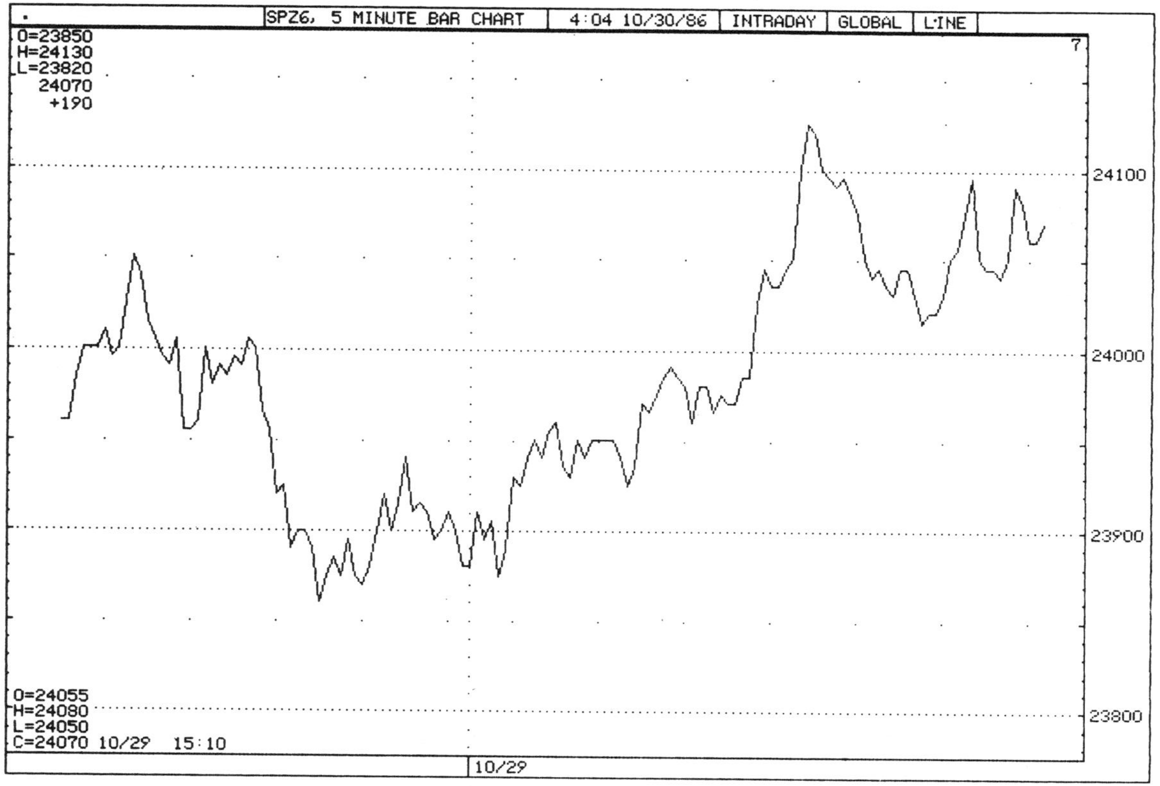

Figure 19.17: CTOD Practice

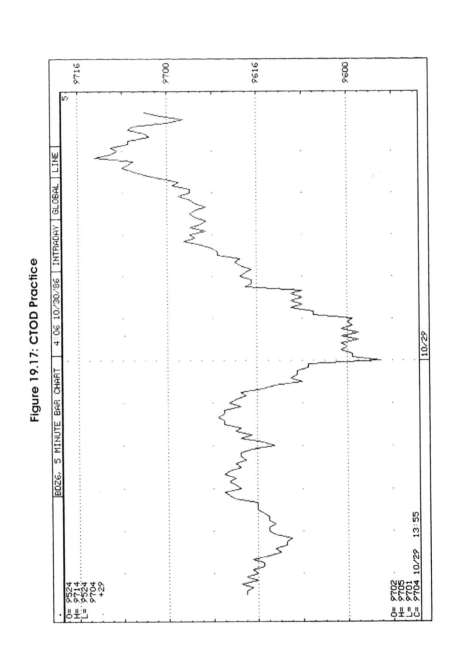

Figure 19.18: CTOD Practice

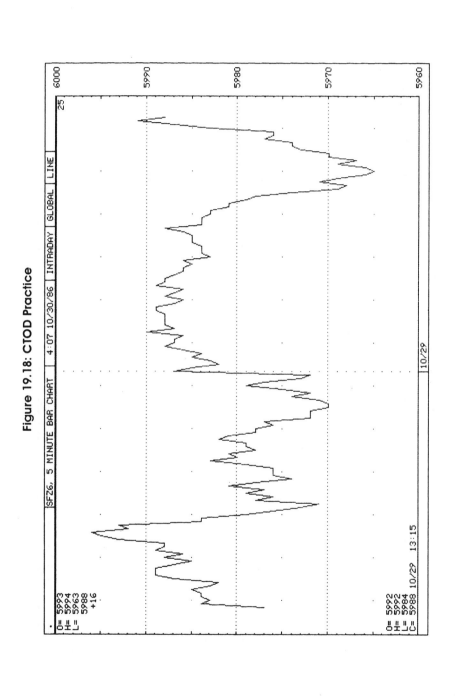

Figure 19.19: CTOD Practice

Figure 19.20: Practice Chart

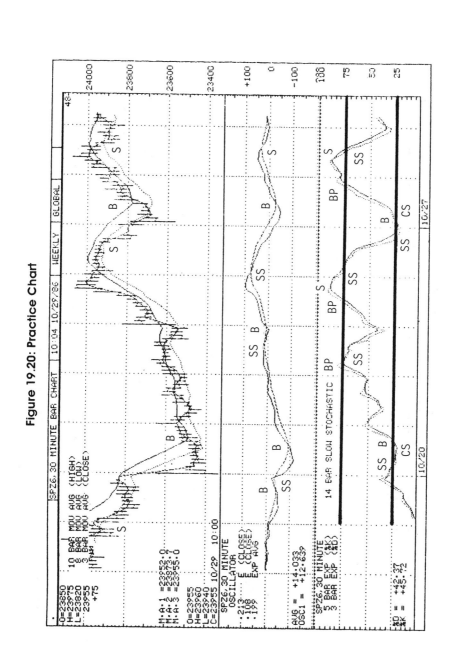

Figure 19.21: Practice Chart

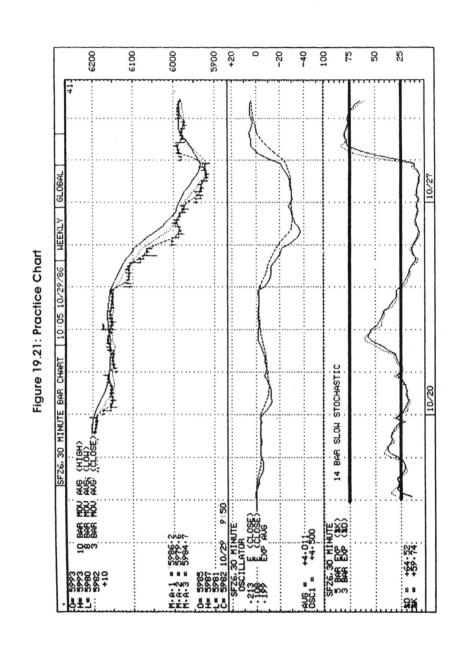

Figure 19.22: Practice Chart

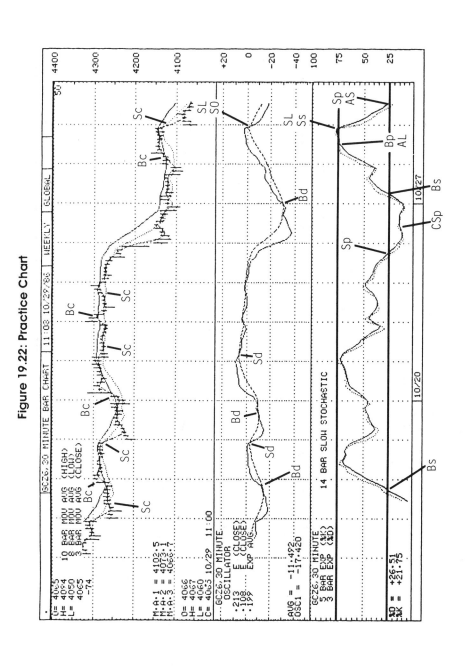

Figure 19.23: Practice Chart

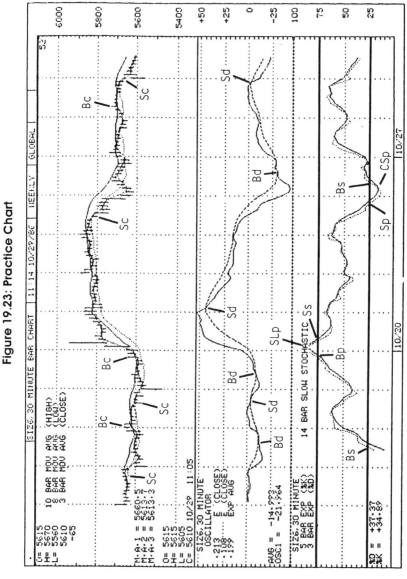

Figure 19.24: Practice Chart

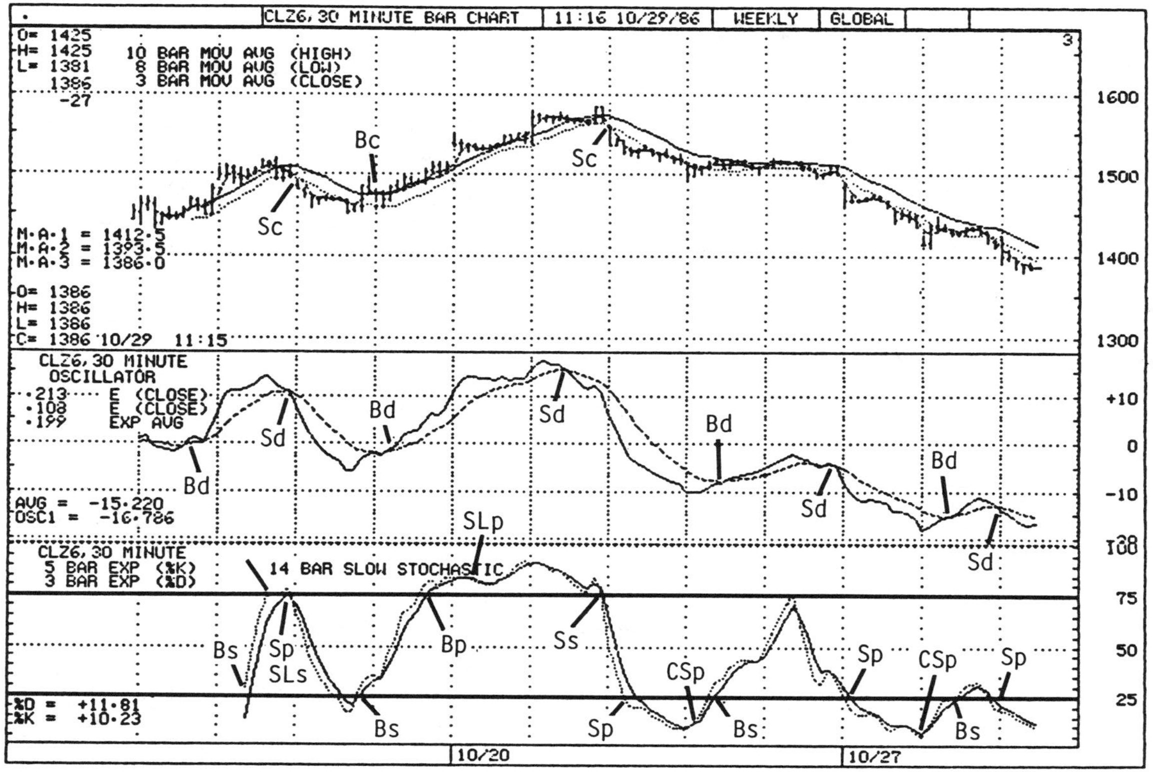

Figure 19.25: Practice Chart

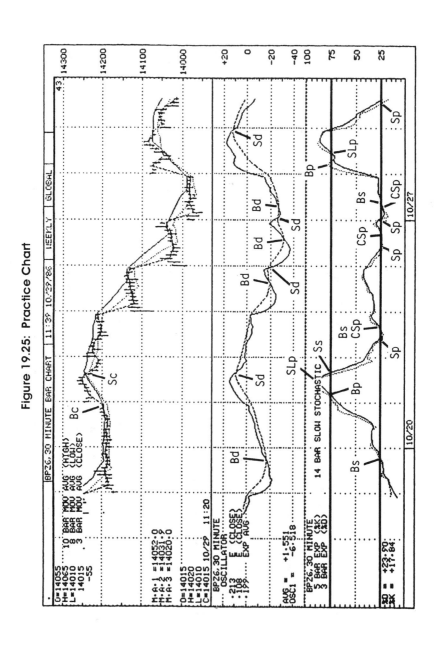

Figure 19.26: Practice Chart

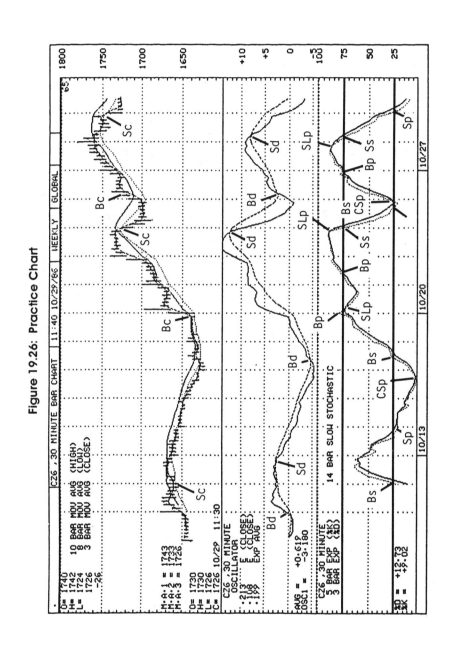

Figure 19.27: Practice Chart

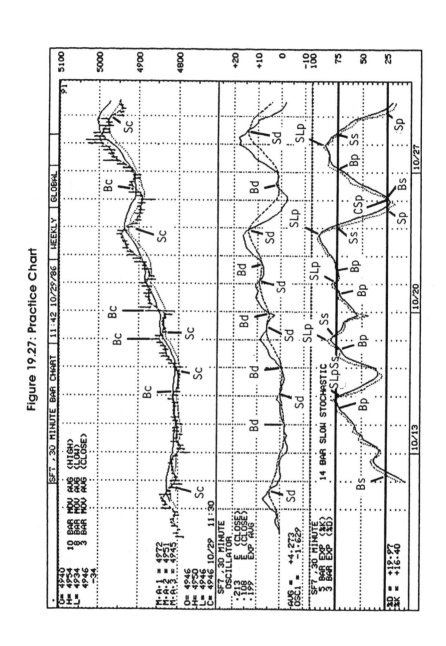

Figure 19.28: Practice Chart

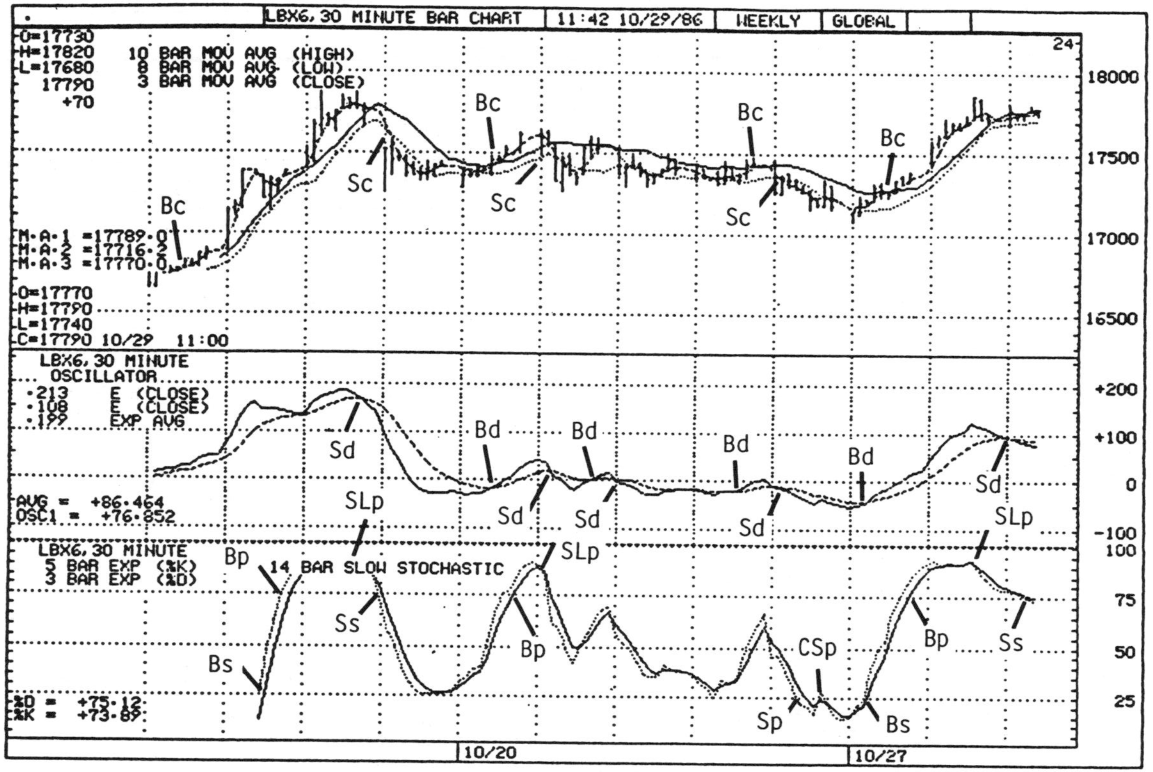

Figure 19.29: Practice Chart

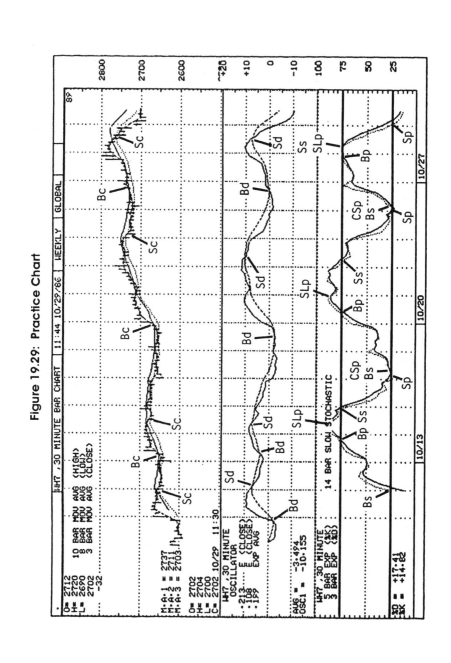

Figure 19.30: Practice Chart

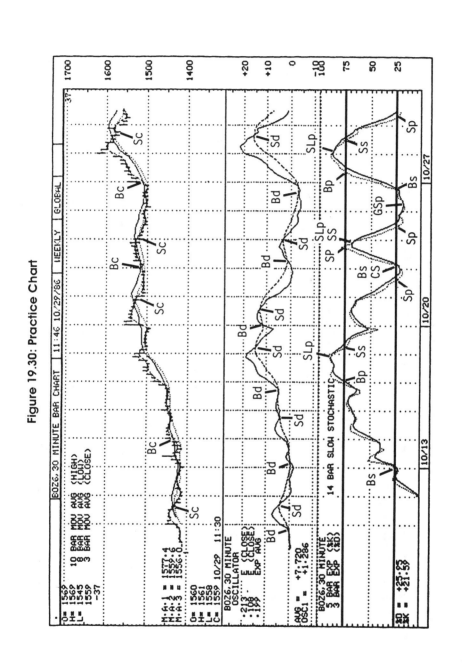

Figure 19.31: Practice Chart

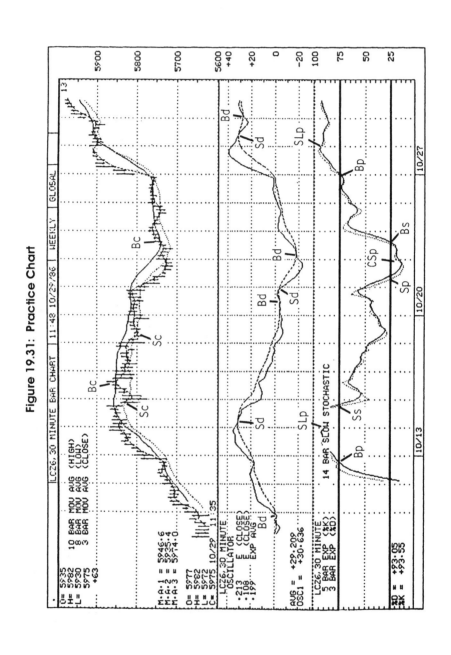

Figure 19.32: Practice Chart

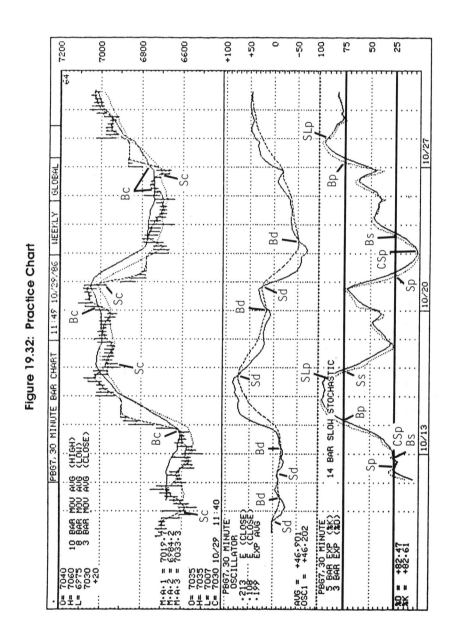

Figure 19.33: Practice Chart

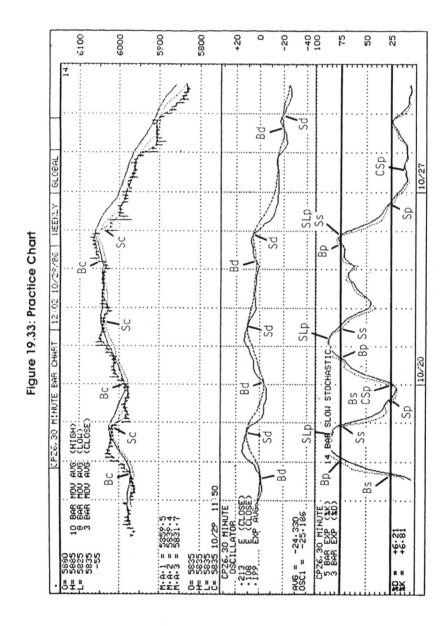

Figure 19.34: Practice Chart

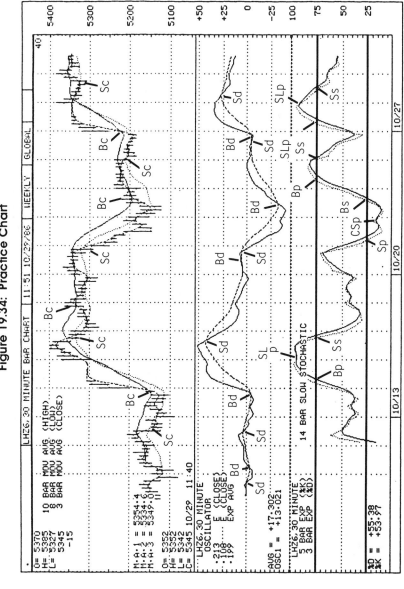

Figure 19.35: CTOD Practice

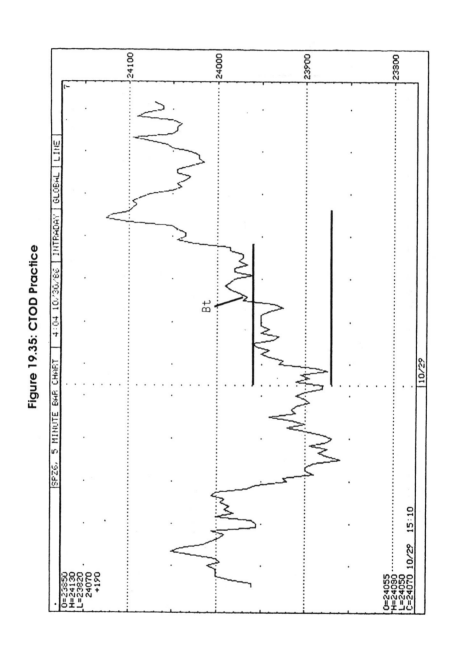

Figure 19.36: CTOD Practice

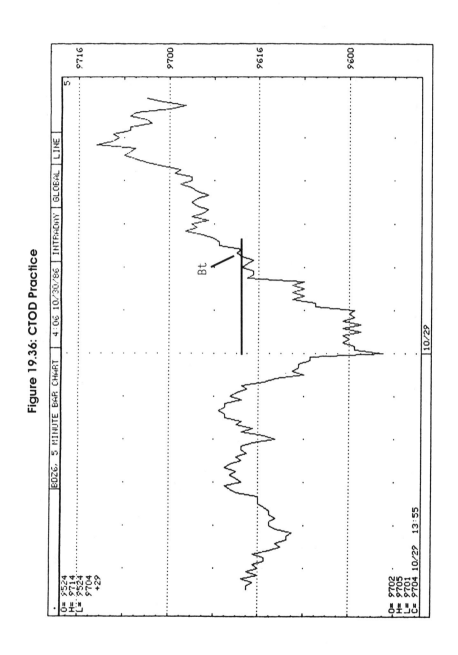

Figure 19.37: CTOD Practice

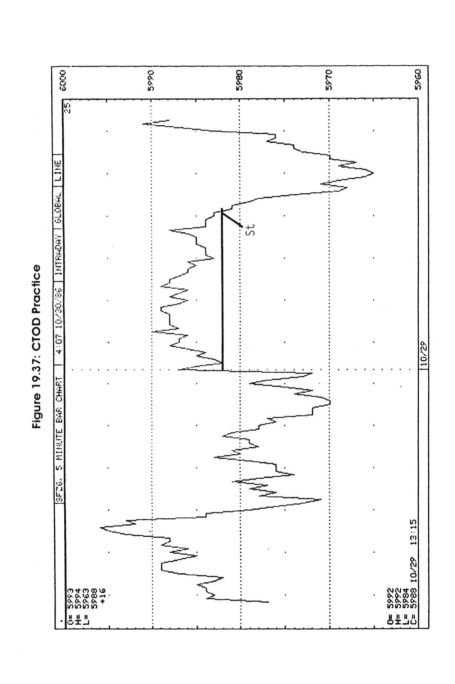

Figure 19.38: CTOD Practice

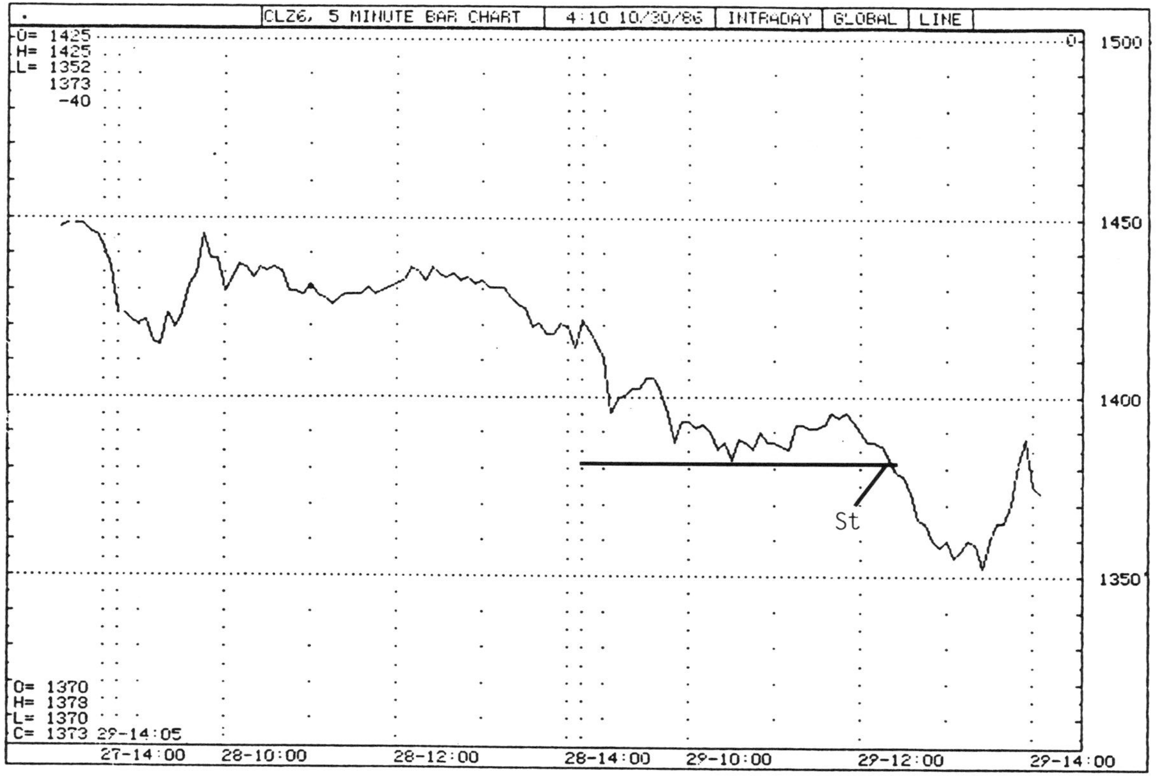

SUMMARY AND REVIEW OF INDICATORS AND TECHNIQUES

The following review of indicators and techniques is designed to serve as a quick reference guide. Note that only the basic ideas and implementations are discussed. Complete discussion, implementation, and caveats are provided in the relevant chapters.

STOCHASTICS—GENERAL DESCRIPTION

The Stochastic Indicator (SI) is basically a price-derived oscillator, expressed in percentages. SI values approach 0 and 100 as limits. SI consists of two values, %K and %D. The SI period can be adjusted as desired. The shorter the period, the more the SI will fluctuate.

Applications

Crossing of 75 percent and 25 percent. If one or both SI lines have been above 75 percent and one or both cross below 75 percent on a closing basis for the given period, then sells can be considered. If one or both SI lines have been below 25 percent and if one or both cross above 25 percent on a closing basis, then buys can be considered. Note that a more conservative variation of this application would be to require BOTH SI lines to cross as opposed to requiring just one line to cross.

Divergence with Price. If price makes a new high for a given time period but SI does not, then a top may be forming. If price makes a new low for a given period of time, and SI does not, then a bottom may be forming.

SI POP. A buy POP is triggered when one or both SI values close at 75 percent or higher for a given period after having been below 75 percent. A buy POP is exited when the SI lines cross again after the buy POP has been triggered. A sell POP is triggered when one or both SI values close at 25 percent or lower after having been above 25 percent. The sell POP is exited when the SI lines cross on a closing basis.

MOVING AVERAGES—GENERAL DESCRIPTION

Moving averages have many and varied applications in futures trading. Basic application involves buying and selling on penetrations of MA. Applications discussed in this manual are somewhat different, as described below.

Simple Penetration of MA. This application is the most elementary. When price closes above a given MA, a buy is triggered. When price closes below a given MA, a sell is triggered.

MA Support/Resistance Method. Two MAs are used, one about three times the length of the other. The longer MA defines trend. The shorter MA is used for buy and sell points. The text describes detailed techniques more fully.

10/8/3 MA Channel. Consists of three MAs, one each of the high, low and closing price respectively. The 10/8/3 channel can be used as support or resistance. The 10/8/3 combination can be used to generate buy and sell points when 3-close MA closes below 8-low MA (sell signal) or above 10 MA (buy signal).

CRITICAL TIME OF DAY (CTOD)—GENERAL DESCRIPTION

CTOD defines the first two hours of trading in all active futures markets as "critical." A five-minute "closing" price plot is used to determine CTOD sell and buy points. After the first two hours, closing above five-minute critical time closing high triggers a buy; closing below five-minute critical time closing low triggers a sell. Various stop, followup, and exit techniques are necessary when using CTOD. See text for complete details.

DUAL EXPONENTIAL MOVING AVERAGE (DEMA)—
GENERAL DESCRIPTION

DEMA consists of three exponential moving averages. The first two are differenced to form the third MA. Signals are generated as buy or sell when the indicator crosses above or below its MA.

Crossovers. Crossovers of the DEMA lines are used as buy and sell points. If trend has been down, then an up cross of the DEMA lines triggers a buy. If trend has been up, then a down cross of the DEMA lines triggers a sell.

Divergence. When DEMA values fail to make a new high with price, then a top may be forming. When DEMA values fail to make a new low with price, then a bottom may be forming.

DEMA Difference. DEMA difference is another way to look at DEMA crossovers and divergence.

TIC VOLUME—GENERAL DESCRIPTION

Each price change is counted as one tic. Tics are cumulated to represent total tic volume. Tic volume does not represent total contract volume, but can be a good indication of approximate total volume.

Application

See text for applications.

DETRENDED OSCILLATORS—GENERAL DESCRIPTION

A detrended oscillator is simply defined as the mathematical difference between price and a given length moving average. Various types of detrended indicators can be computed.

Application

The detrended oscillator is used as a measure of divergence. When price makes a new high but detrended oscillator does not, then a top may be forming. When price makes a new low but detrended oscillator does not, then a low may be forming.

PRICE SPIKES AND PROBES—GENERAL DESCRIPTION

Price highs and lows tend to occur on spikes or "pivots." The lows and highs of important market pivots become important as support and resistance points for buying and selling.

Application

See text. Too detailed for brief description.

About the Author

Jake Bernstein enjoys an international reputation as an educator, contributor of original research, author and futures trader. His books include *Jake Bernstein's New Facts on Futures* (Probus 1992) and *Analysis and Forecasting of Long-Term Trends in the Cash and Futures Markets* (Probus 1989). His articles have appeared in *Futures Magazine, Money Maker* and many other periodicals.

About the Publisher

PROBUS PUBLISHING COMPANY

Probus Publishing Company fills the informational needs of today's business professional by publishing authoritative, quality books on timely and relevant topics, including:

- Investing
- Futures/Options Trading
- Banking
- Finance
- Marketing and Sales
- Manufacturing and Project Management
- Personal Finance, Real Estate, Insurance and Estate Planning
- Entrepreneurship
- Management

Probus books are available at quantity discounts when purchased for business, educational or sales promotional use. For more information, please call the Director, Corporate/Institutional Sales at 1-800-PROBUS-1, or write:

Director, Corporate/Institutional Sales
Probus Publishing Company
1925 N. Clybourn Avenue
Chicago, Illinois 60614
FAX (312) 868-6250